RADICAL

RADICAL

Fighting to Put Students First

MICHELLE RHEE

HARPER

www.harpercollins.com

The names of some of the students featured throughout this book have been changed to protect their privacy.

HarperCollins books may be purchased for educational, business, or sales promotional use. For information, please e-mail the Special Markets Department at SPsales@harpercollins.com.

FIRST EDITION

Designed by Renato Stanisic

Library of Congress Cataloging-in-Publication Data

Rhee, Michelle.
Radical : fighting to put students first / Michelle Rhee.
p. cm.
ISBN 978-0-06-220398-4 (hardback)
1. Public schools—United States. 2. Educational change—United States. 3. School improvement programs—United States. 4. Education—Aims and objectives—United States. 5. Rhee, Michelle. I. Title.
LA217.R495 2013
371.010973—dc23   2012038474

13 14 15 16 17 OV/RRD 10 9 8 7 6 5 4 3 2 1

To the children of Washington, D.C.,
who deserve the best schools in the world

Contents

Introduction: Call to Arms

A few weeks before graduating from college, I faced a choice between two very different paths into my future.

One would take me to graduate school to study labor relations. My mind was brimming with ideas about how to improve manufacturing production through educational incentives for workers and their families. I had been accepted to programs at Rutgers and the University of Illinois.

The other would take me to a public school classroom. I had become intrigued by Teach For America, a relatively new organization in 1992 that trained college graduates to work in public schools in low-income communities.

Graduate school appealed to my practical side, the one that would satisfy my hard-driving mother. Get trained! Get a job! Get married!

Teaching spoke to the part of me that had been growing stronger since I was a teen in Toledo, Ohio, volunteering at a local elementary school. My father always taught my brothers and me that the person who has the ability to do more than take care of her own should give back to the community. "Don't just think of yourselves," he would tell us.

So as my college days came to an end, I was caught between two conflicting choices. I struggled. Two weeks before graduation, I called my grandmother in Seoul, South Korea. My mother's mother had always given me good counsel. I described my dilemma.

"What should I do, *Halmuhnee*?" I asked.

She paused. As a young woman, she had taught kindergarten. I knew she was considering my question.

"Go teach," she said.

But the school was in a poor neighborhood in Baltimore, I explained, a city I knew nothing about.

"It's going to be really tough," I told her.

"It's little kids," she said. "What's hard about that?"

Little did my grandmother know how hard the next few years as a teacher would be for me. Or how rewarding. Little did she know that my experiences in the classroom would lead me on an odyssey, from my rage at the failures of the public education system to my resolve to change that system. Making sure schools in America engage, teach, and prepare students—regardless of where they come from or how they arrive at school—has become my life's work. I am committed to creating a sense of honor for teachers in our country, and to rewarding them for success in the classroom. Somewhere along the way our country has lost the expectations that all children can learn and excel, along with our regard for teachers.

America is the greatest country in the world. But that status is at risk. The United States will not maintain that leadership role—from commerce to military might to moral authority—if we as a nation continue to allow our public schools to deteriorate.

A report by the Georgetown University Center on Education and the Workforce found that the U.S. economy will create 46.8

million new and "replacement" jobs in the next five years, 63 percent of which will require some college education. Yet we're failing to produce the well-trained American workers we need to fill these positions. Half of businesses report that they can't find the workers they need to hire for vacancies they have. And the truth is that when we fail to fill these positions, they'll inevitably have to be outsourced to places like China and India, or other countries where young people have the skills and knowledge they need to be successful in those roles. This is a significant problem that will consign America to decline.

True, America still generates some of the world's best patents, ideas, and businesses—Facebook, Google, and Apple, for starters. But if the programmers are in India, the engineers are in South Korea, and the software developers are in Singapore—where does that leave us?

Two summers ago, I heard the prime minister of Singapore, Lee Hsien Loong, speak before an annual gathering of media executives. When the topic turned to competing in the global economy, he chose to discuss education. He said that when his country set its sights on entering the global market and winning its share, it decided it must first create a strong education system. If its children were not prepared to compete, how could Singapore hope to gain a foothold against the United States, Germany, or China? The country made sure to establish a first-class education system that was linked to the financial and commercial sectors. Seems obvious: invest in education and you ensure a strong workforce and vibrant economy. But in the United States we see education as a social issue, rather than an economic one. When budgets get cut at federal, state, and local levels, education often falls first under the ax. That, too, must change if we hope to compete.

In America in 2012, birth determines possibilities. A poor kid's chances of graduating from college are one in ten. Of all developed nations, America is near the bottom in terms of social mobility. If you told me the race of a child and the zip code in which she lives, I could, with pretty good accuracy, tell you her academic achievement levels. That's the most un-American thing I can imagine! This is supposed to be the land of equal opportunity. But for America's children, it's not. Where you live and the color of your skin largely determine your lot in life. In my mind, that is nothing less than criminal. And it will come to define who we are as a nation unless we do something dramatic—something truly radical—to reverse this reality.

Wealth and class do not ensure a quality public school. Middle- and upper-middle-class children and their parents suffer from mediocrity in the classroom, as well. First-rate suburbs have second-rate schools that are failing to prepare children to get good jobs, create new companies, or innovate. And often, these families don't even know it.

The poorest kids in America (the bottom quartile economically) rank twenty-sixth out of thirty developed nations in math compared with their peers. Our richest kids? They also rank twenty-sixth out of thirty in their peer group. Middling schools are not a problem confined to our ghettos. They plague every neighborhood and community across the nation.

My aim is to bring excellence back to public education by making sure that laws and policies have one goal: to educate students well. What I learned—from teaching at Harlem Park in Baltimore to creating The New Teacher Project to running the Washington, D.C., schools—is that a great teacher can inspire and help any child learn, regardless of that child's circumstances. He or she can come to class hungry from a filthy apartment and a single parent selling drugs, or a posh mansion where the parents are too busy making money to care about their kids. When they get to a good school in front of a terrific teacher, they can learn.

The education agenda in the United States for the last thirty years has been driven largely by the teachers unions and many other special interests, from the textbook publishers to the testing companies. Students have often been neglected in the process, and our standing among other nations has suffered. Students in the United States rank fourteenth in reading, seventeenth in science, and twenty-fifth in math, according to the 2009 study of thirty-four countries by the Programme for International Student Assessment.

The predicament has only grown more desperate in the past two years.

In these chapters you will learn about my awakening to the potential that every child can learn, given a great teacher; my rage at realizing that adults and special interests were blocking change that could bring and keep great teachers in classrooms; and my realization that it would take a grassroots movement to break through the barriers standing in the way of making public schools work for students.

I have separated the book into three sections.

In Part I, "The Journey," I narrate my path to becoming a reformer, from my roots in teaching to my upbringing in the Midwest to the challenges I faced along the way. I hope you will begin to understand how my values and rage developed me as a teacher and a chancellor—a daughter and a mother.

In Part II, "The Movement," I describe the power, the struggle, and the potential of the movement to redirect public education toward the students. You will read my tale through personal stories: from students who have transcended their surroundings—thanks to great teachers—to teachers who have thrived in classrooms and improved the outcomes of their students to parents who have struggled and forced changes to improve their schools.

In Part III, "The Promise," I present my vision for what American schools could be.

My goal is to help create a movement that will remake American public education, so that every child can have the opportunity to learn and excel—and join a workforce that will help the United States compete and win in the global economy. It will not be easy or gentle; it will not be quick. It will require a struggle over power and money.

My grandmother asked: How hard can that be?

Very.

PART I

The Journey

Roots in the Classroom

C hina stared at me, desperate for an answer. I was paralyzed. Excuses filled my mind as her bulging eyes bored
into me.

"Please, Ms. Rhee," she pleaded. "Please!"

We were in my car in front of the notorious Franklin Street
housing project high-rises, one of the most dangerous places in
all of Baltimore. Word on the street was that a dozen murders
and scores of violent crimes had taken place in these towers in
the past year. It was about 6:00 p.m., the sun was setting, and
the situation at the towers was looking sketchier by the moment.
I gazed up at the twenty-four-floor building with its grated and
gated windows and walkways.

"Ms. Rhee, I can't walk up there myself. There are drug dealers everywhere!" She wasn't exaggerating. I could see the young
men with baggy pants and hats on nearly every floor of the tower.
"Ms. Rhee, I'm scared for real!"

My mind began racing with options, but mostly remorse. I often
kept China after school with me to do her homework and help me
prepare for the next day. Usually, though, I dropped her off at her
mother's house on Carey Street, which, though also dangerous,

was filled with neighbors who knew me. "There's that crazy Chinese lady. The one from up over at the school!" they'd say.

Today was different. China was staying with her dad, who lived in the towers; as I pulled up to the entrance, she was begging me to walk her up to her dad's apartment. I didn't respond. While I couldn't imagine sending this tiny eight-year-old up into that building alone, I was terrified of walking into the building and back out again on my own. It was one of those moments that define a person. Half of me wanted to push her out of the car and peel out of the parking lot. The other wanted to grin widely, grab her hand with confidence, and head into the building.

The thought of fleeing was beginning to win out when a loud knock on my window startled the bejesus out of both of us. "HEEEEYYYYYY! Ms. Rhee! What's up, China!" It was China's cousin. "You come to see your daddy? I'll get you up there!" he offered, having no idea what a bullet he was allowing me to dodge. "Great, appreciate it!" I said breezily, as I unrolled the window and flashed him a smile of gratitude.

The minute China got out of the car, I spun out of that parking lot so quickly I might have left tire marks. On my way home, visions of China's frightened eyes kept flashing in front of me. "Good Lord," I thought. "What kind of a world is this? I can't believe this innocent little girl is in these daunting situations on a daily basis."

It made my heart ache, and it made me evermore thankful for the idyllic situation from whence I came.

I GREW UP WITH certainty. I always knew what was expected of me, what I would do, and what would happen to me tomorrow.

The main priority in our family was education. It drove every conversation, admonition, and decision in our household. It loomed over my brothers and me like a smothering cloud.

We were expected not only to put 100 percent of our attention into school, but also to excel. To be number one. And nothing less was acceptable. In fact, anything less was considered a failure.

My first memory of school was not a pleasant one. My parents chose Little Meadows for me, a nursery school in Sylvania, Ohio, a small town northwest of Toledo, near the Michigan line. I remember walking by the staircase one day and overhearing two teachers talking about me. "I think she's slow," they hissed. "She *never* says anything!"

Actually, I was just painfully shy and quiet. But despite my outward appearances, I was sad and wounded just the same when I heard the teachers' assessment of me. "What do they know?" I remember thinking. "They don't know me!"

That feeling, the feeling of being an outsider, persisted throughout my life, mostly because my parents went out of their way to make us Korean. They spoke to us in Korean. My brothers and I went to Korean school every week. There were no Korean food groceries or restaurants in Toledo, so we drove to a suburb of Ann Arbor, Michigan, every week to buy cabbage, tofu, rice, and soy sauce.

My parents were dedicated to ensuring that we knew what being Korean and the Korean culture meant. They doggedly instilled in us the culture of the country they left in the 1960s, which my father described as "education crazy." Both of my parents— Shang and Inza—grew up surrounded by educators.

I come from a family of teachers. Jung Sook Lee, my mother's mother, taught kindergarten in Korea. Four of my aunts on my father's side were teachers. Hae Woo Rhee, my father's father, was a well-known educator in Seoul. He taught for fifty years, starting in primary school, during the Japanese occupation before 1945. He became a principal and served on Seoul's board of education.

When my father was young, everyone knew his dad. Hae Woo Rhee was known as a strict but great teacher and a principal who ran a tight ship. Because his father drew such a hard line for his students, my father was expected to be the model child. The eldest son of the town's most feared and respected educator must be the best, and best-behaved, student. My father fit that mold perfectly.

Growing up among educators, he had a healthy respect for the profession. But he chose to become a doctor. He was a teenager during the Korean War, a time of hardship but also a time when the United States became heroic in his mind for preserving his way of life. He began to consider traveling to the States.

To my dad, America represented hope and promise. Back then, all Koreans dreamed of moving to America because of the freedom and opportunity the country represented. "We all thought in America you'd walk out your door and see Natalie Wood and Sophia Loren strolling down the street. And that anyone could become a Ford or Rockefeller. Anyone could make it if you had the will and a big dream," he'd tell us. My father wanted to be a part of that. Though he successfully lived up to the rigid expectations that his parents set for him, he aspired to something else for his kids. He wanted his children to grow up with the limitless possibilities of America.

MY PARENTS FELL IN love during college and dated while my father studied for his medical degree at Seoul National University. He graduated in 1965. Freshly minted Korean doctors dreamed of completing their postgraduate work in the United States and becoming licensed to practice there. In those days one airplane per week took off from Korea to the States. My dad landed an internship at St. Francis Hospital in Pittsburgh and made plans to leave Korea in July. He asked Inza to marry him and hoped she would join him in America.

"Your *halabujee* [my mother's father] wasn't having that," he told my brothers and me. "He wasn't going to risk having his eldest daughter jilted in a foreign land. Either we would get married in Korea or we wouldn't get married at all."

Needless to say, they married in Korea. After the wedding in June, Shang flew off in July, and Inza joined him in Pittsburgh a month later. My father struggled with his new language and surroundings, but he succeeded well enough that the director of medical education commended him in a letter to the dean of his school in Seoul.

From Pittsburgh, my parents moved to Seattle, where my father started his residency at the University of Washington. My older brother, Erik, was born in Seattle. In 1967, the family of three moved to Ann Arbor so my father could complete his residency at the University of Michigan. I was born there on Christmas Day, 1969. Thus my middle name: Ann. My younger brother, Brian, came fifteen months later.

My dad made $400 a month, minus the requisite amount he had to send to his family back home. So it amounted to a pittance. My mom, unable to speak the language and knowing no one, was bored out of her mind. She spent her days walking the streets of Ann Arbor, stopping in front of the pizza parlor and soaking in the smells of cheese and garlic but unable to ever afford a slice. She would often wander into the A&P grocery store and just walk up and down the aisles. One day she fainted, tired from her pregnancy, and the shopkeeper forbade her from coming in again.

Desperate for cash, my father would drive to Toledo, fifty miles south, once or twice a month, to moonlight—supplement his salary by filling in for doctors at Mercy Hospital. That allowed him to establish a connection with Toledo and Mercy, which offered him his first real job, director of the rehab department, at $2,700 a month when he finished his fellowship. "I thought I was the richest man in the country," he explained to my brothers and me.

. . . .

OUR HOUSE SCREAMED "FOREIGN" from the moment you crossed the threshold. From the overpowering stench of *kimchee* (fermented cabbage) and *ojinguh* (dried squid) to the shoes neatly lined up outside the front door (you could never wear shoes in the house!) to the Asian screen that my mother had custom made for our front entrance, nothing in the Rhee house was normal or familiar to my American friends. You knew from the start that you were about to enter a different world. My friends marveled as they inspected the Korean artifacts that adorned the hallway, the smelly antique Chinese herb chest that was the centerpiece of our living room, and the brush paintings that my aunt had created.

"Weird!" they'd announce gleefully after thoroughly surveying the lay of the land.

But even more foreign than the odors and decor was the way my family operated, and specifically, my role in the family unit. We were living in America but trapped in the landscape and mindset of South Korea circa 1950. That meant that the men ruled the roost and the women served them.

One memory that has stuck with me was when my little brother, Brian, who was not academically inclined, came home with a bad grade. My mother immediately grounded me. He was allowed to go out; I had to stay in.

"You're his older sister," my mother told me. "It is your responsibility to make sure that he is doing what he needs to do." "Whaaaa?" I thought. That was crazy talk! In modern-day America that rationale made zero sense, but to my mother, it was perfectly logical.

Another particularly humiliating experience took place when a friend of mine and I were discussing what back then was dubbed "women's lib." We were talking about how wrong it was for men to think women were inferior. I made a comment about how I would tell any man off who tried to keep me down. *Thwack!* Before I could even get the words out of my mouth my mother had gone upside my head with the back of her hand. "Don't be disrespectful!" she hissed.

It was actually kind of comical, and my friend couldn't pick herself up off the floor from her laughing fit. My mother, however, was unfazed. She was sitting peacefully shucking bean sprouts for dinner one minute and smacking me the next because she didn't like what I said. She returned to shucking without missing a bean.

That's how I grew up.

My parents were very, very strict, especially my mother. My father was a successful doctor and very popular in the community. Everyone knew my dad. He was the liberal one of the two. But my mother ran the show. She was hard-core and strong willed. As my friends would say, "Mrs. Rhee is no joke."

I was allowed out of the house only one night a week and I had to be in by eleven o'clock—no exceptions. I was not allowed to sleep over at friends' houses.

When I complained, my mother would retort, "What good can come of a girl sleeping at somebody's house other than her own?" We ate dinner together around the table every single night. Almost every night it was Korean food.

I had to wake up every morning and pack lunches for my brothers. I set the table and washed the dishes after every meal, cleaning up after my brothers.

"This is what girls do," my mother would say whenever I complained about the unfairness.

The difference between the culture in our house and the one I lived in at school couldn't have been starker.

. . . .

WHEN I WAS GROWING up in and around Toledo, it was a working-class union town built on manufacturing. After World War II, jobs were plentiful in the Jeep plant and the Libbey-Owens-Ford glass company, and the city thrived. Toledo's population reached its height of 383,818 right around when we moved there in 1971. In his practice, my father treated factory workers and plant managers. My friends were the sons and daughters of union members. I grew up with strong feelings of allegiance to unions and the working class.

In the second grade, I asked my father what the difference between a Democrat and Republican was. He said, "Republicans care more about what's happening in other countries. They care about making money. Democrats care more about what's happening in America. They want to take care of the least among us." That settled it for me. I was a Democrat.

LIKE MANY MIDWESTERN MANUFACTURING towns, Toledo went into decline in the 1970s, and continued to struggle into the twenty-first century. It suffered from recessions, plant closings, and white flight to the suburbs.

Toledo public schools had a proud early history, beginning in 1842, when the city council took the first step of voting to build schoolhouses. The first schools operated only in winter and were heated by potbelly stoves. From those modest beginnings, the public schools grew with the city and reached their zenith in the late 1960s, when the school population topped fifty thousand students, educated in sixty-six buildings.

But Toledo schools mirrored the growth and decline of the city. Even in their heyday, the schools struggled for funds. The system depended on local levies, which Toledo residents voted on every year. They were not generous. In fact, the schools starved. In a 1976 report required by Ohio legislators, the schools reported that the system had not had an additional operating levy since 1968. Instruction and facilities languished. Teachers went out on strike in 1970 and again in 1978.

Toledo was hardly an isolated case. The plight of the public schools was the unfortunate norm coast to coast, from inner-city schools to small towns to suburbs. The declining state of public education in the United States during the 1970s and '80s provoked a reaction from Washington. President Ronald Reagan asked his Department of Education to establish a commission to study public schools. In 1983 the commission published *A Nation at Risk: The Imperative for Educational Reform.*

"Certainly," President Reagan said at the commission's first meeting, "there are few areas of American life as important to our society, to our people, and to our families, as our schools and colleges."

For eighteen months, Reagan's commission held hearings across the country and researched schools. Its conclusion: "We report to the American people that while we can take justifiable pride in what our schools and colleges have historically accomplished and contributed to the United States and the well-being of its people, the educational foundations of our society are presently being eroded by a rising tide of mediocrity that threatens our very future as a nation and a people.

"What was unimaginable a generation ago has begun to occur—others are matching and surpassing our educational attainments."

The commission found that twenty-three million Americans were literally or functionally illiterate. Thirteen percent of all seventeen-year-olds were illiterate; the College Board's SAT scores had fallen steadily from 1963 to 1980 by 50 points in verbal and 40 in math; business and military leaders complained they were spending millions of dollars on remedial reading, writing, and math skills.

"The world is indeed one global village," the report stated, concluding: "America's position in the world may once have been reasonably secure with only a few exceptionally well-trained men and women. It is no longer."

Toledo public schools were not what they once had been. Shang and Inza Rhee didn't have to read *A Nation at Risk* to understand that their children might not thrive in public schools and be able to compete with the best. They surveyed their options and evaluated the schools based on their roots in education and the education-crazy country from which they came.

My parents settled the family in Rossford, about five miles south of Toledo, along the Maumee River. We lived in a neighborhood called the Colony, and it was every bit as exclusive and pretentious as it sounds. The sprawling yards separated neighbors at a comfortable distance, and many of the houses looked like mini castles. Good luck trick-or-treating there—the houses were too far apart and the neighbors too crotchety to lead to a good haul. There weren't very many children who lived in the neighborhood, so my brothers and I had to venture outside the stone gates in order to play with our friends. With significant trepidation and skepticism, my parents enrolled my brothers and me in the neighborhood public school, Eagle Point Elementary.

THE TEACHERS AT LITTLE MEADOWS nursery school got one thing right: I was an extremely shy and sheltered kid through primary school. My mother was creating a daughter modeled on her upbringing in Seoul. We weren't Americans. We were Koreans living in America. They were so serious about this that they sent each of us to Korea after sixth grade for a year to be immersed in the culture.

So in the summer of 1978 they shipped me off to Seoul to live with my aunt and her three children. I couldn't speak a lick of Korean. What a shock: I was now living in a tiny apartment, sleeping in a cramped room with my two cousins, and waking up to a breakfast of rice and *banchan* (small plates of seasoned vegetables) every morning.

The biggest adjustment, though, came when I went to school.

Students started every day by lining up and standing at attention. Then we did calisthenics. I remember thinking to myself: "Are you serious? Do I really have to do this?"

I did. Everyone did. I also had to learn Korean, which I nailed down after three months of sitting in class like a dummy. There were seventy kids in my class. They positioned students according to height. Since I was a year older than most of my classmates, I sat in the back. I had no clue what was going on—and I felt like I was a mile away from the teacher.

I got zero special treatment, because in Korean schools, competition ruled. Every child was ranked by his or her grades, from one to seventy, and the rankings were posted. I couldn't believe they told everyone how they measured up against one another!

But rather than damaging the souls of the less accomplished, the rankings focused every family on moving their children up the ladder. The question Koreans asked was "How can I get my kid ahead?" They made their children spend more time in class. They tutored them. If they were seventeenth, they competed to be sixteenth or fifteenth. Every family pushed their child to be closer to number one.

I saw that it was not only okay but essential to compete. I also started to understand where my mother got her strictness and her discipline. Compared with my American friends' moms, Inza seemed militaristic. But living with her was a walk in the park compared with these Korean mothers.

That year in Korea changed me in profound ways. I lived in a society where competition and excellence were rewarded, and attended a school that demanded hard work and dedication from every child. To do well was a symbol of your family's commitment and accomplishments. To do poorly was a blemish on your family. Everything a kid did was a reflection of his family and nothing was more important than maintaining their honor.

While all of this was foreign to me, one thing that I relished was the fact that for once in my life, I was in the majority. Having kids tug their eyes up into slits and being taunted with "Chinese, Japanese, dirty knees, look at *these*" was commonplace in my life back home. But in Korea, as long as I kept my mouth shut I looked like everyone else. In a strange way, that anonymity was empowering.

For the first time in my life, I did not feel like an outsider.

THE NEW SENSIBILITY CHANGED my life at home in Toledo.

In grade school I had been a hanger-on, someone who attached herself to the popular girls and tried to not look conspicuous. My parents were dissatisfied with that and with our overall experience in public school. They wanted more. They wanted the best.

When I returned from Korea my parents enrolled me in Maumee Valley Country Day School, a local private school. Established in 1884 as a school for girls, it had stayed small and accepted fewer than five hundred students from grades kindergarten to twelve, though it had become coed. The campus was arrayed over seventy-two wooded acres close to the Maumee River. Most of my classmates were the children of doctors, lawyers, or professors at one of the local colleges.

At Maumee Valley, I wasn't the most popular kid at first, but I started to hone my skills as a leader. I was the girl who was in the middle of everything. I knew everyone's business. I became the fixer.

When I was in seventh grade, the middle school took its annual trip to Washington, D.C., to see the sights and tour the monuments. After three action-packed days, it was finally time to board the buses back to Ohio. After surveying the scene, I wasn't happy. There weren't any seats left on the bus I wanted to ride on, the one with the cool and popular kids. Somehow a small group of nerds had gotten seats on that bus. I sprang into action.

"Move!" I demanded. They scoffed and looked at me as if to say, "Make us." I held sway in the school, but I certainly wasn't the prettiest or most popular girl, so a bat of the eyelashes wasn't going to help me here. Once I realized the confrontational approach was not going to work, I decided to try a softer one.

"Hey, don't you guys want to ride on the other bus with your friends? That would be so much more fun!" I cajoled.

"No way!" answered back their spokesperson. "If you haven't noticed, we scored seats on the cool bus." The task went from difficult to impossible. The nerds hadn't landed there by accident. They knew exactly what they were doing.

Looking dead in the eye of the King of the Nerds I said, "I'll give you twenty dollars for your seat."

"What? No way—are you crazy?"

"Nope," I replied, "take it or I'll offer it to someone else."

"I'll take it!" said another nerd.

"I'll give you my seat for fifteen dollars!" said another.

Within minutes I was brokering seats for all of my friends, with money exchanging hands at a frenetic pace. After we were all happily seated and about to take off, the head of the middle school, Laszlo Koltay, stormed onto the bus.

"*Everyone get off now!*" he boomed. We knew we were in trouble. Once all of us were assembled in the parking lot he said, "It has come to our attention that people are *paying* other students for their seats on the bus. This is absolutely unacceptable. I need to know who is involved. Right now."

Busted. Mr. Koltay was looking for names. He glared at his prize pupils, me included, assuming one of us would come clean and give up the culprits. None of the faculty would have guessed that I was involved in a million years. I was a Goody Two-shoes. Too nice to be involved in such unsavory acts.

And everyone knew that. We stood in preteen solidarity with no one uttering a word. When it became apparent that they weren't going to get anywhere with the inquisition, Mr. Koltay exacted his toll on us. We would be riding back to Toledo seated in alphabetical order by last name. "No one," he explained, "will be having an enjoyable ride home."

This kind of maneuvering became commonplace for me. I would use my reputation as the good girl to my advantage throughout my young adulthood. The sweet-girl facade belied the rebel brewing inside. My friends would say I was always bossing people around and telling them what to do. Whether it was the question of whom to catch a ride with, whom to date, or what to wear to the party, I became the go-to girl in our class. The dynamic became formalized as I ran for and won student council representative each year in school.

While my social life was improving, at least by preteen standards, one thing I began to realize after my time in Korea was that not everyone lived the sweet life in Rossford, Ohio, and I had it pretty good. My father often said, "You have what you have because you were lucky to be born into this family—not because you are particularly smart or special."

In high school I performed a broad range of community service, but I focused most of my volunteer time on children. Every January all students participated in a monthlong study or project outside school called Winterim. I spent my most memorable Winterim at the Child Life Center at the Medical College of Ohio, where I helped care for terminally ill children.

I remember one little girl I'll call Rachel, maybe four or five years old, with a beautiful, cherubic little face, and long, wavy blond hair. She had leukemia. My job was to play with her, and every day we would meet in the playroom. I remember she would lie down on the floor and gyrate and make sexual sounds.

I found it troubling, and she wouldn't talk about it. I approached the director of the program.

"Why does Rachel behave like that?" I asked.

She explained that Rachel came from a really troubled home, where she had been sexually molested. It was my first exposure to anything like that. I had grown up in such a sheltered, loving home, I could not imagine a child of this age being the victim of sexual abuse, but I could see all the manifestations of it coming out.

It made me sad, but it also drove home my father's words. I was lucky by birth.

I WAS ALSO LUCKY enough to meet Mary Weiss, the mother of my tenth-grade boyfriend, Adam. I didn't know it at the time, but Mary was my model teacher.

Mary and her husband, Steve, were the exact opposites of my parents. My parents were tough and strict; the Weisses were liberals, hippies back in the day.

Their daughter, Sarah, had died when she was in the sixth grade. They had adopted Adam when he was an infant, and in a way, I felt like they had adopted me, too. I would eat dinner at the Weisses' a few times a week my senior year of high school. We talked politics, business, and music, but mostly Mary talked about the trials and tribulations of the classroom. What I learned and heard at that table formed my sense of an ideal teacher.

Mary Weiss was born in Buffalo, New York. From an early age, she told me, she wanted to be a teacher. In high school, she taught at a Bible school and wound up getting a history degree at the University of Toledo. She and Steve married in college and settled in Toledo. Mary got a teaching degree and chose to teach at Martin Luther King Elementary, in Toledo's inner city.

Mary didn't have to teach, especially in a rough part of Toledo. For her, teaching was a calling.

"I want to make a difference in my students' lives," she said.

She celebrated her students who went to college, and she fretted over the ones who went to jail.

"I have the same expectations for all of my students," she said. "Each one is capable of doing anything. I want them all to be somebody, whether their father is a college graduate or never went to high school."

Mary invited me to volunteer in her class during the spring of my senior year, so I would leave school early and drive into inner-city Toledo. When I first saw Mary's classroom, it looked chaotic. The walls were plastered with her students' work. The children were busy at their wooden, flip-top desks, or they were reading in small groups.

"It might not look organized," Mary told me, "but I run a tight ship. I know what every child is doing. We have a routine. These kids might not have a routine at home, but they're going to get it here at school. Every child knows what's expected of them."

I worked one-on-one with the children. If a student needed extra help, Mary sent him or her to me. We read; we talked; we worked on math problems. On Valentine's Day, I showed up with a card and candy for each student.

I came away from my time at Martin Luther King with a few things: I witnessed what a great teacher could do. I thought about teaching for the first time. And I was angry that these children came every day to a school with a decrepit playground and a school building that was falling apart.

My father's words rang true, once again. I was lucky.

ONE DAY, A RUMOR raced through Maumee Valley's pristine Upper School: one of our classmates was pregnant. Faculty, parents, and students were in shock. Maumee Valley girls didn't get pregnant! Because Maumee Valley girls didn't have sex . . . or so we thought.

Every year Maumee Valley would offer scholarships to students from Robinson Junior High, a school in one of Toledo's poorest neighborhoods. Dede Barnes was on full scholarship at Maumee Valley, and she was pregnant.

Dede and I were not close, but we were acquaintances. We ran with different crowds. I was president of the student council and a very social animal. She kept to herself. We were both good students. At the same time, I was never fully part of the cool crowd, in part because I was Korean. That made me an outsider and often put me in the position of being able to glide between cliques. I became a peacemaker, a bridge.

I gathered a few of my buddies together and said, "Let's throw Dede a baby shower."

"Are you crazy?" one asked. "How would we do it? Who would come? What purpose would that serve?"

I got the same reaction from some teachers who wanted Dede's problem to quietly go away. I was determined to embrace her and let her know that we accepted her predicament. I can't say that I was bent on making a dramatic statement about race and class. I was neither reflective nor focused enough to arrive at that conclusion. But I did know how it felt to be excluded. The least we could do as a community was alleviate Dede's sense of isolation.

With friends and parents, we reserved a room at a restaurant. People arrived with gifts. We had a great time. Dede beamed.

After Dede left school to have her baby, we never saw her again on campus. We assumed that the school had not invited her back. We also assumed that Dede would become a statistic: a single, teenage mother who dropped out of school and went on welfare. It would be a tragic and cautionary tale of a promising life gone wrong.

Except it didn't.

When I arrived at Wellesley College my freshman year, whom did I run into but Dede! Not only had she made it through high school and continued to achieve, but she did so in such a way that earned her admission to one of the most prestigious colleges in the country.

Seeing Dede buck the system and defy the stereotypes and assumptions changed me. She came from one of the city's roughest neighborhoods. She had all of the odds stacked against her. But through her experience, I began to realize that environment did not determine fate. At least, it didn't *have* to.

I was lucky to be born into my situation. She was unlucky to be born into hers. Did it have to stay that way? Was her fate sealed because of her circumstance? As it turned out, school determined her future possibilities. If kids had the will and the potential, and they had the opportunity to attend schools with good teachers, they could become great successes despite the obstacles.

Dede's story confirmed what I learned from Mary Weiss—that education could make a difference in a child's life, regardless of how she comes to school.

If MY COMING-OF-AGE WAS a gradual but steady change from a shy Korean child to an independent, perhaps bossy teen, I truly left my comfort zone in Saskatchewan.

During my junior year in high school, I worked at a summer camp for kids on a Native American reservation in Canada. I had no idea what to expect. The first morning I woke up, and I couldn't find a plug for my blow-dryer. And the people were laughing at me, because we were in a trailer on the Indian reservation. "Sweetheart," one said, "there are no plugs to plug in your hair dryer. You can put that thing away for the rest of your trip!"

No hot showers, either.

It was the first time I had seen and experienced abject poverty. Children were living as they might have in the nineteenth century. It was so foreign to me.

Some of my counselor colleagues were foreigners, in fact. I got to know Manny, a German man whose specialty was clowning, so he wore different clown costumes around the reservation. Helen was a Canadian athlete who taught the kids how to play soccer. What could I teach them? I fretted until I came up with something we could do without needing too many supplies (which were in short order): origami.

Every day I set up a table and invited children to make swans that we would string up in trees, or frogs that would jump, or intricate squares we could blow up into spheres. First the young ones would take seats, then the older kids would drift over, and pretty soon I would have a full table. Teaching the kids to make these shapes taught me my first lesson about good instruction— clear instructions. When I told the kids, "Fold the paper in half," they'd do so somewhat haphazardly. That would cause the figure not to come out correctly. So I had to learn to give really specific directions about making the corners line up and monitor them as they were doing so.

I gravitated to the little ones. Every morning I would lead a small group into the meadow, where we would sit in a circle and play "Doggie, doggie—where's your bone?" One would sit in the center with his or her eyes closed; the rest would pass around a spoon behind their backs. I would call "stop," and the one in the center would have to guess who had the spoon. They never tired of the game.

After two months I truly believed that I had touched these kids and was having an impact on their lives. I thought I had formed tight bonds with them, that they loved me, that they couldn't wait until I came in the next day, and of course, that they'd miss me desperately when I left. They would remember me fondly as the woman who taught them how to make origami swans one glorious summer.

As camp came to an end, all of us counselors embarked on a weeklong canoe trip. We made our way up to a remote launching point, and then we canoed back to the reservation. We stayed in tents. When we returned from that trip, we had to spend the night at the reservation before we left the next morning for home. I walked through the reservation, hoping to have one last visit with the children on whom I had had such an impact.

"Hey!" I said to one group of kids I'd recognized.

They looked at me as if I were a stranger!

The look on their faces was "Who are you?"

After one week, they didn't remember me. What a wake-up call. Had it not been for the brief layover back on the reservation, I would have left there believing that I had made an impact on these kids' lives. But a week later, not only could they not care less about me, but they didn't even remember who I was.

The message to me was clear—little girl, this is not about you. This is about you coming and doing your little community service and feeling good afterward that you helped the poor little Indian kids. You didn't help them. Their lives suck right now. And it wasn't made any better by you, coming for a few weeks and running a summer program.

You're not even a blip on the radar in their lives. It was humbling.

I GOT MY FIRST glimpse of the importance of being humble in the workplace during my summers working at Grumpy's, a deli near the Toledo Zoo. I started in 1988, after my junior year in high school, the year that China loaned pandas to the Toledo Zoo. It was pandemonium.

Jeff Horn and his wife, Connie, owned and managed Grumpy's. Jeff named his sandwich shop as a warning for customers. If you were looking for good food, this was the place for you. If what you were searching for was a feel-good lunch spot, not so much. Jeff screamed at customers, and he wouldn't hesitate to fire employees. During the first summer I worked for him, he opened his "annex" by the zoo. He started off with about twenty employees. By the end of the summer, I was one of only two left. I did it by keeping my mouth shut and my head down, and working my butt off. Grumpy and I got along.

Jeff's mind-set when it came to employees was simple. "I have to make money, and I can't sit around and let the ineptness of minimum-wage workers make me less successful."

Translation: He would fire you in a heartbeat.

I can't tell you how many salad makers I lived through. One woman finished making a bowl of tuna salad but neglected to scrape off every ounce of tuna from the spoon. Grumpy saw her dump the spoon in the sink.

"You're fired!" he screamed.

Come in late? Don't bother coming in at all.

"You're fired!"

Bad attitude? There was room for only one of those.

Bye-bye.

My sophomore year in college, when I was nineteen, Jeff and Connie opened a Grumpy's in Port Clinton, on Lake Erie east of Toledo. They asked me to be the manager. Their daughter Jennifer ran the business on the family side. We hired sixteen teenagers, opened for the summer season, and business was good. Connie came by often to make sure all was going well.

One particularly hot day I asked four of the girls to clean out the trash cans, which were smelly and gross. One of the girls, a cute one with swagger because she was the leader of the pack, declined. Connie already didn't like her.

"What are you going to do about it?" Connie asked.

"I don't know. What *should* I do about it?" I responded.

"Fire her!" she said. "You have to send a message."

I had never fired anyone before. And I had definitely never "sent a message" to anyone. I was a little scared, but I knew I couldn't show any hesitation or weakness. I would have to follow Grumpy's lead. I did what I was told and fired her.

The girl threw a hissy fit. She looked around at the other workers. Her eyes pleaded for solidarity. There was a moment of silence. I looked around at the other girls.

"Anyone else have a problem?" I asked.

No one replied. Instead, they walked outside to clean the trash cans. They got the message, and I learned a useful lesson: firing people never feels good, but there are times when you have to show an employee the door.

I HAD HAD MY own taste of rejection.

When it came time to apply for college, my first choices were Princeton, Brown, and Harvard. I applied to all three. The responses: no, no, and no.

The only two schools that I got into were Wellesley College and University of Miami, Ohio.

My boyfriend, Adam, was going to the University of Cincinnati, which is very close to Miami, and they offered me a scholarship. I told my folks that I was going there. My parents basically said, "Abso-freakin-lutely not. You are going to Wellesley. All-girls school, we're good."

So there you had it. I was going to Wellesley. At the time I didn't fully appreciate the all-women's environment and transferred to Cornell after my freshman year. I think my parents assumed that at an Ivy League institution, where they had always dreamed of sending their kids, I would get a staid, conservative education. They were wrong.

When I got to Ithaca, New York, I was overwhelmed by the size of the school. I felt like I was getting lost and realized I had to find a niche, a community. So two friends—Heidi Moon and Jenny Hahn—and I formed RAW, short for "Radical Asian Women." We designed a little sign with a yellow fist. But I still had no idea why I would have reason to be a radical, until I took a few specific classes.

Asian American History was a shock. I had thought that Asians were the model minority, different but in some ways better than white Americans. The course taught me that Asians had faced harsh discrimination building the railroads, that many had come over as indentured servants, that Japanese and other Asians had been essentially jailed in camps during World War II. It was all new to me.

That triggered my radical Asian woman phase, in which I didn't like white people, since they were the oppressors. Call it the next stage in my breaking away from the submissive Korean woman that my mother had hoped to create. I took courses in African American history too, which deepened my sensitivity to discrimination.

I landed a work-study job with an organization called Peer Educators in Human Relations, or PEHR. It was a pretty un-usual program. Our job was to go out onto campus and conduct peer facilitations and trainings of other students in bigotry and oppression.

Before we could go out and train anybody, we had to go through the training ourselves. So I went through this life-changing set of training sessions where people got right in my face and essentially said, "Little Asian girl, let me tell you why you're always trying to make nice. Because you are scared of facing confrontation. If you want to really be who you are, you need to stop this charade of trying to make people feel good all the time. You're just fitting into the mold of what an Asian woman is supposed to do. Break the mold!"

I had yet another awakening. I vowed, "I am not doing that anymore."

I wasn't the only student going through changes. There was a group of us who went through the training: some radical black people, some really radical Latino and gay students, and then a few radical lesbians—and me.

There were a few painful moments. I used to do things like say the word *chicks*, and the lesbians in the group would just rip into me. "We are *not* weak, little, helpless, cute animals. We're *women*!" they'd yell. And I'd say, "I got it, I got it. Sorry!"

But Inza Rhee's good little Asian girl still had her place. During the day I was the radical student, but at night I would work at a Japanese restaurant. I'd put on this kimono and be the nice, cute, subservient Asian woman so that I could get a lot of tips. The owner came up to me one night and said, "I've got to tell you, in eighteen years of running this restaurant, you are the best waitress I ever had!" I played the part well.

As I completed my senior year at Cornell and prepared to graduate, I imagine my classmates saw me as an enigma—with good reason.

I had cultivated my radical side. And by the time I had taken more courses in the history of oppression, I had the substance to support my innate rebelliousness. At a rally for gay pride, I was in the crowd when one of the speakers asked if anyone had something to say. I surprised myself by taking the microphone and telling Asian gays to come out of their shells and free themselves from the bonds of their upbringing. It was time, I said, to speak out, for ourselves and other oppressed people.

But I was also a sorority girl, albeit not a very good one. I was a member of Kappa Alpha Theta, the nice girls' sorority.

And I was the perfect, subservient, demure Asian waitress at night—because I needed cash.

An enigma to some, perhaps, but I didn't feel a tension within. The radical and the practical never seemed an odd combination to me. They were different parts of my personality. Somehow they would come together—in the classroom.

2

The Heart of Teaching

I t was a blessing in disguise. I had been called down to an administrative meeting for one of my special-needs students. Usually teachers abhorred these bureaucratic meetings, and I certainly didn't relish them, but I needed a break. Day in and day out, I struggled with my students. It seemed like it didn't matter what I said or did. . . . Nothing worked with my kids. They simply wouldn't listen. I would routinely spend the day alternating between screaming at the children, bribing them, and giving them the silent treatment for their misdeeds. None of it worked.

So when the office called me down for the meeting over the intercom and sent the librarian in to cover my class, in all honesty I almost did a little jig. "A break!" I thought, and I grabbed my folders. As I was getting organized, the librarian walked in. The kids were going nuts as usual, and she raised her eyebrow as she cased the joint. Her mere presence caused the children to calm a bit.

"Unfortunately, I have to go to this special education meeting," I explained. "I shouldn't be more than an hour. Thank you so much for doing this."

"No problem," she answered back, cracking her gum. "Take your time. We'll be just fine."

"I'm not sure if you've heard or not," I half whispered, "but my kids are kind of difficult. They can get unruly."

"Oh, don't worry about that. These children know who I am. And they know I don't play that," she replied.

"Yeah, right," I thought. "You don't know my kids."

I scurried through the door and down the stairwell into the meeting room. After approximately sixty mind-numbing yet strangely joyful minutes, the meeting was over, and I headed back to my room. I walked slowly, steeling myself for reentry. When I got a few feet away from my classroom door, I paused. Oddly, there was no noise coming from the room. No screaming, no yelling, no crashes.

"Did she take them outside?" I wondered.

I walked into the room and was startled to see my entire class hard at work. They were copying down on their paper sentences that the librarian had written on the board. The librarian was sitting at my desk, leafing through a pamphlet, cracking her gum.

"Uh . . . how were they?" I asked, with some trepidation.

"Oh, they were great. Just great. Weren't you, children?" she asked.

"Yes, Ms. Blackwell," they singsonged in unison.

Ms. Blackwell picked up her purse and headed out the door. She hadn't even crossed through the door when my kids started up again. They were yelling at each other, hitting one another, and throwing things across the room in record time.

"Wait a minute!" I screamed at the top of my lungs.

Interestingly, the children ceased fire long enough to hear my plea.

"Can someone please explain to me why it is that you can behave like that for Ms. Blackwell but you can't do that for me?" I asked.

Anthony, one of my chief mischief makers, stood up. "It's because she knows what she's doing," he said matter-of-factly. And then turned to his neighbor to resume their arm-wrestling match.

. . . .

THE WINTER BEFORE I graduated from Cornell, while at home during break, I had a rare day off from serving sandwiches at Grumpy's and decided to relax at home. I grabbed a Snapple and a bag of Doritos, switched on the TV in the family room, and became one with the couch.

We had four channels in those days, and my parents must have been watching the Public Broadcasting Service station, so that's what came on as I relaxed. The little screen showed scenes from a school where young people my age were teaching. It turned out to be a documentary on a brand-new outfit called Teach For America. That it even caught my eye was pure luck.

One of the first scenes showed a principal taking a young guy out into the hallway.

"You're not very good at this," she told him. "Maybe you're not cut out for teaching. I'm afraid I have to fire you."

But what really got my attention was the next scene: It showed a young Korean guy teaching science to a class of mostly African American students. He was conducting an experiment where he poured water into a tube half filled with sand and rocks. The rocks settled to the bottom first, demonstrating how heavier material settled.

"He's really good," I thought to myself. "Here's this nerdy Korean guy rocking it in the classroom. I figured he'd be the one getting fired."

Back at Cornell, I started to see posters for TFA information sessions. They showed a young African American guy teaching kids. It asked: "How Can I Afford Not To Make This Work?"

That touched my twenty-one-year-old soul. It took me back to my days volunteering in Mary Weiss's classroom. It spoke to my father's constant advice that we give back to the community. Perhaps I could put my newfound social consciousness to the test in the classroom. I loved being around children. I decided to give TFA a shot.

"Oh," said my friend Jenny Kim. "That's kinda weird, isn't it?" She was being the good Korean girl, heading to med school. Many of the friends I had taken Japanese language classes with were going to Japan to take jobs in the private sector. They had taken that class with that end in mind. Their response to TFA: "Hmm."

Missy, my college roommate, was the most supportive of the idea. "You should absolutely do it," she said. A couple of my do-gooder friends were applying to TFA, too. So I signed up for an interview and prepared to compete for a job.

I had to design a lesson that I would teach to the other interviewees and TFA staff, who would listen and grade my skills. I chose to teach a lesson in how to say "Hello" in Japanese, which isn't that simple, since there are two forms of speech: formal and informal. I launched into the lesson by using two of the students interviewing with me as subjects. Even then I had a knack for hooking in the class. I held their attention, made them repeat the phrase in various ways, and came away feeling pretty good.

The second part of the application process didn't go so well. I had a one-on-one interview with a TFA staffer named Regina Sullivan. I left the interview thinking she didn't like me. We just didn't hit it off.

"I'm not going to get that job," I told my roommate.

I started reviewing my graduate school options when . . . to my surprise, the acceptance letter arrived from TFA.

Inza was surprised, too.

"Are you crazy?" she asked. "We didn't send you to an Ivy League college so you could become a teacher! This is absolutely unacceptable. There is no way that we will allow you to do this!"

I couldn't believe it. I looked toward my dad plaintively. He had always been my champion, and he was much more civic-minded than my mother. My mother and I both held our breath as we waited for him to weigh in. He thought for a few minutes with a pensive look on his face. Finally, he spoke.

"This would be a good thing for you to do. Give it a try," Shang said.

"*Yuh-Bo!*" my mother shrieked, hurling "honey" in Korean as an epithet. They left the room, and I could hear them going at it. Shang returned.

"She's going," my father declared. And that was that. My father had spoken, and his word was the last.

The problem was, I was ambivalent, too. I am not much of a planner. I never knew what I wanted to do from one stage in life to another. I always admired people who, from when they were very little, knew they wanted to be a doctor or a writer or a teacher. That has never been me. When I was in high school I didn't know where I wanted to go to college. When I was in college I didn't know what I wanted to do after graduation. But I knew that I liked working with children, I believed that public education was important, and I figured this would buy me some time. I accepted the job.

AFTER A QUICK BREAK at home in Toledo for two weeks, I boarded a plane from Detroit to Los Angeles, where I would spend the rest of the summer training to be a teacher—kind of.

I remember getting off the plane and seeing people with TFA signs. We were funneled onto buses. I got into one of the front seats and stared straight ahead. Behind me the bus was packed with white kids flirting and yammering. I rolled my eyes and thought, "Good Lord, this is like summer camp."

We arrived at California State University's campus at Northridge, where TFA held its summer institute. At the dorm I lugged my bag into a two-bedroom "pod" with a common room. No one was there, but one bed had bags and stuff on it. It looked to me, based on the pictures on her desk, like it belonged to a preppy white kid, so I moved my things into the other bedroom. My eventual roommate, Deepa Purohit, turned out to have come from Cleveland, and we even had a few friends in common. The white girl was Liz Peterson, a true California girl from Long Beach. She roomed with Rosemary Ricci, who was from outside of Philadelphia. Within a few days together, I had thrown my juvenile biases aside, the four of us grew very close, and Liz Peterson became one of my best friends.

We were in TFA's third cohort, and the program was still evolving. It was neither efficient nor particularly effective. We woke up every day at 5 a.m., boarded buses, and rode for hours through traffic to Pasadena. We did practice teaching for a half day and then returned to Northridge for more training and seminars. I'm not sure I learned much that summer, and I didn't feel prepared for what was to come. If you put five hundred recent college graduates back in dorms for the summer, what you get is indeed summer camp. It was a scene. Sure, it was grueling, and we did get exposed to the classroom, but we mostly had a lot of fun.

At the end of the institute, we started to get our teaching assignments. Liz, Rose, Deepa, and I were all detailed to Baltimore, so we headed east and found a house together. One by one each TFA corps member was offered a position in a school and prepared for beginning the school year with their class. I waited. And waited. Baltimore was not a city where I especially wanted to wind up. Still, I was a bit disappointed and worried when everyone got a job but me. Even two days before school started, I had yet to be hired. I figured it was mostly because I was Korean. Korean-black dynamics have always been a bit strained. If you are the African American principal in hard-core Baltimore, you are not thinking, "Yeah, that Korean girl is the one I want to hire. Let me take her!"

The day before orientation for the school year, a woman from the central office called and said, "Well, you still haven't been placed as a teacher. But you have to go someplace, since we are paying you. So go to this address: 1401 West Lafayette Avenue. The school is Harlem Park. They will be waiting for you."

They weren't.

I WILL NEVER FORGET pulling up in front of Harlem Park. The school was in the middle of a very downtrodden, dangerous neighborhood. It looked large and impenetrable from the outside. Bars on dingy windows. Trash blowing up against chain-link fences. I was terrified. I found my way to the office and told them I was reporting there until I was assigned to a teaching position. They had no idea who I was or why I was there, so I sat for an hour in the ninety-degree heat in the waiting area. I must have looked pretty pathetic and bedraggled when a teacher walked in the office and took pity on me.

"Well hello there," she said. "What brings you to Harlem Park?"

It was Everlyn Strother, a Harlem Park veteran and one of the school's best teachers. I said I was waiting to be assigned to a school and that the central office had sent me here.

"C'mon, c'mon, come with me to my room. Follow me, baby," she said.

Her room was a model of organization and preparation. She sat me down and started moving around books, setting up workstations, and making sure posters were secured to the walls. As she did her thing, she asked me about my training and what I hoped to accomplish. And why I was so scared.

"Look, baby, you gotta know what you're getting into here,"

she said. "You can't look as scared as you do now. You have to be confident. I remember being in your shoes when I first started teaching. I was just as scared. Be patient. Hang in there. Remember, they're children. And come to me if you need help."

Hmmm. Just like my grandmother said, "Little kids. How hard can that be?"

The principal finally swept through and motioned me to her office. I tried explaining the situation to her, that I wouldn't be there long—only until the central office found a school for me. After my long-winded speech she looked a little exasperated.

"Second or fifth?" she asked.

"Excuse me?" I responded.

"I have two openings. Second grade or fifth grade. Which one do you want?"

I quickly had to switch gears.

"This summer I student-taught in a second-grade classroom in Los Angeles," I said. "I was pretty effective with the students and thought they responded well to me, so I think second grade is probably better."

"Fine," she said, looking wholly unimpressed and uninterested in my rationale. "Second it is."

The truth was, of course, I was worried and figured second graders were a lot smaller and younger than fifth graders, so I stood a better chance.

Harlem Park was a huge school and had four second-grade classes. They assigned students to different classes according to their academics and behavior, a practice called tracking. It was a rite of passage that the new teachers were assigned to the students on the lowest track. Therefore, I was assigned second grade, track four: the students with both the lowest achievement and the highest discipline problems. They had been together since kindergarten. And there were thirty-six of them in the class.

The classroom was worse than dingy. The windows were

protected on the outside by black steel grates. The windows were so dirty and yellowed that light barely came through. But at first things went relatively well. I had my kids sitting in nine clusters of four desks each to foster cooperative learning, a popular strategy at the time. Over the course of the first few weeks I came up with fun and engaging lessons, and the children seemed to respond well.

There was only one problem. All classrooms at Harlem Park were assigned a teacher's aide. Mine was a gruff woman who clearly had seen her fair share of young teachers pass through. Too intimidated to give her any direction, I pretty much let her do her own thing. Or maybe I should say, she just did her own thing. She'd come and go as she pleased, sit in the back of the room, cut out letters, or do other things she felt were appropriate.

The other thing she did was yell at the kids. I remember teaching a lesson where I read the book *Caps for Sale*. As I read the book and chanted the refrain, "Caps! Caps for sale . . . fifty cents a caaaaaap!" the kids started to join me, singing at the top of their lungs. The aide thought the children were being much too loud.

"Stop that silliness!" she screamed at the children.

I was shocked and chagrined at the same time, but mostly I was a new teacher who didn't know how to react. I thought it was great that the children were so engaged. Why squelch a student? That could ruin their enthusiasm for learning! Call me clueless. But I didn't have to worry about my aide for long.

Kurt Schmoke—a dynamic, young African American leader—was starting his second term as Baltimore mayor. He devoted himself to reforming his city's dismal public schools. The summer before I started teaching, Schmoke contracted with Education Alternatives, a consulting company, to take over some of the city's worst-performing schools. Harlem Park was among them. The company fired the aides from these schools because they didn't have college degrees. My new aide was an older white guy, very tall, dumpy, tousled hair, brushy mustache, square-framed glasses, and generally unkempt. He looked like he was at least seventy. He did not belong at Harlem Park, in the ghetto, trying to connect with second graders. Not only did he not make my life easier; he made it harder. He became a target for the kids. They threw stuff at him. They made fun of him. I lost absolute control of the class when my first aide left. While I'd initially thought she was a problem, I quickly came to realize that she was the only reason my classroom was under control.

My once-angelic students, who I worried might have their enthusiasm crushed by a harsh word, were all of a sudden spewing harsh words of their own. "Punk-ass bitch!" they'd call out to one another, as they threw pencils and books at one another. Or worse, "Screw you, Chinese bitch!" they would yell at me. Once they realized that the aide was gone and I had no classroom-management skills, the kids took over.

It was unlike anything I'd ever experienced. I remember walking down the steps to the cafeteria one day when one of the kids tripped and fell. Every kid who passed him kicked him, like it was a natural thing. I ran back up the stairs and said, "What are you people doing? This is crazy! Stop it!"

As I dropped the students off at lunch in the cafeteria one day, two boys started to fight. One kid had the other in a choke hold. The eyes of the kid being held were bulging out. It looked as if his blood vessels were going to pop. He was about to pass out.

"Stop!" I yelled. I tried to jam my hip between them to get some leverage to pull them apart. I couldn't imagine the level of violence eight-year-old kids were capable of.

I was helpless: I had zero respect from the kids and zero ability to strike fear into their hearts. How could I win back something I never had? What could I use as a threat? That I would tell on them to their moms? That they would get bad grades? That I would send them to the principal? They feared none of those things.

My class was infamous at a school that had experienced its

share of violence and misbehavior. The kids would walk down the hallways and rap on doors and push around younger kids.

"That's Rhee's class," the other teachers would say, with palpable distaste.

I have gone through some difficult and painful times in my life, but nothing compares to my first year as a teacher. It was the hardest time of my life, period.

Back at our home on East Baltimore Street, my friends and I commiserated and compared notes on the trials of teaching for the first time. Liz, Deepa, and Rose all had been assigned to tough inner-city schools. But Harlem Park was a special case, the worst case. My friends had more supplies, smaller classes, and better support from the administration and parents. It was a pretty well-established fact within TFA that my assignment was extremely difficult. Doubts began to creep into our conversations. We started to voice the dark side of young, idealistic college grads faced with the reality of attempting to engage and teach disadvantaged students for six and a half hours a day.

"There's nothing I can do," I remember saying after one particularly rough day of being screamed at. "I am a well-meaning person. I work my butt off. I care about my students and their futures. But it doesn't matter."

As HARD AS IT was to take the daily frustrations and feelings of helplessness, the hardest thing was coming to the realization that, in fact, I was the problem. This became abundantly clear to me with the transformation of Tameka Tagg.

Tameka was a teeny little girl; she was also one of the main rabble-rousers in my class. She interrupted lessons and instigated trouble for the entire class. She drove me crazy. After one particularly difficult morning, I gave up and sent her to another classroom. The teacher was Bertha Haywood, a thirty-year veteran and a great teacher. She also had top-tier students. Whenever I peered into her class and saw all of her children paying rapt attention to her, I assumed it was because she had the highest-performing and best-behaved class. As it turns out, that wasn't the case.

When I walked down the hall later in the day to pick up Tameka, I stopped and looked through the little window in the door to Bertha's classroom. And there was Tameka Tagg, sitting with her hands folded, raising her hand to answer questions, smiling and keeping quiet.

And it struck me at that point: It's not her—it's me. It's not just about kids who come to school hungry, from families who don't care about education, through streets with a gauntlet of drug dealers. I was creating the kind of environment where they could act up and be crazy, but if they were in a different environment with a different teacher, they could be calm and learn. It was me!

This point was driven home by mentors from the University of Maryland, Baltimore County, who came to observe my class as part of our certification program. Two of the faculty pulled me aside after one class.

"You should think about changing your profession," they said. "This classroom is not safe for the children. This environment is not good for them. They are not learning anything."

WHEN I WENT HOME for Christmas during my first year as a teacher, my mother took one look at me and said, "You don't look so good."

I had developed a condition—when I scratched myself these huge, crazy red welts appeared. My roommates affectionately referred to it as "the Itch." My mom saw them and said, "There is something seriously wrong with you! This is *not* normal."

She took me to the doctor.

"Is there any stress in your life?" he asked. "Usually these symptoms are a sign of extreme anxiety and pressure. You should avoid that to the extent possible."

"Are you kidding me? My entire life is stressful," I answered.

On the way home from the doctor's office, my mother said quietly, "Don't go back. Stay here. You weren't supposed to be a teacher anyway. You went to an Ivy League school. Cornell, for goodness' sake! Apply for law school in the fall and just stay with us. You'll be fine."

Sounded good to me. Law school rather than Harlem Park? Why not?

The way I rationalized it in my head was that my kids were not better off with me in the classroom. I told myself I wasn't quitting because I couldn't handle it; I was quitting for the good of the children.

Besides, word through the first-year TFA corps was that teachers dropped out on a regular basis. Some lasted a few weeks, some a semester, many left after the first year. Maybe I just wasn't cut out to be a teacher. I started warming to the idea.

"No, lady," my dad said as I was explaining my change of course. "You are going back. Pack your bags."

I tried to protest. But as always, my dad's word was the last. Shang packed my bags, loaded them into the car, and sent me on my way.

WELTS AND ALL, I returned to Baltimore an obsessed lady.

My new strategy was to throw spaghetti against the wall, hoping something would stick. I tried everything. I changed seating configurations. I tried every discipline system in the book. If one system didn't work, I'd introduce another a few days later. The constant changes weren't good for the kids, but I was a woman possessed. I was bent on figuring out a way to be successful.

Eventually I found a seating arrangement that actually worked.

Instead of having kids sit at tables, I had them sit in a big U so that I could see what everybody was doing at all times. I could put the troublemakers in the middle, too.

Harlem Park had some excellent teachers. Their students walked through the halls in quiet, straight lines. Their kids did their homework. They were quiet in class. Bertha Haywood, who had taken Tameka Tagg into her classroom for an afternoon, was perhaps the best teacher in the school. I was reluctant to bother the veteran teachers, but one day I stopped into Ms. Haywood's classroom after school.

"Okay," I said. "I just don't understand that child. Tameka was wreaking havoc in my class all morning. She spends a few hours in your class, and she's an angel. She returns to my room, and she's making the class nuts again. What's your secret?"

"No secret," she said. "The first thing you have to do is establish your authority. You're the boss. They need to know that. Next, you have to keep things interesting for the kids. A classroom should be exciting for students. Every day I have one surprise planned for class that I know the children will enjoy. It keeps them engaged and motivated. They expect something fresh every day."

"Like what?"

"Take today," she said. "We made finger puppets. These children had never made finger puppets before. We made them to mimic characters in the book we were reading. They were totally engaged—in making the puppets and acting out the scenes in the book. And now they can take the puppets home with them. It's something they never would have anticipated."

I was in awe. Ms. Haywood had been teaching for thirty years, and yet each night she was up trying to figure out new ways to make her kids excited about her lessons. Amazing.

That night I went home, sat in front of the TV, and made pizzas out of yellow and red paper: yellow for cheese and red for sauce.

Brown paper in the shape of mushrooms and little green squares to look like green peppers. I was doing a lesson on fractions, and I wanted to surprise the kids with paper pizzas they could place into halves and quarters. Roger Schulman, another TFA teacher, came over to watch TV with us.

"What on God's green earth are you doing?" he asked.

I explained.

"You are insane," he said. "For one lesson, you are making thirty-six individual pizzas? Each with individually crafted pepperoni and olives? Have you lost your mind?"

"Yup," I said. "Every student gets a pizza."

I had taken Bertha Haywood's words to heart. The next day was my first truly calm day in the classroom. The kids were fascinated and delighted with the pizzas. And they started to understand fractions.

When it came to discipline, I set up a simple rewards system. I had two chalkboards. The larger one I would use for lessons, and on the smaller one I would put the students' names—not when they were bad, but when they were good. And if they did something good, I would put a star next to their name; if you did something bad, I would erase the star. For the kids I knew were troublemakers, I would have to put their names on the board as soon as they walked in.

"Oh, thank you for putting your jacket up!" Quickly put their name on the board.

Now they had something to lose. If there was nothing to take away, then it wouldn't work, right?

And then I set up a whole economy, where at the end of the day I gave tickets for the number of stars that the kids got during the day. At the end of the week students could trade their tickets in for candy or stickers or erasers or toys.

Finally, Rhee's class was no longer wild. Well, less wild, at least.

. . . .

FROM EARLY IN THE school year, Rhoda Jones, the assistant principal, was sure I was going to quit. She saw me struggling to maintain order. She saw that frightened look in my eyes. I guess she marked me down as a lost cause and didn't bother to offer much help.

One day when I was at school late, planning, I snuck into the supply closet to look for some construction paper. Teachers were not permitted in there. Rhoda Jones saw the door ajar.

"What do you think you're doing?" she asked.

Busted.

I apologized and explained I needed the paper for a project I was planning for the kids.

"Next time, ask," she said.

I walked away, downcast.

"Hold on," she said, handing me a package of construction paper. "I see you here after school every day working on lesson plans. You are here before I arrive in the morning, too. I can tell you are trying hard, and you have lasted far longer than I had expected, to be honest. But, child, you need help."

"Tell me about it," I said.

"You spend all your time here inside the school building," she said. "You have to let our children know you are part of the community. You can't be afraid of going to their houses. Show up at their door. Let their parents know what their kids are doing in your classroom. Make yourself a real part of their lives."

The next day Craig Washington refused to stop talking during our math lesson and pinching the girl in front of him.

"Keep it up," I said, "and I am going to walk you home after school. Let's see what your mother has to say about how you behave in our class."

He laughed and kept cutting up. I guess he figured it was another one of my empty threats.

When school let out I found Craig, tapped him on the shoulder, grabbed his hand, and said, "Let's go, son," just like I imagined Rhoda Jones would.

We started walking. Much as he tried to maneuver out of my grasp, I kept his hand in mine. His buddies along the way stopped and watched.

"Hey," one said, "there goes Craig with his teacher. She has to hold his hand. Little boy needs to have his hand held!"

Craig was pained the entire walk home. I, however, took pleasure in the taunting, hoping it might dissuade Craig from taking actions that would warrant further hand-holding. "I ain't no little boy!" he argued back to his friends. "I don't even know who this crazy lady *is*!"

It was a long way to Craig's house. He lived out of the neighborhood. Sweating profusely, I knocked on the door. His mother answered. I explained that her son had been acting out in class and making it hard for me to teach.

"He's ruining it for the rest of the students," I said.

"Don't worry, Ms. Rhee," she said. "I'll get on him. Trust me, this won't happen again. Right, Craig?"

"Yes, ma'am," Craig replied.

And it didn't.

I visited more homes. In some I met with parents willing to help. Others were too surprised to comment, and a few wouldn't even open their doors. But I came away from each visit with a better understanding of my students and what they were up against. I adjusted my teaching accordingly.

Once word started to get around that Ms. Rhee was out in the neighborhood, and that I was often the first one in the parking lot and the last car out, even the drug dealers and the older kids who hung out on the corners and stoops started to take notice. I tended to park on the street, rather than in the teachers' lot. One evening I left school just before dark and walked to my car. I passed a few men sitting on a stoop.

"Hey, Ms. Rhee," one of them said. "Don't worry. We're looking out for your car."

I smiled and wondered how they knew my name.

At the end of April, when the monitors from the University of Maryland, Baltimore County, came back to my classroom, they said, "These kids are actually learning something. This is not a great classroom yet, but you have definitely turned it around."

After the doubts and the welts, I was relieved. I had never failed at anything. For me, quitting was failure. I understood how difficult and depressing teaching could be, but I also caught a glimpse of its rewards.

DURING THE SUMMER AFTER my first year, I didn't work another job. Liz, Deepa, and Rose were driving cross-country to California. I chose not to join them. I spent all summer preparing to teach again.

A few of my aunts were visiting from Korea, so I put them to work cutting out shapes for my students. It was a little sweatshop of Korean ladies. They gabbed and gossiped and made bags of shapes that I could use to teach math.

At Harlem Park we didn't have a lot of books, so I went to my dad's medical office every day and photocopied books. I made lesson plans. I kept Bertha Haywood's advice in mind and tried to come up with surprise lessons. And then in August, I shoved everything in my car—the photocopies and the bags of shapes— and drove back to Baltimore for my second year.

I arrived early to set my whole room up. I was big into colors and making the room super exciting. And so I had made all these posters with bright colors, and I set up beanbag chairs so it was the kind of place you would want to come into. It was a place of learning and fun and surprises.

I had changed, as well. My new students would see a different Ms. Rhee. This time around, Ms. Rhee was not going to play. When I met my students for the first time, I wore my game face. No smiles, no joy; I was all thin lips and flinty glares. I made them line up and walk in and out of class.

"Nope," I said. "Not good enough. Try again."

They lined up in the hall again and walked into the classroom.

"Again," I said. Four times.

My mistake the first year was trying to be warm and friendly with the students, thinking that my kids needed only love and compassion. What I knew going into my second year is that what my children needed and craved was rigid structure, certainty, and stability, as well.

OVER THE SUMMER I had taken some time to attend a professional development seminar set up by the educational consultants who had taken over the school. It was about how to teach math to kids. I am not mathematically inclined, so I thought it would be interesting but not very useful. But that professional development wound up changing my life.

I believe that if you give engaged, motivated people a kernel of crucial information, they'll take the kernel and grow it into something ten times more valuable. But you've got to give them something. That summer math course became my kernel. I learned how to teach Calendar Math, a system that launched a whole array of teaching tools and activities based on the numerical day of the week. The kids took it from there. They soaked it up.

Every day we did an exercise called Incredible Equations. We would take the number of the date (8 if it was March 8) and the kids would have to come up with different equations that equaled 8. At first, they'd come up with simple ones, like 4 + 4 or 8 + 0, but then some of them would get creative.

"One hundred minus ninety-two," they'd say.

I would respond: "Great! You know what? There is another way to write one hundred, and that is ten times ten." So I didn't teach them the concept around multiplication; I just showed them another way to write 100, and they latched on to that. And then I taught them to put a parenthesis around it and subtract 92, which gets you 8. Which is algebra. And so they just picked up on these things very naturally. Then we learned that 10 x 10 x 10 is 10-cubed, and we went on from there.

Year two was my first successful year in the classroom.

THAT SECOND YEAR, WHEN I relied on Calendar Math, the teachers in our grade decided to do something a little different. We each wanted to be able to focus on a smaller number of subjects so we could really concentrate on becoming an expert in that arena. I had teamed up with Michele Jacobs, a first-year teacher, who would also teach math while the other two teachers taught language arts. Michele had graduated from Morgan State, where she had played basketball. She stood about six two and cut a commanding figure, so the students didn't mess with her. For me, she brought a sense of humor and enthusiasm and became a kindred spirit in the belief that all kids could achieve. We hit it off and coordinated all of our lesson planning.

The following year, my third, Michele and I teamed up again. We decided to go one step further and bring seventy kids together into one classroom. Instead of trading classes back and forth, we were all going to be in the same space with two teachers. We also had two wonderful "interns," Deonne Medley and Andrea Derrien, who worked alongside us very effectively.

We ran our entire classroom using a different model. We evaluated each student's progress academically, since we had some advanced kids and some kids who were really far behind. We tailored lessons for every single student. It was part of the Education Alternatives Inc. model that we were supposed to be implementing. We did everything in small groups. We set up this system and bought seventy Tupperware tubs, one for each student. The kids filled the tubs with their notebooks, pencils, books, and other supplies, then slid them under their chairs. They moved from station to station with their tubs. I would set an egg timer. Ten minutes . . . boom. Once the students heard the egg timer go off, they knew they had thirty seconds to grab their tubs and go to the next station.

Each station had a table, and the group of tables was arrayed in an oval in the large classroom. Each table had ten chairs. One station was devoted to journal writing. Every Monday, they would respond to the journal prompt. That night, Michele and I would read the drafts and correct every paper, and the next day return it to the student for a rewrite. It was immediate and time-intensive for us—no chance to slack off if we weren't feeling like correcting seventy papers—but it worked. The children understood and followed the writing process and became good little authors.

At the listening station, students could hear chapters of books they were reading. Michele would follow at another station where the students would read from their assigned books, and she would instruct them in specific reading skills. At another, I would use flash cards to teach phonics.

It ran like clockwork. Students who were way behind made quick progress; decent readers got better. Even after just the first semester, every student was reading at a higher level, and by the end of the year, they were far ahead of their peers.

I had added reading to math in my instructional expertise the summer after my second year. The folks at Teach For America had gotten wind of my success at Harlem Park, and they invited me to be an instructor for new corps members in Texas. While I was in Houston, I met Kevin Huffman, who gave me pointers on reading. He also won my head and heart. We started dating and knew from early on that we would get married. Kevin taught me how to teach reading through a program called Direct Instruction. I photocopied all of his materials, brought them back to Baltimore, and put them to use. I created small, flexible groups. If a student was in one group and started doing really well, he could move up to another group. Things were very fluid. That's how we did everything; we were able to tailor instruction for each student. Some were learning how to spell *rat*; some were knocking out *meticulous*. Some could read picture books, and others could read *James and the Giant Peach*, by Roald Dahl.

It worked. We could see improvement immediately.

EDUCATION ALTERNATIVES INC., THE private education company Mayor Kurt Schmoke had brought in to improve Harlem Park, offered seminars on new teaching tools it had developed. Because I attended some of the seminars and used a few of their methods, which most of the veteran teachers scoffed at, I became a poster child.

When word got around that I was having success, Education Alternative executives started showing up to observe my classes. They liked what they saw and asked if I would accompany them to speak with teachers at public schools on the East Coast about their model. Why not? We gave presentations in Hartford, Connecticut, where Education Alternatives was trying to contract with the public schools. The presentations went well. Then we traveled to Washington, D.C., for a community meeting with teachers.

I remember pulling up to Clark Elementary School, a low-slung building on Kansas Avenue in a middle-class, African American neighborhood. The parking lot was jammed. The auditorium was filled, mostly with teachers. The Washington Teachers' Union had packed the hall. Jimmie Jackson, union president at the time, had primed her teachers to pounce.

When I got up to describe how I had used the math tools to improve my students' skills, Jackson stood up and accused me of buying into the profiteers' propaganda and ploy to try to take over the schools.

I was a bit shocked. I had seen a fair amount of pushback from some of my colleagues at Harlem Park. But the level of animosity directed at me seemed over-the-top.

I continued to talk about lesson plans and new tools for teaching.

"Whore!" someone yelled from the audience.

"Okay," I thought—"that's a first." I finished my presentation and sat down. I was uncomfortable. The rudeness and flat-out verbal violence were shocking, but it didn't seem endemic of the teachers union. I attributed it to rigid bureaucracy—to old-school people who were resistant to change.

WHEN MY CLASS BEHAVED well for an entire week, I would often reward a group of students with a trip to another Baltimore neighborhood. Some of my students rarely ventured more than ten blocks from their homes, so this was always a treat. We would go to Chuck E. Cheese's for lunch or spend a Saturday afternoon at National Harbor. Early in my third year, I got the bright idea to take the class on a real trip.

"Who's been on an airplane?" I asked the class.

We were reading a book about the Wright brothers and early air travel at the time. Not one hand went up.

"Really?" I asked. "No one in this class has been on an airplane? Okay! Who *wants* to go on an airplane?"

There was a buzz in the room. "No way!" some said. "We could fall out of the sky!" "I'm too scared!" said others. "YEEE-AAAAAAH!" screamed some of the boys.

Eventually, every hand shot up.

Southwest Airlines was just starting up in Baltimore at the time, and they were advertising round-trip flights from Baltimore to Cleveland for forty-nine dollars each way. Cleveland is not far from Toledo. I thought, "Why not raise funds and take the whole class there?"

Our class held raffles and sponsored carnivals and put on bake sales. I convinced Education Alternatives to front a few thousand dollars for the airline tickets. My father's doctor friends agreed to sponsor students. We planned a three-day trip for the third grade. We bought plane tickets, rented hotel rooms, and organized ferry rides. The kids were excited out of their minds. And scared.

Some of the parents were scared, too, at first. "You're not taking my baby on a plane," one mom said to me. But most relented, and quite a few said, "I'm coming with you." So we had plenty of chaperones, but the trip required much coaxing and explaining.

The kids knew I was from Ohio. "How are we going to talk with the people out there?" one student asked. "We don't speak Ohio."

I laughed. Since I was Korean, they had assumed Ohio was full of Koreans who looked like me and spoke a different language. I set them straight about that. And off we went: about ninety-five students out of a class of 110, and nearly twenty chaperones, mostly parents and a few teachers. We went to the Cleveland Metroparks Zoo, ate all we wanted at the Old Country Buffet, went to see a movie, and spent an afternoon at the Children's Museum of Cleveland. We had a blast. By the last day everyone was exhausted.

My parents had driven from Toledo to see us in action and come along on some of our adventures. I remember walking into my parents' motel room Sunday morning. Inza and Shang were asleep—with one of my students dead asleep between them.

Everlyn Strother, the teacher who swept me into her room my first day at Harlem Park, came along as a chaperone.

"I knew you had the potential to be all right," she said. "But this—this was something else."

By the end of my time at Harlem Park, my kids who had been with me for the second and third year were soaring. I would have put them up against kids from any private school in Baltimore. One student's mother was dying of AIDS. Another student had been sexually abused by multiple men over many years, and now she was living with her drunk grandmother, who neglected her. More than a few came to school hungry. These were children who had life stories that I couldn't even imagine. Despite all that they came to school every day. They'd come early, and stay late. They came on the weekends. They worked hard. They fought through all the noise and the people telling them, "Don't do what that Chinese lady is telling you to—come out and play instead." They'd do their two hours of homework. And they went from being at the bottom to being at the top academically.

It was then that the light went on for me: I realized that their low academic achievement levels weren't about their potential or their ability or anything else. It had to do with what I was doing as a teacher, what we were doing as a school, and the expectations that we set for them. That's what it was all about.

The parents understood. When I was a first-year teacher, the savviest parents took their kids out of my classroom. They knew my classroom was out of control. But by the end of my third year, the parents were requesting their kids be assigned to my class. When word got out that I might be leaving Harlem Park, many said, "You can't leave. My baby is coming into the third grade. You *have* to teach her."

I GOT SERIOUS ABOUT leaving Harlem Park in the winter of my third year.

I was happy and doing well as a teacher. My principal, Linda Carter, recognized our success and appreciated our work. Wyatt Coger, principal of the entire Harlem Park campus, which included a middle school, offered me the chance to become a lead teacher. I could stay and improve outcomes for students, one class at a time.

But I was unsettled by much of what I had experienced at Harlem Park. I was outraged at the condition of the school, the low expectations for the students, and the poor quality of education in some of the classrooms. On one hand, I was happy that I was able to make progress with my students, but I wondered, "Why isn't this happening everywhere?"

I also started researching urban schools nationwide, and what I found disturbed me even more. There were Harlem Parks in every city across the country. Generations of children were getting shortchanged. I could not stand for that.

I started considering graduate school. I wrestled with the decision and applied to several law schools and, on a whim, Harvard's Kennedy School of Government. I knew I could stay in Baltimore and have an impact on this group of kids, but I began to believe that public policy had to change: how we run schools and select our teachers, how we train them, how they relate to the students—so much had to change for all kids who look like my kids to have an equal shake in life.

The Kennedy School admitted me, and I decided to accept. I knew I wanted to have a broader impact on education reform and policy. I also was terribly sad, especially during and after the Cleveland trip. I had gotten to know the kids and their parents better. It focused me on how much the kids deserved and how they could blossom, if they were given a chance.

I had no idea what the Kennedy School would bring, but I came away from Harlem Park with a combination of rage at the broken system and belief in every child's ability to learn—with a great teacher.

3

Recruiting Teachers

I figured I had complied with my mother's wishes—twice—when I earned degrees from Cornell and Harvard. But when I described my plans to start a business that would supply teachers to public schools, Inza was not impressed.

"What do you know about starting a company?" she asked. "Why would someone think you could do that?"

Many American mothers today would see this line of questioning as hurtful, certainly not confidence building. Not so with Inza. She was a pragmatist. She asked the questions that other people were thinking but were too polite to ask. Rather than cheering me and my brothers on blindly, she was always shrewdly skeptical. It kept us on our toes and taught us to defend our ideas intelligently.

"Are you sure this is a good idea?" she asked. "Maybe you should stay in school."

My father supported my devotion to public education. Shang, son of an educator, always honored teachers. "You can do this," he said.

This time, though, Inza had a point. I knew absolutely nothing about starting a new organization. But that didn't mean I *was going to take her caution to heart and wilt. Instead I went to Barnes & Noble and bought as many books as I could find on starting a business, including* Business Plans for Dummies. *Not the most illustrious start ever, but a start.*

Who would be right: Inza or Shang?

WENDY KOPP, FOUNDER OF Teach For America, came to speak at Harvard sometime toward the end of my second year. I had managed to navigate my way through the Kennedy School, meet people who would become important in my future endeavors, and hone my skills in statistics. I was twenty-six but didn't know what my next step would be.

"What are your plans?" she asked. "I'm curious about your next move."

I told her I was thinking of working for a foundation that gave money to education reform initiatives.

"You don't want to do that," she said. "That's not where you're going to have the kind of impact you want. Trust me."

And I did. Five years earlier I had put my life in Wendy Kopp's hands. I had left the prestigious halls of my Ivy League university, and instead of heading to Wall Street or graduate school, I went to teach in inner-city Baltimore. I wasn't the only one who cast practicality and her future aside to follow Wendy Kopp's vision. Five hundred other recent grads from the best colleges across the country had made the same choice.

Why?

When you meet Wendy, you don't think she's the type to start a movement. She grew up amid privilege in Highland Park, Texas, a wealthy suburb of Dallas. She's smart as a whip and driven, but she's not a particularly inspiring orator. So why were so many of America's most talented twentysomethings willing to toss it all in for Wendy? Simple: Because she had an incredibly compelling idea.

During her senior year at Princeton, Wendy turned an idealistic notion that she had been harboring for years into her thesis. She wrote about the need to inspire the next generation of leaders to be focused on fixing public education. The way to do it? Recruit, select, and train the most outstanding young people in our country to spend two years teaching in some of the most troubled urban or rural public schools. While they were in the classroom, they would fill a huge need for talented new teachers. After their two years—and whether they stayed in teaching or went to law school, medical school, Wall Street, or Capitol Hill—they would be lifelong advocates for public education.

Wendy was one of us. She had graduated from college only three years before I had. She knew that many college graduates were seeking meaning in their lives in a way that taking a regular job couldn't provide. In forming the concept of Teach For America, she tapped into that search for fulfillment beyond the almighty dollar.

Wendy is an odd duck—a painfully shy woman who has become a truly effective leader. During our summer training institute she was a bit like Mr. Snuffleupagus from *Sesame Street*—a mythical creature whose sightings would be tracked by corps members trying to determine whether the legend was real. She was only twenty-five at the time.

The first time I laid eyes on Wendy we were at a dance party at the Teach For America Summer Institute, toward the end of our training. We were cutting loose, celebrating and preparing to leave for our placement sites. Wendy is a notorious workaholic. Apparently, on this evening, her staff had convinced her to let her hair down and party a little. In hindsight, it probably wasn't the best idea for the founder of Teach For America to be cavorting with the corps, but the staff advising her were twentysomethings with a burning desire to have some fun.

I remember dancing with my roommates when the room

started buzzing. The crowd parted like a scene out of a movie, and in came Wendy with some of her trusted staff. I couldn't take my eyes off the woman who had inspired so many. There she stood, in the middle of the dance floor, looking unbelievably uncomfortable. As she started to dance, she nervously jerked around to the music for a moment, without much success at rhythm, and then her bra strap slipped off her shoulder. She tried to push it up. But with the herky-jerky of her body, it fell down over and over again. Finally, thinking better of it, she slipped behind one of the large speakers to fix her bra.

"Really?" I thought. "That's our leader?"

But Wendy's tentative moves on the dance floor were no reflection of her tenacity as a leader. She proved to be an incredible advocate for her program—a woman who got things done. She was absolutely relentless. TFA suffered in its first few years from a lack of funding and a vicious attack from the education school elite who wrote mercilessly about how Teach For America allegedly damaged kids. She braved her way through what she calls "the dark years," talking wealthy donors into shelling out millions of dollars to build the program. She tried her best to stave off the criticisms that TFA was an ineffective program that did nothing more than make do-gooders feel good about themselves and pad their résumés.

All the while she not only built a brand—she built a movement.

Today, nearly 20 percent of the graduating classes of Harvard and Yale apply to Teach For America, and most get rejected. TFA alumni can now be found running school districts, leading the best charter schools in the country, working in leading think tanks, serving as governors' education advisers, and even taking on the call of elected office.

The shy, awkward girl from Highland Park, Texas, had created a popular phenomenon.

So when she asked to meet with me in Cambridge, Massachusetts, I was eager to hear what she had to say.

. . . .

AT HARVARD I HAD enrolled in the master's in public policy program, with a concentration in education policy. When I enrolled,
Harvard didn't have a stand-alone concentration in education
policy, so I made one up. There was an approved concentration
in health, human services, and education, so I tweaked that by
taking all the education-related courses at the Kennedy School
and some at the Graduate School of Education.

Harvard was a foreign world to me, almost as strange as Korea
in some respects. I had never experienced anything like it. It made
my years at Cornell seem like a walk in the park. I was not an
outstanding student and never had been. Harvard, I quickly found
out, was full of people who have always been the smartest kid in
the class.

On the first day, we had been assigned a case to read before
class, and I watched the nauseating ritual of students working
overtime to make a good first impression on the professor and
their peers. In graduate schools like the Kennedy School and law
schools throughout the country, students form study groups.
These groups serve both academic and social purposes. People
jump to form groups as quickly as they can, but it has to be done
carefully. The goal is to identify the smartest people possible and
form a group with them.

I sat in the classroom the entire day without uttering a word or
impressing anyone. Despite that, I was invited to attend the first
session of a study group by Michael Simon, a guy I vaguely knew
from the Teach For America Summer Institute. I thought it might
be a mistake to completely eschew the ritual, but I joined it with
a dose of skepticism.

The group that convened was large. Too large. Clearly the
leaders had decided to treat the first session like a tryout. A bit
annoyed, but still wanting to prepare for the discussion of the case

the following day, I dug in and participated during the group. I'd read the paper carefully and brought up a few insights.

As the session was drawing to a close, a small Latina woman approached us.

"Hey," she said. "My name is Layla. I'm in your section. Do you mind if I join your group?"

Obviously, they did.

"Actually, I think the group is too large already," one of the students replied. "I don't think we have room. Sorry!" Everyone turned their heads to their papers.

"Well, if we don't have room for her, I think I'm going to join her and start a separate group," I said quickly.

"Uh . . . ," said the spokesman, having to calculate the benefits and risks quickly. "I guess one more person can't hurt."

And with that, my friendship with Layla Avila took root. In my eyes they were judging both her and me on our race. They figured an Asian student could keep up, but a Latina might be a drag. They didn't want her to join our group, because they didn't think she'd add value.

They ended up being wrong. Very wrong. Layla was brilliant. She and I got along so well that after that first semester—both of us still bitter from the interlude that brought us together—we decided to break off from the group and form our own. We always worked together and then picked up strays here and there, depending on the class and who might be left out.

Layla and I could not have been more different on paper. She was born to a Mexican mother in East Los Angeles. Her father wasn't in the picture, and her mom had multiple sclerosis. Layla spent much of her childhood taking care of her mom, often skipping school to do so. She lived in one of the toughest sections of Los Angeles and attended one of the most notoriously bad middle schools, Stevenson Junior High.

It was there that a teacher, Don Mitchell, took notice of Layla's undeniable intellect. He saw how easily she grasped concepts, how diligent she was when motivated, how well she completed her assignments. Mitchell also knew that if no one intervened, Layla would attend Roosevelt High School, the worst-performing high school in the city, where she'd likely become a statistic.

He told Layla about a program called A Better Chance. It plucked kids like Layla out of the ghetto and sent them to private schools throughout the country. Mitchell knew this was Layla's only chance. He convinced Layla and eventually her mom that she should apply. She was accepted into ABC and was placed at a private school in Colorado Springs, Colorado. Deciding to leave her sick mom was tough, but even back then she knew that if she got a great education, it would make all the difference—so off she went.

Fountain Valley School of Colorado could not have been more different from East Los Angeles. Layla was one of the few minorities in the school and—as would become the pattern in Layla's life—she was underestimated. When she arrived she heard murmurs of "affirmative action kids" who were taking spots away from other, more deserving students. But Layla did her thing, unfazed by the unwelcoming climate.

She studied alone and kept to herself. She didn't make many friends. She focused on proving everyone wrong. At the end of her first semester, she was ranked number one in her class. Her classmates were stunned.

She remembers mumbling to her detractors: "Affirmative action my ass."

DESPITE NEVER HAVING BEEN a great student, I found my stride at the Kennedy School. Layla and I took an almost identical course load and did all of our work together. We did well. Probably the most surprising thing to me about my experiences at the Kennedy School was my affection for statistics.

In high school I had struggled through calculus. I never liked math at all and completely avoided it in college. Logarithms, sines, and cosines made absolutely no sense to me. So when I saw that we were required to take quantitative classes as part of our course of study, I shuddered.

But statistics spoke to me in a completely different way. It wasn't about abstract concepts; it was completely logical and concrete. I quickly learned the value of statistics. We read the newspaper, see stories about a study showing that eggs are bad for our health or that kale is good for us, and take them as fact. We might believe what we are reading and change our behavior based on the information, often based on statistics.

What I learned at the Kennedy School is that data can be manipulated. Two academics can look at the same set of data and come to two wildly different conclusions based on the biases they bring to their research. The most valuable skill I learned at Harvard was to never take numbers at face value, to always dig in and analyze to see what's really happening in any given situation.

WENDY KOPP AND I had kept in touch during my time at Harvard. She was aware that I had done well at Harlem Park and that I had decided on graduate school. We had emailed a few times and followed one another through friends. She knew I was clearly still committed to working in public education in some capacity. I had applied for fellowships that would have allowed me to work for a foundation on education reform, but nothing was panning out.

Out of the blue, I got a call from Wendy's office. She was in town giving a speech in Boston and wanted to meet with me. They wanted to know if I was available.

We met for lunch. She wore that intense look on her face. I detected that distinctive cross-armed lean-in that she does when she's trying to talk someone into something. I'd seen her turn on her persuasive, almost magnetic charm before—usually to wring something from funders or school district officials. This time I was the target.

"We have all of these school districts that are begging us for more teachers," she said. "At TFA we can't recruit and train them fast enough. The school districts are asking, 'How do you develop these teachers? Bring us some more.' "

She paused. She sipped her water. She leaned in.

"We are not growing at Teach For America," she said, "so we can't fulfill their needs. We have no plans to grow anytime in the near future. School districts need some help. So why don't you start an organization that could help them recruit more and better teachers?"

It made sense. After my experience in Baltimore, I knew that excellent teachers could make all the difference for students and schools. I agreed to start an organization that would help school districts and states find the best teachers.

Wendy managed to get a grant of $50,000 to pay my first year's salary. She gave me a desk and an office at the Teach For America headquarters on Wall Street.

Each day I would trudge into the office, read my books, and try to figure out what I was doing. After a while, I felt that I needed to start producing something, so I began to write the business plan for the new venture.

By the time I finished what I thought was a solid draft, I decided I needed some feedback. I was reluctant to take it to Wendy until I got some validation that it was a decent start. I did some research and found an organization, called SCORE, that matched fledgling entrepreneurs with retired business executives. One morning I went to the New York SCORE office, where I was given a number and asked to wait. About thirty minutes later I was seated across from an older gentleman who had been an executive in the textile industry. He was short, wiry, and condescending.

His tiny bow tie was knotted high on his neck, like a nut and bolt with wings.

"Where's your stuff?" he demanded gruffly.

I pulled out my draft plan and handed it to him. He flipped through the pages.

"Young lady," he said, "I have no idea what it is that you are trying to do here."

I said, "I'm trying to start a new company. A nonprofit organization that helps school districts and state departments of education hire new teachers."

"Who are the shareholders?" he asked.

"There are no shareholders. It's a nonprofit organization."

"You have to have shareholders. If not, you have no equity."

"We don't need equity; we are a nonprofit organization."

"You don't want to make a profit?" he asked, shaking his head and looking at me like I was a moron.

"No. This is a *nonprofit*!"

We were fifteen minutes into what was scheduled to be a forty-five-minute session.

"Young lady," he said, "you are wasting my time. You can't sell a business plan that has no profits attached to it. No one is going to invest in that. I don't know why you're here, but come back when you have a real plan."

I am not a violent person, but I wanted to punch the guy. I'm also not a crier, but at the same time, the exchange almost brought me to tears.

"Really?" I thought. "Is it that hard to understand?"

He stood up, shook his head, shook my hand, and said, "Good luck."

As it turns out, my concept was hard to understand, but I knew in my core that it made sense. I was trying to start a nonprofit organization, but I didn't want to do it in the traditional way. I hate asking people for money, and I didn't want to spend all of my time fund-raising. So I decided that the organization should be a revenue-generating, nonprofit organization.

I'd been around education long enough to see a huge number of nonprofits whose leaders spent inordinate amounts of time explaining how their do-gooding was doing someone some good. If it was that hard a sell, I thought, then you had a problem. My idea was to start a business where we would sign contracts with school districts that needed our services. They would pay us to provide great teachers. Our model would charge the district only for the amount it cost to do the work, no profit added. If we were providing valuable services for the district, it would be willing to pay for them. If we weren't, then we didn't need to be in business, and we would fail.

People didn't get it, but it seemed crystal clear to me. And since it made sense in my head, I pursued it. The first order of business was to lay my hands on some start-up capital.

DON FISHER, LEGENDARY FOUNDER of the Gap, was beginning to invest in a major way in education reform. He was a big supporter of Wendy and Teach For America as well as the KIPP (Knowledge Is Power Program) charter schools, and Wendy thought he was the ideal candidate to become our angel donor.

I continued working on the business plan, made it as good as it was going to get in my hands, and went to meet with Scott Hamilton, the head of Fisher's foundation.

Scott was a jerk to me. He was skeptical, dismissive, and condescending—a younger version of the elderly fellow with the bow tie. During the course of several meetings he poked holes in all of my assumptions and berated the plan. He was arrogant and a pain in the butt, but he had my money, so I suffered through it.

My idea was definitely unconventional. Wendy had established TFA based on the goodwill and good faith of rich donors. They operated in a world where everything was done by grants. Philanthropists gave money based on compelling ideas they felt would help the world become a better place. The nonprofits would do the work and then try to convince the donors of all the good their donations had brought and ask for more money to do more good work.

I wasn't trying to convince Don Fisher and Scott Hamilton that I was doing good for the world. I was trying to convince them that I had a viable concept for a self-sustaining organization and that I had the ability to lead that organization and bring my off-the-wall idea to fruition.

After weeks of meetings and what he called due diligence Scott Hamilton called Wendy Kopp.

"I'm not sure I have confidence in Michelle as a leader—or in her plan," he said.

"I do," Wendy said. She called and appealed directly to Don Fisher.

He was inclined to give me the money, only because he believed in Wendy. Scott still thought it was a bad idea. So he fashioned a compromise.

"Fine," he said. "We'll give you the $833,000 in start-up capital."

I knew there was a catch.

"But," he continued, "if this revenue-generating concept of yours actually pans out, then that means you should be recouping those dollars. We'll give you the money as a *loan*, not a grant. And we'll expect repayment. With interest."

I saw Wendy lean forward in her chair ready to push back and push for a grant.

"Done," I said, without skipping a beat. "When can I expect the check?"

. . . .

MY FIRST TASK WAS to find some clients. But to attract them, I had to make it seem as if I ran a viable business.

With the first installment of Fisher money in the bank, I set to work designing business cards and letterhead. Okay, *designing* might be a stretch. I tried out different fonts and colors and ended up with a clean green logo that read "The New Teacher Project." I never liked the name, but I didn't have time to mess around, so I went with it.

I had originally wanted to come up with a cool name. I created a list of hundreds of options. At an afternoon meeting with Wendy and Fiona Lin and Karolyn Belcher—two friends from TFA who had become trusted advisers—we tried out all the names on the list for size. The candidates ranged from "TEACH!" (a failed earlier TFA effort) to "The Woodhull Group" (after Victoria Woodhull, the first woman to run for president) to "Teacher Recruitment Services." But Wendy kept returning to "The New Teacher Project."

"The name has to explain what we do," she said, "but it also has to be different and innovative."

Karolyn and I weren't buying it, but we both knew that arguing with Wendy once she got something stuck in her head was a waste of time and sanity. After two hours of idea after idea being shot down I said, "Okay, we'll go with this for now. New Teacher Project it is."

"*The!*" Wendy insisted as I was walking out of her office. "The *The* is critical. It's not 'New Teacher Project'; it's '*The* New Teacher Project.'"

And The New Teacher Project was born. But if I wanted it to survive its first month, I needed to find some clients and bring in some revenue.

I had absolutely no idea where to start and less of an idea of how to sell our services, but I was fortunate. Wendy, in her travels coast to coast building TFA, had established good relationships with school districts and foundations across the country. She used those contacts to get me some initial meetings, and I hit the road. In the first month I traveled to Houston, Dallas, Austin, Boston, Philadelphia, Compton, Los Angeles, Sacramento, Kansas City. I met with anyone and everyone who would meet with me.

In the process, I watched myself develop some skills as a persuader. Things started out a bit rocky as I tried to explain what it was that TNTP was trying to do: provide a steady supply of quality teachers, for a fee. I could read what resonated with people and what didn't. I honed my pitch quickly. By the end of the first month, I had a solid sell down. And even though I hated asking people for money, I began to revel in the pitch sessions. Here I was asking established school district officials to spend money on a person with no track record and a business model that was untested. I found it both perilous and exciting—and I was getting better at each meeting.

That year, 1997, there was a significant teacher shortage crisis. School districts were having trouble staffing their schools, and urban school districts were hit particularly hard. They often opened the school year with hundreds of vacancies. We found ourselves selling into a buyer's market.

In relatively short order, we had two contracts, with the School District of Philadelphia and the Austin Independent School District. David Hornbeck was the superintendent in Philadelphia at the time, and a TFA alum, Ben Rayer, had become his special assistant. Hornbeck had just hired Marge Adler, a professional from the corporate world, to run his human resources department. She was amenable to the idea of hiring consultants but skeptical about our ragtag new operation.

"So who exactly *is* this organization?" she asked. "Where are you headquartered?"

"You know," Hornbeck said, "Wendy started Teach For

America in her dorm room at Princeton. This is probably like that, and look how successful Wendy was!"

With that, they signed the contract. Our job was to consult with the school district to design better recruitment and selection functions that would generate a larger and higher-quality teacher applicant pool.

Needless to say, Marge Adler was a little shocked to see me show up as their consultant a few weeks later, but she went with it at her boss's insistence.

The third contract was a bit tougher. I was close to closing a deal with the Compton Unified School District, just outside Los Angeles, but state-appointed superintendent Randy Ward proved to be a difficult negotiator.

In Compton, we had proposed starting a new program, Teach Compton!, that would recruit one hundred midcareer professionals to Compton to become teachers.

"Yeah, yeah," Randy Ward said, "I know what you *say* you're going to do. But what if you don't? Then I'm out one hundred thousand dollars with no new teachers, and you've got my money in New York City taking Wendy out to lunch!"

"I assure you, Dr. Ward," I said, "that will not happen. That's not how we operate. We deliver."

"Listen, honey, you're good. You talk a good game but that is not going to help me if I shell out my money, and you don't deliver me any teachers. I need a guarantee!"

"What kind of guarantee?" I asked.

"A guarantee that I don't get screwed!" he boomed.

"Okay," I said.

"And show me what you're actually going to do first. All this talk better not just be talk!" With that, he left the room.

That night I got on the phone with my team. I had hired my first four employees, and their paychecks depended on my bringing these contracts in.

"No way," said Tracy Spitzberg and Jennifer Rose, two women from the corporate world I'd brought on board. "We can't sign a performance-based contract!"

They argued that we would have to spend money to recruit teachers. If we didn't deliver the teachers, he would want his money back, but it would already be out the door. We wouldn't be able to repay him!

"We can't take on that kind of risk!" said Charity Mack, my director of operations, who was responsible for tracking our finances.

"We won't have to repay him because we are going to get the teachers," I responded, "and if we don't, we're losers and deserve to go out of business anyway.

"Oh," I added, "and he wants to know what we're actually doing. Let's show him a mock-up of the recruitment ads we'll be doing."

We spent all night on the phone coming up with potential ideas. None worked. As it neared 1 a.m., the group was getting tired, and I was getting frustrated. After more bantering back and forth, we stumbled on it: "Compton's Kids Deserve a Beverly Hills Education." I don't even remember who came up with it, but it was brilliant. Since we were short on cash, we skipped the idea of a full graphic presentation and mocked up a sign on paper with a black background and white letters that spelled out the phrase.

I loved it. So did Randy Ward.

I hired Layla Avila to run the contract, and we were off to the races. In weeks we were fielding dozens of requests for future teachers.

The last contract of that first year was the Massachusetts Department of Education. Commissioner David Driscoll and his young deputy, Alan Safran, had set up a meeting with Wendy to help replenish their teacher ranks. Wendy said she couldn't do it. She suggested TNTP and opened the door for me. I went in for the sell.

"I can't believe Wendy pawned us off on you!" I remember Safran saying. "I mean, no offense, but come on! I want TFA, I need TFA, and now I've got some unproven, new project?"

I can endure plenty of abuse, especially when I have a lot on the line, but this guy was making me mad.

"Look," I said, "if you don't think we can help you, that's fine. I am not going to try and talk you into working with us."

"What are you talking about? Isn't that why you're *here*? To convince me that you're as good as Wendy?" he said. "What have you got? What can you do?"

Safran started talking like a man possessed.

"I want something big," he continued. "I want something better than TFA! TFA is small potatoes. TFA is so yesterday. I want something new and fresh and exciting. I want to take all of the candidates away from TFA!"

In the midst of the rant, I realized I kind of liked Alan Safran. I appreciated his wild energy and decided to add my own. We started to exchange ideas. After an hour, we came up with the plan. We would start the Massachusetts signing bonus program. The first of its kind, the program would offer $20,000 bonuses to people who came into the program and agreed to teach in a low-performing school district. The bonus would be paid out over four years, but that was a detail we didn't trumpet. Instead the $20,000 number was the headliner.

It worked! This fourth and final contract of TNTP's first year was an instant hit. It attracted national news coverage and garnered thousands of applications. The participants were dubbed the "bonus babies."

We worked frantically that first year and accomplished a tremendous amount. We found that the challenges in the school districts were immense. It wasn't just that they couldn't attract good candidates. It was that their systems didn't treat candidates well. In many cases, no one would return an applicant's calls. Their applications would be lost. No one contacted them after they had applied.

After trying to change the way some HR staffs operated, we decided the best remedy would be to try to conduct these functions ourselves. We created separate Teaching Fellows programs in each school district to take applications from midcareer professionals who wanted to become educators. The TNTP staff would review teacher applications, interview applicants, communicate the requirements to them, train them through a summer program, and deliver them to the district in time for the start of school.

It worked! So well that it surprised us. We got applications for our programs from rocket scientists, investment bankers, and judges. All of these people were willing to leave their jobs for the opportunity to teach.

As we were closing out our first recruitment season and gearing up for our summer training programs, I got a call that changed the trajectory of The New Teacher Project: Vicki Bernstein, with the New York City Department of Education, was on the line.

"We need three hundred teachers for the start of school," she said. "Can you help?"

The assignment was nuts. The New York system was gargantuan: the largest in the nation. It included more than a million students, in 1,700 schools, with nearly 75,000 teachers. In the other programs that we'd run, we were hiring 100 teachers on average, and we had nine months to run our entire process. Vicki wanted 300 teachers, and we had three weeks to recruit them before the training program.

"We have never recruited this many people before in ideal circumstances, much less three weeks," Tracy said. "*And* if we screw up, we screw up with the biggest and highest-profile school district in the nation. No way!"

"Who is going to run the thing?" Charity asked. "We're

already all working beyond capacity. This is a major undertaking, and we'll need an entire team to pull it off!"

There was no shortage of good reasons not to take the project on. But I knew we had to do it. For all of the risks, there was tremendous upside. A foot in the door with the New York City public schools would create opportunities nationwide.

"We are taking it," I said. "We can pull this off."

The first order of business was assembling our recruitment materials. After another marathon late-night session we landed on another gem: a grainy black-and-white picture of an adorable young Latina child. Above her the caption read: "Four out of five 4th graders in the city's most challenged schools can't read and write at grade level." At the bottom of the page: "Are you willing to do something about it?"

We loved it.

The New York City department hated it. The powers that be felt the message was too negative. They wanted something more positive.

I argued that facts are facts. We didn't make that statistic up. Moreover, a message that says, "Hey, everything in the school system is great—come be a cog in the wheel!" is not very compelling. Tell people they can make a difference, and they will come.

Karla Oakley, the woman I'd hired to run the contract, took our argument to Harold Levy, the new chancellor. He was a bit of a maverick. He green-lighted the idea. The response to the pitch was immediate. *New York Times* editors were so intrigued by the ad that they assigned a reporter to cover our campaign. The article ran with a picture of the ad.

Within days we had thousands of applications.

RUNNING THE NEW TEACHER PROJECT made me realize that we *could* make a real difference. Quickly, we were working with most of the large urban school districts across the country and hiring thousands of teachers a year. We partnered with the Chicago Public Schools, Miami–Dade County Public Schools, Los Angeles Unified, and many others. Our experience base was growing exponentially.

And so was my rage.

Our job was to work with the school district bureaucracies. They were our clients. And it was uncanny how they simply couldn't manage to do what a competent organization should do. In fact, they did the opposite of what must be done to recruit and hire the best teachers. It was maddening.

When we began our work, we figured that there simply weren't enough people out there who wanted to teach, so we had to inspire people to do something they hadn't thought of doing before. I quickly learned that we could get huge numbers of very qualified people to apply for teaching jobs.

Attracting candidates wasn't the problem. But we found that the school districts couldn't hire them—or wouldn't hire them. They had set up systems and processes that made it impossible for them to hire the best teachers. We were so frustrated that we decided to try to document the problem by thoroughly examining how school districts responded to applicants, cataloging the processes and compiling the results in a report.

At first we couldn't convince anyone to fund the project, but we thought it was so important that we started the research on our own dime. Jessica Levin, our chief knowledge officer, led the effort, along with Meredith Quinn, whose research and writing skills made the project a success. They asked all our site managers who were embedded in HR offices in districts across the country to begin to track who applied for teaching jobs and when they applied. We also monitored whether they were ultimately hired.

The results were shocking. They totally smashed the myth that there was a shortage of urban teachers. To the contrary, we found that experts in math and science were banging down the doors to get hired, but the school systems were turning them away. It made me crazy!

How could schools deny the best candidates? First, school budgets were often not finalized until summer, leaving many principals uncertain of how many staff they would have to hire. Second, the districts often did not make structural decisions—school closures and consolidations or changes to staffing plans—until summer. That combined with the unresponsive and unaccountable nature of the HR departments equaled disaster. Third, even if a school district could usher a new teacher through the process in time for them to show up in the classroom at the start of the school year, the union contract mandated that no new teacher could be hired into the system until all of the current teachers had been placed.

Potential teachers were essentially stiff-armed before they could get in front of the students.

Lots of politicians have stories about constituents, relatives, or friends of friends who applied for teaching jobs and became so frustrated by the process and bureaucracy that they decided to do something else. Those, however, were just anecdotes. Our report put numbers behind the anecdotes in a compelling, sixty-three-page document supported by graphs, charts, and case studies of three school districts.

We named it "Missed Opportunities" and went public in April 2003.

We were very excited about the report, but we had low expectations. Who would care? We printed a couple of hundred copies. Requests poured in. Within weeks we had to print more. Because it confirmed the suspicions and anecdotes of so many people, "Missed Opportunities" resonated. Requests came from think tanks, institutions of higher education, states, and lawmakers on Capitol Hill. Investigative journalists devoured it.

TNTP's first foray into the policy world was a success, but we didn't want to be known as one-hit wonders. The report and its reception made us hungry for more. We understood the impact and value of a document that presented live data and broke new ground. Lawmakers began using it to guide new policy, which had been our hoped-for ideal outcome. But we also knew that "Missed Opportunities" barely began to delve into a deeper set of obstacles. We wanted to expose more problems and recommend solutions.

Jessica Levin and I wrestled with the remaining roadblocks to hiring great teachers. We decided that the first two problems of HR processes and budget timelines could be addressed by good leadership and planning. The third issue, the requirement that school districts hold open spots for all current teachers without assignments, before offering spots to any new teachers—was a much tougher problem. This issue revolved around collective bargaining agreements and so it touched on a series of sensitive, sacred cows in public education.

"There's no doubt about it," said Jessica, "the union issues are the seemingly intractable ones. Those are the ones that would be most interesting to delve into."

"Okay," I said, "let's do it."

"Are you crazy?" she said. "The unions would go ballistic. And they are not people you want to be on the wrong side of."

"We have to solve the problems," I said, "right?"

"Of course," she replied.

"And you just told me that the budget and HR issues are more easily solvable."

"Correct."

"Then we have to pry into the guts of the union contracts," I said.

"Oh, honey," she said, "do you realize what you're getting us into?"

Here's how Sandra Feldman, the well-respected head of the American Federation of Teachers, reacted to "Missed Opportunities."

"If these transfer policies are getting in the way of recruiting new teachers in a timely fashion, labor and management should get together and create a better way of dealing with it."

If Sandy Feldman was willing to say that, how mad could the teachers unions be with us?

AND WITH THAT, WE embarked on our second major project. It required two years of research and evaluation. We collected data in five urban school districts. In November 2005, we published "Unintended Consequences." The report enumerated in exacting detail the rules and regulations embedded in collective bargaining agreements that prohibit school districts from hiring the best teachers. In fact, we showed that union contracts required school districts to give jobs to teachers who had demonstrated their failure at teaching.

Take what school districts call "voluntary transfers." If a teacher lost a job at one school because of budget cuts or poor performance, he or she was not fired from the system. Under the contract, they were considered "excessed." Translation: If a teacher failed or was deemed unnecessary at one school, he could be first in line for a job at another school in the district. There was often nothing voluntary about the transfers. Bad teachers were often forced out of one school, only to be foisted on another.

"Voluntary transfer rules often give senior teachers the right to interview for and fill jobs in other schools even if those schools do not consider them a good fit," we concluded. Most principals reported that they didn't want to hire those teachers. But contract rules forced them to accept teachers they neither wanted nor needed.

Under contract rules, terminating a teacher requires weeks of time in writing reports and evaluations and holding meetings. Often principals simply "excessed" bad teachers and passed them from school to school, a ritual some referred to as "the dance of the lemons."

Contract rules often put promising young teachers—and their students—in a precarious position. A more senior teacher could bump a new teacher from a classroom, even if the more experienced teacher was known to be a lousy educator who had failed to teach students effectively for decades.

In reporting on these issues, we knew we were challenging powerful unions and liberal dogma.

"We hope that this report will initiate a discussion not on the merits of collective bargaining as a whole (which we support), but on the effects of the specific contractual requirements governing school staffing," I wrote in the foreword: "When these rules were adopted in the 1960s by newly formed teachers union locals and school boards, they were an important and legitimate response to widely perceived arbitrary and poor management. Based on the now four decades of experience with these provisions, however, we believe it is time to find a new balance between protecting teachers from past abuses and equipping schools with the necessary tools to achieve excellent results for their students."

"Unintended Consequences" also presented very specific recommendations for change. We gave districts a road map for a better teachers union contract. Among our recommendations: Teachers could transfer from one school to another, but they could no longer force a school to accept them. If a teacher lost his or her job at one school—for poor performance, falling student enrollment, or any other reason—he could apply for a job at another school, but he was not guaranteed a position. Promising new teachers would not be the first to be laid off, and senior teachers could no longer bump those with less experience. Contracts would include procedures for evaluating teachers, training those who were not measuring up, and rewarding the best ones.

The report got the attention of teachers unions. They went on the attack. We also got the attention of Joel Klein, who had succeeded Harold Levy as chancellor of New York City schools. New York was one of the districts that we had gathered data from for "Unintended Consequences." Klein was doing battle with the unions at the time. After two years of negotiating unsuccessfully with the United Federation of Teachers (UFT), the school system and the union were heading toward binding arbitration. The UFT is the New York affiliate of the American Federation of Teachers. Randi Weingarten, already a powerful and legendary union boss, ran the UFT at the time.

Many of the disputes revolved around staffing and seniority, matters we had investigated at TNTP. Klein asked for my help.

I loved Joel Klein from the moment I first spoke with him. Upon Harold Levy's departure, New York mayor Michael Bloomberg had named Joel his new chancellor. The choice was a total shock to many. Klein was not an education professional—not even close. He had worked in the Clinton administration and as the CEO of the U.S. corporate arm of the Bertelsmann media conglomerate. But he was a New York kid, the son of first-generation Americans. He grew up poor and attributed his success to the great education he got in New York public schools. Still, he was an unlikely candidate for the head of the largest school district in the country.

Before Klein started his new job as chancellor, he called me to have a conversation. By that time, we were the largest supplier of new teachers to the New York public schools, supplying two thousand new Teaching Fellows every year.

"What's wrong with the way we hire teachers?" he asked.

At first I was a bit skeptical, so I stayed on the reserved side, unsure of what his reaction would be. But we connected, and I warmed to the task. I ran down what we had found with "Missed

Opportunities" and our theory on union contracts. I told him how we had structured our Teaching Fellows program to work around the bureaucracy, and I described our success to date.

"Okay," he said, "can you do more?"

"More Teaching Fellows?" I asked.

"No, more to solve the fundamental problem. I get the Teaching Fellows piece, that's great. Keep doing it. But you're saying that the HR function for hiring traditionally certified teachers is broken. Why can't you start a program like Teaching Fellows to go after those folks? Circumvent the system again."

"Umm," I mumbled, "your HR department may not be so excited about that."

"I'm not worried about them," said Klein. "Can you do it or not?"

"Okay," I said tentatively. "How many do you want?"

"How many can you do?" he asked.

"I'll have to talk to my staff and get back to you," I said.

"Yeah, get back to me," he said, nonchalantly.

I went back to my staff and relayed my conversation with the new chancellor.

Karla Oakley quickly chimed in. "I don't think that's a good idea."

"Why not?" I asked.

"The HR department barely tolerates us as it is. This would put us in direct competition with them. And that would not be good."

"Why not?" I asked again.

"'Cause we'd probably kick their butts," she replied, "and *that* would not be good."

After some rigorous debate, we decided to put together a proposal to locate another five hundred recruits for the new program. I sent it to Klein but half expected the idea to die on the vine. After all, the guy was about to take over a system of 1.1 million kids. He was having conversations with hundreds of experts in school law, finance, special education, food service, and transportation, just to name a few. He probably wouldn't even remember our conversation.

In what I would later learn was true Joel Klein fashion, he got back to me immediately.

"Let's go" was his answer.

This guy was no joke. He totally won me over.

IN 2005, KLEIN AND his labor negotiator, Dan Weisberg, asked me to get involved in their stalemate with the UFT. I agreed immediately.

By then Klein had been battling for two years to change the union work rules, such as the one that forced principals to hire incompetent teachers. But Klein had unearthed another outrage. Teachers who had been deemed incompetent or unsafe—some because they had been accused of abusing students—were still on the payroll. The disciplinary system to assess and perhaps dismiss failed teachers was so cumbersome and lengthy that hundreds of teachers caught in the process were warehoused in what was dubbed "the rubber room." Rather than go to a classroom, they came every day to bare rooms in school buildings. They read, they ate, they slept. And they cost Klein's system $40–50 million a year.

Klein and the UFT were at war. Under state rules, deadlocked negotiations with public unions come before an arbitration panel of three judges. Klein and Weisberg figured I could help their case. I had no idea that the stage was set for the first skirmish in what would become a wide-ranging battle over the union's grip on public education.

"You sure?" he asked.

"Yeah, what do you mean?" I replied.

"It's just that most of the people whom we've asked to testify at the panel have turned us down. They're all terrified of the UFT."

Indeed, elected officials and education experts alike knew that supporting Klein and the schools against Randi Weingarten and her union was tantamount to excommunication from the UFT's good graces—and campaign cash.

"I'm good."

IT WASN'T THAT I was being brave. It's that I had absolutely no idea what I was getting myself into.

Several weeks later I was asked to report to the offices of Proskauer Rose, a top Manhattan law firm. I was directed to the room where the arbitration was taking place. It was set up with four sets of tables forming a square. The head table was the arbitration panel. The UFT and New York public school teams were set up facing each other, perpendicular to the panel. The fourth table, facing the panel, was set up for the witnesses.

I slid into a seat behind the school system's table. One of Klein's staffers tapped him on the shoulder, whispered into his ear, and motioned toward me. Joel turned around, smiled his broad smile, and leaned forward. I leaned forward to meet him.

"Welcome to the madhouse. Thanks for coming, kiddo," he said, and then turned back around.

I listened for a while and then was called to give my testimony. My part was pretty simple. Since we had gathered data directly from New York City schools, I was not hypothesizing about what might be happening. I was presenting facts.

I talked through "last in, first out" policies, by which promising new teachers could be let go if a veteran teacher wanted his or her job. I described the time-consuming thicket of rules a principal had to follow to fire an incompetent teacher. I walked the panel through the forced-placement rules, which required principals to hire teachers who had failed at other schools—"the dance of the lemons," in the words of some principals. I ran through other provisions of the union contract that were detrimental to creating successful schools.

With each example, I presented data to show the negative impact on students.

At the conclusion, I shared our recommendations. I laid out five changes that should be made to the union contract to make it better for kids.

Then came the questions. The panel asked me a few. The school's lawyers also asked me a couple. Last was the UFT's turn.

"Ms. Rhee," one union lawyer asked, "isn't it true that you run an organization that has a multimillion-dollar contract with the NYCDOE? And that your organization would stand to benefit by helping the DOE?"

"Yes, we do have a contract with the DOE, but my testimony is not about helping the DOE, it's about the facts."

Randi Weingarten shot me a level stare. If looks could kill, I would have been dead.

I stood up, grabbed my things, and exited the room. Joel came out after me.

"You were dazzling, kid. Really good. You're ballsy."

The panel ruled for Klein and the New York public schools. It struck down forced placement and replaced it with mutual consent, which meant a principal had to agree to accept a teacher from another school. The arbitrators accepted four of my five recommendations.

Compared with Randi Weingarten, I considered myself a peon at the time. I had no idea that I had created an enemy.

4

The Road to D.C.

Toward the end of my first meeting in Washington, D.C., about running the public school system, I was trying to figure out how to break it to the city administrator that I didn't want the job. A trim fellow with a shaved head walked in.

"Hi, I'm Adrian Fenty," he said. "How are you?"

"Fine, sir, it's an honor to meet you."

The new mayor of the nation's capital seemed young and energetic but not particularly impressive. He was wearing a white shirt, blue tie, blazer, and rumpled khakis. He looked like a mayoral aide, rather than the chief executive of a city with a $10 billion budget.

"As you know, I'm taking over the schools and I'm looking for a chancellor to lead the district. I don't want one of the usual suspects. I'm looking for someone with a different profile."

He looked around a lot and seemed distracted. He had two BlackBerrys going at once.

"We went up to New York, and I was incredibly impressed by Joel Klein," he continued. "I told him I needed someone like him, and he recommended you." Klein, Fenty said, had described me as someone who knows education and how school districts work, but that I came with a fresh perspective from outside the system.

"That's exactly what I'm looking for," he said. Then he typed an email on his BlackBerry.

"I appreciate the chancellor's kind words," I responded, "and while I do know education and understand how some aspects of school systems work, I have a specific expertise in teacher quality and HR. I don't have a broad base of experience in running a school district."

During our first meeting, Adrian Fenty failed to impress me. I wasn't sure that I wanted to run a school district for him.

TWO YEARS AFTER MY initial run-in with Randi Weingarten in New York, I was getting restless.

TNTP was doing well. By 2007, we had built a staff of about 150 people and had an annual budget of more than $20 million. And I had long ago paid off the original $833,000 loan from Don Fisher at the Doris and Donald Fisher Fund. I should have been thrilled and content. I had a great job where I was doing meaningful work and was my own boss. But I kept getting the nagging feeling that it was time to go. I just didn't know where.

I had read somewhere that well-organized leaders always plan for their succession, and that they do it well in advance of their departure. My departure was not imminent, or so I thought. I couldn't imagine another job where I'd feel like I was having nearly as much direct impact as I was having—and not have to answer to a boss. That was an important piece to the puzzle. I am not great at taking orders, and in most jobs, you have a boss. So what could I possibly do next?

Without an answer to that question, I started planning. My number two, Ariela Rozman, was an incredibly competent woman. We complemented one another perfectly. I would go out and do all of the external work, like closing contracts and making presentations. Ari was a taskmaster. She made the trains run on time, and there was no one better at it.

I'd originally brought her in to be the vice president of marketing. It wasn't a great fit for her, but I immediately saw her gift. She became the chief operating officer, which was the perfect role for her. As I considered her, I thought she had about 80 percent of what it would take to be a great CEO. But what about the other 20 percent? We needed someone to be the face of the organization to represent us to the outside world. I thought about the rest of the management team. All of them were incredibly talented and driven. There was Victoria Van Cleef, my vice president of marketing; Robin Siegel, my chief financial officer; and Jessica Levin, my chief knowledge officer. But none of them was exactly right. I considered people outside the organization, but I didn't love the idea of bringing in a stranger.

Then my thoughts turned to Tim Daly. We had hired Tim when he was twenty-three. I still remember interviewing him to this day. He knocked my socks off, and I watched him ascend from selection coordinator to selection manager to program director with our New York City public school system contracts. He was incredibly impressive, and I thought he had that presence that one would need to wow the clients.

However, he couldn't hold a candle to Ari on the management and operations front. Also, I would probably have a mutiny on my hands if I promoted a kid four levels down as the new CEO. I wasn't sure what to do. I scheduled a one-on-one dinner with Ari to talk about her future.

"I'm succession planning," I said.

"*What?* Where are you going? You can't leave!" she screamed.

"I'm not going anywhere," I responded. "At least not yet. I just feel that it's time to move on, but it's a little terrifying because I don't know where to go. Anyways, this is a few years off."

. . . .

IN MAY 2007 I went down to New Orleans for the NewSchools Venture Fund Summit, education reform's version of the World Economic Forum, held every year in Davos, Switzerland. The buzz was all about Washington, D.C. The nation's capital had just elected a new, young mayor—Adrian Fenty. Word was that he wanted to take over the schools, and he wanted to push through bold reforms. I was invited to a late-night brainstorming session with about two dozen reformers to discuss what the new mayor might do.

The session was a total snoozer. The usual suspects said the usual things. Nothing new or innovative emerged. I remember leaving thinking, "Jeez, these people have no clue what they're going to do."

The next day Victor Reinoso, D.C.'s deputy mayor for education, who had led the previous night's session, found me.

"Hey, I need to talk to you!" he said.

"Sure, what do you need?" I asked.

"A superintendent. We need a rock star. You've worked with all of the best people across the country. I need you to tell me who's good and who's not. Can we discuss it over dinner tonight?"

"No problem," I said. "See you then."

We went to Jacques Imo's, a favorite New Orleans haunt, and over alligator cheesecake, I gave him four names.

"If anyone can turn that crazy system around," I said, "these are your best bets. I just don't know that you can talk any of them into doing it!"

I left feeling good. I'd sung for my supper and gave them the only people who might have a shot at turning around the D.C. schools.

I knew what I was talking about, too. TNTP had been working with the District of Columbia Public Schools (DCPS) for years.

We had profiled it in our studies. The school system was one of the worst bureaucracies we'd run across. In fact, we were about to pull out of our contract. Given that we worked with all of the most dysfunctional school districts in the country, you knew that meant DCPS was a whole different level of bad.

IN THE WEEKS LEADING up to the summit, I'd had some tense conversations and communications with Clifford Janey, the superintendent in D.C. He was a good guy, and we actually liked him. He seemed focused on kids, and he was thoughtful.

But Cliff Janey was not a quick decision maker. He moved slowly, and it was causing us problems. We'd recruit all of these great teacher candidates and have them ready to hire. Then at the last minute he would make a decision to hire math coaches for all the schools, or to close a few schools, and that would throw all of the staffing functions into turmoil. He would make the decisions so late in the game that it would push hiring new teachers back until right before school, making our jobs impossible.

"It just isn't a good use of their money," explained Kaya Henderson, our vice president, who oversaw the D.C. contract. "We charge them money to source these candidates, and we find the best. But they can't hire them in a timely manner, so they all leave. What's the point? If all we cared about was making money, we could have a contract here forever without having to produce any results."

"But that's not us," I said.

"My point exactly," Kaya said.

So we decided it was best to terminate the TNTP contract. We wanted to give Janey a heads-up so, I called him. He didn't want us to leave. I explained our rationale, and we had some conversations and left messages back and forth. I was still pretty sure that we were going to quit working with his school system.

In D.C., I had gotten to know Jim Shelton, program director for education at the Bill & Melinda Gates Foundation. Jim had grown up and lived in D.C. and was incredibly frustrated with how the public schools were operating.

"Don't leave," he pleaded. "You have to hang in there." He also told me that mayoral control under Fenty could be a game-changer. "Don't end the contract now. Just wait a little while," he said. "As soon as the mayor makes the transition and hires a chancellor, it'll be a different ball game for you guys. I promise."

I was skeptical. I'd seen my fair share of superintendents come and go. Each transition brought the promise of a new way of op-erating, but it rarely panned out.

THE NEXT MORNING VICTOR REINOSO sought me out again.

"Hey, can I grab you for a minute?" he asked.

He led me into a side room off the conference's main corridor.

"What about you?" he asked.

"What *about* me?" I asked him back, confused.

"You becoming the chancellor in D.C.!" he said excitedly.

"Abso-freakin-lutely not. No way!" I answered.

"Why not? Last night you said it was a once-in-a-lifetime op-portunity for the right person."

"Right, the operative term being *right person*. I am the *wrong* person."

"Aw, come on, you wouldn't even think about it?" he pleaded.

I was thinking, for starters, about how hard it would be to uproot my family from our base in Denver, where Kevin Huffman and I had settled down after being somewhat nomadic.

"Nope," I told Victor. "I have two kids in Denver."

Kevin and I had married in the mid-1990s and moved to D.C., then to Toledo to be near my parents. In 2004 we moved to Denver, again to be close to my parents, who had moved there once Shang retired. They were helping us raise our two daughters: Starr, who had been born in D.C. in 1998, and Olivia, who came along in 2002 when we were living in Toledo.

Kevin had gotten his law degree and was working for Teach For America. Working out of Denver, I was on the road much of the time, which took a toll on our marriage but not on our focus on the girls.

"Really?" Victor said facetiously. "Because we have a lot of schools in D.C. that they could attend."

"Seriously, Victor, give it up. Being an urban superintendent is the worst job in the world. Your hands are tied so you can't actually do anything, but you get blamed for everything. Not gonna happen."

"Would you just come out and meet Mayor Fenty?"

"I'll meet with the mayor but not about the job. I'll meet with him to tell him how critical it is that he not hire a bozo and tell him what needs to happen in the district with HR."

"Okay, fine," Victor said. "I'll take just that."

A COUPLE DAYS BEFORE the D.C. visit, I was in New York with my entire family to attend the Teach For America annual gala dinner. The board had decided to establish an award in honor of Peter Jennings, the legendary ABC News anchor, for TFA alums who had demonstrated leadership and accomplished significant education reform after leaving the corps. The selection committee had chosen me as the first recipient.

My parents were thrilled. Shang and Inza flew to New York with Starr, Olivia, and Kevin Huffman. Though we had grown apart and would later divorce, Kevin and I were still friends and confidants.

Meanwhile, Shang and Inza were about to understand what their crazy daughter had been up to. My folks would have asked the same questions that came from the retired businessman who called my idea nuts before I even started TNTP. They never really knew why I was flying all over the country to talk to school administrators. But being in the Waldorf-Astoria ballroom with a thousand people watching their daughter receive an award by Peter Jennings's widow—*that* they could understand. Even my girls, who were too young to grasp school reform, were impressed.

I was scheduled to sit at the head table next to Joel Klein. When he saw me approach, he came over and kissed me on the cheek.

"Some of the others were advocating for other candidates," he whispered. He had been on the selection committee. "I told them they all paled in comparison to you. No one has your kind of guts. Congratulations."

I went onstage, gave a short acceptance speech, and returned to my family's table. Shang and Inza were beaming. The girls were digging into chocolate-covered strawberries. All was right with the world.

THE NEXT MORNING MY phone rang. It was Victor. He was frantic.

"What's the matter?" I asked him.

"A few weeks back, we had taken the city council up to visit New York, speak with Mayor Bloomberg, and see what mayoral control of the schools looked like. Fenty fell in love with Klein and said, 'I need the next Joel Klein.'"

"Good for him!" I said. "You absolutely do!"

"Well, this is where it gets tricky. Joel Klein called the mayor this morning," Reinoso said. "He told him he should hire you!"

"What?" I asked.

Klein and I hadn't even talked about D.C. the night before. "Why would he do that?"

"I don't know. All I know is the mayor woke me up at five a.m. this morning saying, 'Who's Michelle Rhee? Joel Klein says I should hire Michelle Rhee. If she's that good, why isn't she on any of these lists you gave me, and why haven't I met her yet?'" Victor paused. "And . . ."

"And what?" I demanded.

"And I told him not to worry because you were already slated to come in and meet with him next week," Victor blurted out.

"Victor!" I was pissed. "I told you that my meeting with him was not to interview for the job. I'm not interested in being chancellor."

"Well—it is now!" Victor replied and hung up.

THOUGH I WAS A bit nervous that the mayor would be mad that I was not interested in the job, and that I might be wasting his time, I figured he'd take one look at me and dismiss the idea anyway.

I showed up in D.C. in the middle of May, went to my conference, and called Victor to get the details on the meeting with Mayor Fenty. There was tremendous speculation about whom the mayor was going to choose as the city's first chancellor. Reporters were watching his every move. Fenty's aides arranged for me to come in to City Hall late at night, and not to sign in. They directed me to enter through a side door, under the cover of darkness.

Who were they kidding? Was I the only one who realized that I could sign in and out of that building fifty times and no one would ever conceive of the idea that I might be a candidate for the position?

Abby Smith met me at the door. Abby was a TFA alum I knew who was now working with Victor and Eric Lerum, Victor's chief of staff. On the way up to the mayor's office, I was joking around. They wore game faces. It became clear that for them this was a big meeting. Abby had sung my praises to the mayor. If I bombed, her credibility was on the line.

"Hmmm," I thought. "It might be harder to get out of this than I figured."

I entered the conference room of the Bullpen, Fenty's take on Bloomberg's open-office model. There were no walls in the office, just a large open space with everyone sitting at desks. Fenty believed it would lead to transparency and good energy.

I sat down. Fenty wasn't there, but the interviews commenced. Dan Tangherlini, the mayor's city administrator, grilled me for a half hour. No introductions, no niceties; he just started pitching questions.

"Where would you send your kids to school?"

"What would you do in your first hundred days?"

"What's your assessment of what's wrong?"

I answered his questions matter-of-factly. In my mind, I wasn't interviewing for the job. I still had no intention of being a school superintendent, but he caught me off guard, and I just reacted.

Then Mayor Adrian Fenty abruptly walked into the room, introduced himself, and started asking questions. After we exchanged pleasantries, he started in with some questions of his own.

"Tell me what you're like as a manager."

I told him I was good at sniffing out talent. My staff jokes that I have a "seven-minute interview"—that after seven minutes I can tell whether someone is good or not. I said I try to hire people who are a lot smarter than I am.

"I see my job as manager as knocking down the barriers that stand between my staff and their doing their jobs well," I said. "I try to create the environment where the people I hire can be successful."

"That sounds great," Fenty said. I wasn't sure he had paid much attention. "Is this job something you'd consider?"

"Actually, Mayor, I agreed to this meeting not to interview for the job but to tell you about The New Teacher Project. I live in Denver, have two kids and a tough personal situation. I'm not really certain that I could even honestly consider this job."

"Well," he said, "I think it's a great opportunity, and I really think you should consider it."

And with that, Mayor Fenty left the room.

I picked up my things, and Abby walked me out of the build-ing. I went back to my hotel room and called Klein.

"Well?" Joel asked excitedly.

"Eh," I said. "He didn't knock my socks off. I don't think I can take this on, and I don't know that I even want to. In the back of my head I sort of wanted him to inspire the heck out of me. If I was ever really to consider taking on a job like this, I would want to be working for someone who is really exciting."

"Can I be honest?" Klein asked. "You're an adult now. You don't need your boss to inspire you. You can be the inspiring leader. What you really need in this situation is a mayor who will back you up one hundred percent. You're focused on the absolute wrong thing."

"I don't know," I said. "The bottom line is I don't think we really connected. I wouldn't be surprised if this thing ends here."

"Well, get some rest. Sleep on it," Klein said. "We'll see."

I woke up at four the next morning so I could catch a flight to Denver to get back in time to attend my daughter Olivia's pre-K graduation ceremony. When I landed, I turned on my phone and checked my messages. The first one was from Klein.

"Joel Klein. Call me as soon as possible," it said.

I called.

"Well, he didn't knock your socks off, but you knocked his socks off. Fenty called me first thing this morning. He wants you to be the first chancellor of the Washington, D.C., public schools."

"Holy crap" was the only thing I could get out of my mouth.

FOR THE FIRST TIME, it dawned on me that the possibility of running the D.C. schools was real. Despite my genuine efforts to downplay my desire and capacity for the job, Klein had advocated for me, and Fenty was ready to offer up the position.

And for the first time, I started to imagine myself as chancellor.

True, it would put stress on my daughters and Kevin. We would have to pull up stakes again and move to D.C. I was reluctant to add strain to an already shaky situation.

But if I were at the helm of a public school system, I could put into practice many of the recommendations TNTP had proposed to other school districts. Perhaps I could bring along some of my best staff from TNTP. Perhaps we could put in place a process to evaluate teachers. We could gather data to measure student achievement. Maybe we could streamline the way the system terminated incompetent teachers. We could reward the best teachers. We would start making students—rather than adults—the top priority.

It was definitely intriguing. The first conversation I had was with Kevin. Though we were essentially separated, we were still living in the same house. And while our marriage was on the rocks, we talked constantly and trusted one another. I told him what was happening.

"Wow! What a story," he said. "This is unbelievable!" As an education reformer himself, Kevin understood the challenges and the opportunity. He was incredibly excited by the prospects. We talked for a couple of hours.

"Look," he said, "the bottom line for me is that I think this is a nearly impossible job. But if *anyone* can do it, you can. I think you should do it. I would be willing to move across the country so you can take it."

That conversation made the prospect a reality for me for the first time. It allayed my greatest fear. If Kevin was willing to move back to Washington, D.C., with me and our daughters, maybe I could actually make this work.

NEXT I MET WITH Kati Haycock and Jan Somerville from the Education Trust, an organization that had supported TNTP. They were two of my most trusted confidants.

"No freaking way!" said Kati, voicing her disbelief and her dis-
approval at the same time. "You know this city and its school district are on a completely different level of dysfunction. Don't do it."

"Come on," I pleaded. "We always sit around lamenting about
what superintendents *aren't* doing. This is a chance for us to put
our money where our mouths are. We could walk the walk!"

"She's right, Kati," said Jan. "It would be pretty spectacular!"

"Absolutely *not*," said Kati. "You'll get slaughtered by the
racial politics. It won't even matter that you're smart and capable
with all of the right ideas. The racial politics will do you in, and I
care about you and your career way too much to let that happen."

Her thoughts definitely gave me pause. I thanked them both
and hugged them as I left the dinner, even more confused than
before. As I turned to leave, Jan gave me a half, knowing smile. I
think she sensed I was inclined to do it, and she was already wish-
ing me luck.

Then I called Kaya Henderson. Kaya was one of my favorite
people in the world. Her mom, Kathleen, was an educator in their
hometown of Mount Vernon, New York, and became a school
principal at thirty. Kaya excelled at Mount Vernon High, got a
degree in international relations from Georgetown University, and
later got a master's in leadership there. Education was her passion.
She taught middle school Spanish in the South Bronx, where she
became enraged by the raw deal that poor kids were getting in
public schools. She joined Teach For America, where we met and
became kindred spirits. I brought Kaya into The New Teacher
Project. She rose to become vice president of strategic partner-
ships and ran Teaching Fellows programs, including the one in
Washington, D.C. Kaya knew D.C., the schools, the unions.

"You are never going to believe this," I told her.

"What?" she asked excitedly. She knew I wasn't one to exaggerate.

"They want me to become the chancellor of the D.C. schools,"
I said.

"Shut up and stop messing with me," Kaya retorted.

"No, I'm serious!" I said.

"Okay, that's crazy! This is crazy! Oh my dear sweet Jesus!" She was yelling.

When she calmed down she asked, "Are you going to do it?"

"That depends on one thing," I said.

"What?"

"You have to come with me. I won't do it without you. You have to bite off your pinkie."

At TNTP I'd told the senior staff an old Korean story about a group of rebels who'd gone off to fight during the Japanese occupation. In order to prove their loyalty, they each bit off the top of their pinkie and wrote their name in blood on a banner. When TNTP was entering into a new three-year strategic plan I told the senior management team they all had to bite off their pinkies and sign up for three years.

Kaya knew what I was talking about.

"Lord help us, this is so nuts," she said.

"Well?" I asked.

"I'm in, mama! Let's go!" she said.

MY LAST MEETING WAS with John Deasy. He was the head of the Prince George's County, Maryland, public schools and one of my favorite superintendents. He was unapologetic about his focus on closing the achievement gap, so I felt a kinship with him. We met for dinner on Pennsylvania Avenue, a few blocks from the White House.

"Do it!" he said. "You *have* to."

"Ugh, I don't know," I lamented.

"What's not to know? This is what you've been waiting for your whole life."

"I don't know this guy, the mayor. I mean, it would be one

thing if we knew each other and I trusted him, but I don't know him from Adam. What if he turns out to be a flake?"

"Let me tell you one thing. I've been watching this whole scenario unfold, being right across the border. This guy, Fenty, he is putting his entire political life on the line to take over the schools. And he wants you to be his chancellor. And you're asking whether or not you can trust him? He's putting his political life in your hands, for God's sake! Have a sense of perspective!"

In our first meeting, I had not connected with Adrian Fenty. He seemed distant and cold. With Joel Klein's and John Deasy's encouraging words and Kaya's commitment to join me in mind, I returned to D.C. to meet with Fenty one-on-one. I needed to look him in the eyes, measure his words as he asked me to be his chancellor. And I needed to ask him a few essential questions.

This time Fenty ushered me into the cavernous mayoral suite, in the top floor of the John Wilson Building, on Pennsylvania Avenue between the White House and Capitol Hill. This time he was dressed in a dark blue suit, crisp white shirt, and polished black cap-toe shoes. His head shone. His eyes burned.

"You don't want me to take this job," I said.

"Yes, I do," he responded. "I am certain that you are the right person to help our children. We need you."

"Your job, as a politician, is to keep the noise levels to a minimum. There is no change without pushback. In order to really fix this system, we'd have to do really radical things that would undoubtedly cause you a lot of headaches."

"As long as what you do is in the best interests of the kids, I don't mind the noise."

"Why me?" I asked. "In any world, it doesn't make sense."

"I'm looking for someone who has a passion for educating children and will work long and hard to improve achievement.

I've been living in D.C. my entire life. I know that we will never be a great city until we have a great public school district for *all* of our kids."

"What," I asked, "would you risk for a chance to turn this system around? Because I can't make any guarantees. . . ."

He considered the question. He paused. His eyes relaxed.

"Everything," he replied.

I believe he smiled. He had me at "everything."

5

Breaking Barriers

n taking the D.C. job, I had my sights set on breaking through barriers in a school system that had resisted reform for decades. Reporters presented a more immediate hurdle: could I open schools on time? The questions cascaded the day we discovered a warehouse where books and supplies had been languishing—for years.

"Mayor Fenty!"

"Chancellor! Chancellor!"

"Chancellor Rhee! Can you answer a few questions?"

The mayor and I were touring the warehouse jammed with boxes upon boxes of unopened textbooks, notebooks, and unused classroom furniture. I looked at the mayor out of the corner of my eye, but neither of us broke stride. He signaled to me that we should stop. We both pivoted and grounded ourselves for what we knew would be an onslaught of questions.

"Is this what you thought it would be, Chancellor?"

"How bad is it?"

"Are you going to be able to open schools on time?"

"We need to know if schools will be opening on time, Chancellor!"

*I had been on the job for two months, with most of that time
spent trying to get ready for school opening. Every day and everywhere I went, reporters and parents asked whether schools
would open on time. I didn't understand it. Schools were slated
to open on August 27. That was the first day of school. Why was
there so much confusion about that?*

*As it turned out, for years in Washington, D.C., judges had
ruled that because of violations to health and fire code standards,
the schools could not be opened. Whenever that happened, city
officials would scramble to meet a minimum threshold of accept-
ability. It often resulted in school opening being delayed two to
three weeks.*

*"I guarantee you," the mayor said with authority, "that
schools will be opening on time this year."*

*"How, Mayor? Are all the books delivered? Are all the build-
ings ready? How can you be sure?" they asked.*

*"I'll let the chancellor answer your specific questions," the
mayor said.*

*"Yes," I wondered to myself. "How indeed?" And then I
stepped in front of the cameras.*

ON THE MORNING OF Tuesday, June 12, 2007, Mayor Fenty
asked me to meet him before eight o'clock in his private office
in the John Wilson Building, D.C.'s city hall, around the corner
and down the street from the White House. I dressed in a cream-
colored jacket, black and cream skirt, and black heels. Fenty's
people had set a press conference for nine thirty to introduce me
as the first chancellor of D.C. schools.

"Let's go down and meet the city council members," he said.

Every Tuesday the city's thirteen council members gathered
for an informal breakfast near their grand, ornate chambers in

the Wilson Building. What a lovely way to meet the legislators, I thought, right? Wrong.

My official introduction to the city was unorthodox at best. It had begun two days before, when I arrived in the city on Sunday morning with my two daughters and my parents. As we walked off the plane, we passed a newspaper stand. The front page of the *Washington Post* asked, "Can D.C. Schools Be Fixed?"

"Oh, Lordy," I thought.

Starr, my eldest daughter, was right behind me reading the same headline.

"Yes!" she shouted. "My mommy's going to do it!"

I clamped my hand over her mouth and shuffled us to baggage claim.

Once settled in the hotel, I got a call from Mayor Fenty.

"Hey," he said, "how was the trip?"

"Fine, sir," I answered.

"The kids and your parents settled in?"

"Yes, we're great, thanks," I said.

"Okay, okay, good," he continued. "I'm thinking about meeting with an editorial board writer tonight. Not sure if I should have you come or not. What do you think?"

My mind was racing. I'd never been in this kind of situation before.

"Well, it might be better if you laid the groundwork without me. But if you think I should attend I'm willing," I said.

"Yeah, yeah," he said, mostly to himself. "I'll get back to you." And he hung up.

A short while later I got another call. This was from Victor Reinoso, the deputy mayor for education.

"The mayor wants you to come to the meeting. Carrie Brooks will be at the hotel in fifteen minutes to pick you up," he said.

"Victor!" I said. "We haven't even prepped or discussed what he wants me to say! Shouldn't we be a little more prepared before my first major interview?"

"It'll be fine," Victor said. "You'll do great!"

He was about to hang up.

"*Wait*, Victor!" I shouted into the phone.

"Yes?" he asked.

"Who's Carrie?"

I ARRIVED AT CITY HALL early that Sunday afternoon and sat in the mayor's waiting room for a few minutes. Then I was motioned to come back in the room where the mayor had been meeting with the *Washington Post* writers.

Fenty was sitting at the head of the table. Jo-Ann Armao and Dave Nakamura were sitting in the two seats to his right. Armao wrote most of the *Post*'s editorials on local matters; Nakamura covered D.C. politics. I filled the seat to his left and started talking.

"In my core, I'm a teacher. That's why I'm so excited about this opportunity. I realize that I'm a bit of an unconventional choice, but I know schools and I know school districts."

Armao and Nakamura were looking at me as if I were purple.

"Why don't you back up," the mayor said, "and tell them who you are and why you're here."

Are you kidding me? I figured the mayor had been prepping them, teeing up the conversation and explaining why they were sitting there on a Sunday afternoon. The announcement of the new chancellor was the biggest scoop in the city. But apparently the mayor had just been engaged in small talk. They had no idea who I was.

"Of course," I said. "I apologize. My name is Michelle Rhee. I am the new chancellor of the Washington, D.C., public schools."

Jo-Ann Armao's jaw dropped.

David Nakamura smiled. He knew he had a scoop.

. . . .

LATE MONDAY NIGHT, THE day before the scheduled announcement, the mayor called Clifford Janey, the sitting superintendent,
to tell him he was fired. Then he called District of Columbia
Council chairman Vincent Gray to ask for a meeting. It was at
11 p.m.

"Are you people insane?" I asked Victor and his chief of staff,
Eric Lerum. "Who calls for a meeting at eleven p.m.? And who
takes a meeting at eleven p.m.?"

"Oh, trust me," Eric said, "the chairman will be in the office.
And he'll take the meeting."

The mayor and I walked up to Gray's office. It was four minutes after eleven o'clock.

When Fenty had proposed his takeover of the schools in January and guided the legislation through the city council, he had
agreed to collaborate with the legislators in searching for and
choosing the first chancellor. That's not exactly what transpired.

"I would like to introduce you to Michelle Rhee, our new
chancellor," Fenty said.

Though I could tell he was shocked, Gray tried not to show it.
I'm sure his mind was racing, and he was paying scant attention to
my introduction of myself and my experiences. After a few minutes of small talk he stood to shake my hand. "It was a pleasure
meeting you, Ms. Rhee. I look forward to working with you."

THE NEXT MORNING, AS we huddled in the mayor's office shortly
before the announcement, the staff guided George Parker and
Nathan Saunders into the room. Parker was president of the Washington Teachers' Union; Saunders was the VP. I had had some
experience with George through my work at The New Teacher
Project. I knew him to be a fair and reasonable guy.

"Hey, Kaya!" he exclaimed and kissed Kaya Henderson on the cheek as he entered into the room.

"So you know Kaya, that's great!" the mayor said. "And that must mean you know our new chancellor, Kaya's boss, Michelle Rhee."

"Uh, yeah, Michelle, nice to see you," George sputtered.

"As you know," the mayor continued, "the Public Education Reform Act requires that you have the opportunity to meet the chancellor candidate. So here she is."

George, like Vincent Gray, was stunned.

"I think we're ready to go down to the press conference now, Mr. President," the mayor said. Then he asked, "Are you comfortable?"

"Uh, yeah," Parker said, and we headed downstairs to stop at the council breakfast, before the press conference.

The *Washington Post* had blasted the news of my nomination on the front page that Tuesday morning. When we got downstairs, the council members had already read the paper, and the press was buzzing outside of city hall.

The mayor introduced me to the council members one by one. I shook hands and tried to make small talk. More thin lips and stunned expressions.

"We would love you to join us for the press conference," Fenty said. At 9:15 a.m., we all filed out and stood in front of the Wilson Building, the sun splashing across the steps, a bank of cameras staring at us.

As the mayor stepped up to the podium, a reporter spoke first.

"Mayor Fenty! Mayor Fenty!" she screamed. "Why do you insist on showing favoritism to the *Washington Post*? There are many media outlets in this city! It is unconscionable that you would repeatedly show favoritism to the *Washington Post* alone!"

He ignored her.

"Within the past hour," Fenty said, without skipping a beat, "I have signed a mayoral order appointing Michelle Rhee acting chancellor."

No one could even hear what he was saying because this woman was screaming over him. Yet he continued as if nothing was happening. Is that what I'm supposed to do, too? Just pretend I don't hear this lady screeching in my ear?

I stepped to the microphone. I smiled. Silence. "Good morning," I said. Some clapped, tepidly. I looked up. My family and friends were the only ones putting their hands together.

"Thank you, Mayor Fenty. I see this as a tremendous opportunity. . . ."

We smiled. We shook a few hands. It seemed like a dream.

THERE WOULD BE NO opportunity to mend fences or smooth ruffled feathers.

After a brief stop at District of Columbia Public Schools (DCPS) headquarters, we hopped in a van for the first foray in a summer-long tour of the District of Columbia, from border to border. Aboard the van were Tim Daly and Ariela Rozman, my successors at TNTP. They were helping to staff me for the first few days because they knew me best.

Our first stop was Benning Elementary School, on D.C.'s east side. We headed away from downtown and the National Mall on Pennsylvania Avenue, drove up Capitol Hill past the House office buildings, the U.S. Capitol to our left, and crossed the Anacostia River to Ward 7, home to D.C.'s black working and middle class. I started to see firsthand how much my new home—the city behind the monuments—was starkly divided by race, class, and power.

The Founding Fathers created the District of Columbia in 1790, fulfilling plans spelled out in the Constitution. They envisioned a federal enclave that would house the government, but they wanted to separate it from the state politics of Maryland and Virginia. It was placed under federal control in 1801, with

Congress and the president to run the city. They didn't anticipate the population that would come to live in the city around the government. Waves of residents have since flocked to the District of Columbia, especially during the two world wars. Many African Americans migrated up from North Carolina and formed a solid middle class, nurtured by jobs in the federal government. Under segregation, schools such as Dunbar High were among the finest in the nation.

For more than 150 years, except for a brief period after the Civil War, the District of Columbia suffered without an elected local government. It failed to develop a homegrown political class. White supremacists in Congress ran the city as if it were a plantation. They disregarded the health, welfare, and education of the black underclass, which grew and eventually settled in neighborhoods east of Rock Creek and across the Anacostia River.

When President Dwight Eisenhower desegregated the D.C. schools in 1954, many whites moved to the suburbs. By 1960, D.C. had become the first majority African American city in the nation.

President Lyndon Johnson started the move toward limited self-government in 1965, which paved the way for local leaders and civil rights activists to run for local office. Marion Barry was among them. Barry's first step into elective politics was a run for school board president in 1971. D.C. schools were already among the worst in the nation. Barry vowed to improve the schools and campaigned across town in a Camaro with the poster "United To Save the Children." He won, but rather than improve the schools, he used the post as a stepping-stone.

Home Rule—with an elected mayor, city council, and school board—took effect in 1974, under President Richard Nixon. Barry was elected mayor first in 1978, and then three times after that.

As head of the school board and in his four terms as mayor,

Barry paid scant attention to the schools. When pressured to reform education, he said that schools were under the control of the school board, which was statutorily accurate. For the next twenty-five years, school buildings fell into disrepair, the Washington Teachers' Union controlled the classrooms, nepotism ruled the central administration—and generations of African American students were not taught to read or write, add or subtract. The dropout rate was above 50 percent.

But in white neighborhoods east of Rock Creek Park, some schools were among the best in the nation. Elementary schools prepared students to excel. Each year top graduates of Wilson High, an integrated school in Tenleytown, went to Harvard, Princeton, and the Massachusetts Institute of Technology. The achievement gap was a canyon.

WHEN WE PULLED UP to Benning Elementary, I saw the results of that quarter century of neglect. The one-story, tan-brick building looked more like a jail than a school. A low concrete wall surrounded it. It had no grass or playground.

I might well have been the first superintendent to set foot in Benning, and the administrators had set up a table with cheese and crackers. I was more interested in checking the classrooms than chatting. Benning was hot and dark inside, the lights turned off to keep it cool since the air-conditioning wasn't working. The school seemed empty, because it was operating at half capacity. Benning was designed for the open classroom model, and the few students I saw seemed distracted.

Principal Darwin Bobbitt walked us past the library. I stopped.

"There are no books in here," I said. "This is supposed to be the library. What's going on?"

"We didn't have enough books," he said, "so we took down the shelves. Why pretend to have a library?"

. . . .

THERE WAS NO PRETENDING that D.C. schoolchildren weren't in dire straits.

Low-income black children in the fourth grade scored the worst in the country on federal reading tests. Eighty-eight percent of eighth graders scored below proficiency in English. In the nationwide report card—the National Assessment of Educational Progress—children that I would be responsible for were scoring far worse than their counterparts in other cities. Their performance was the worst in the country.

Most people blamed poverty for the low academic achievement levels of the children in D.C. They were wrong. The federal report card showed that poor African American students in New York City were two grade levels ahead of the poor black kids in Washington, D.C. On average, fourth- and eighth-grade students in the District of Columbia were about a year behind students in similar straits nationwide, in cities such as Houston and Boston. There is no doubt that poverty and home environment have an impact on students and schools, but clearly there was something terribly wrong with the D.C. schools.

I was not the first leader to promise reform, and I was not the first outsider. The district had churned through six superintendents in the ten years before Fenty asked me to step in with the new title of chancellor. I saw a cautionary tale in retired general Julius Becton, who had taken over in 1996 and promised change. "Failure is not an option," he said. The general never got control of the central administration or the schools. His administration failed to open schools on schedule. The bureaucracy couldn't come up with an accurate count of students. He said trying to run D.C.'s public schools was harder than fighting in a war. He resigned after sixteen months.

I was convinced that the culture of the school system and the quality of instruction in the schools had combined to frustrate superintendents and fail students. The national studies proved my case: it was not just the poverty or drugs or broken families or violence that made it hard to teach kids.

To paraphrase Clinton adviser James Carville: It was the schools, stupid. And the mind-set.

Tim pointed out a sign he'd found in Slowe Elementary, one of the stops on the tour of schools that first day: "Teachers cannot make up for what parents and students will not do."

Wonder why I was enraged?

THE EVENING OF MY first day on the job, after visiting Benning Elementary, we pulled the van up to Angela Copeland's house on W Street, in D.C.'s Anacostia neighborhood, around the corner from Union Temple Baptist Church. Copeland's row house was painted pastel blue with white pillars. The plants on the porch gave it an inviting feeling, but I didn't feel too welcomed when I first got out of the van. Conversations stopped. People stared.

I could tell what they were thinking. "What's this Asian lady doing here?"

As an outsider in so many ways, I was determined to show up in neighborhoods and homes across D.C. and make myself accessible to all. The visit to Copeland's house was the first of four meetings in living rooms that first week. At every home—and at every encounter at every school thereafter—I would give out my cell phone number and invite people to call.

"Are you sure you want to give your number to everyone?" Eric Lerum kept asking. He was the mayoral aide Fenty had assigned to me for my first month on the job.

"Absolutely sure," I responded. "Parents, teachers, students— they all have to know that they can reach me, get a response and reaction, that we can try and answer questions and fix problems."

But no cell phone contact could fix the problems I knew I would encounter inside Angela Copeland's home. There were about fifteen parents waiting for me in her front room. Copeland introduced me. I smiled. No one smiled back. No one was rude, just skeptical.

I sat down on an ottoman in the middle of the room, looked around, and set my eyes on a woman whose lips were pursed and eyes most doubtful.

"Now, I know what you all are wondering," I said. "What does a Korean lady from Toledo, Ohio, know about running schools, and why did Adrian Fenty pick her? Am I right?"

I stopped. I smiled. I could tell I had disarmed them. They weren't expecting me to talk about the elephant in the room.

"Have you ever had a schools superintendent ask to meet with you in your homes?"

"No" came the chorus.

"Well, I'm here. My job is to ensure that every kid in this city is in a great school so that all of them are getting an excellent education. What do I need to do to accomplish that?"

Hire teachers who will challenge our kids. Bring art and music back in the schools. Repair the buildings, enrich the after-school programs, enforce discipline.

When I left two hours later, I might not have converted the group, but I had established a connection, offered up my cell phone number, and promised to return. I also got my first sense of the sameness and separation that I would encounter among parents from different parts of the city.

On my second night on the job, after meeting with council members and telling a cadre of top principals that I was committed to supporting them, I met with parents at a home all the way across town, in the Palisades neighborhood of Northwest D.C. The Koczela home was a lovely house set back on beautifully landscaped grounds. There was a Volvo wagon in the driveway and a BMW parked across the street. I could have been on another planet.

Here there was standing room only in the living room. There must have been at least fifty people. They seemed relieved to meet me and adored Kaya Henderson. I didn't feel the need to break the ice, but when I asked for questions, they sounded very much like the ones I had heard the night before across town in Anacostia: better teachers, more art classes, courses in Latin and French, and more than once: "Please rebuild the schools and fields."

My promise to these parents was simple: "I am about preventing the district school bureaucracy from impeding your plans to improve your schools. I know it has been a drag in the past."

Most of these parents left happy, but I was left with a quandary. Here in this wealthy, white neighborhood, I was accepted and welcomed. Yet these parents and their kids and their schools didn't need much from me. I wasn't planning to devote as much time and energy to them. Most of the schools west of Rock Creek Park were in fine shape compared with the ones east of the Anacostia. My challenge and my passion was around raising achievement for the children of the folks I had met the night before. I was intent on improving their schools, their teachers, their outcomes. Yet those parents were so skeptical of me.

How could I bridge that gap?

THE BEST PLACE TO start was from the pulpit.

"Church," Kevin Johnson told me. "You gotta go to a black church."

Kevin Johnson—or KJ, as his fans called him—had become a friend and confidant. We'd met at an education conference a few years back, and he'd convinced me to sit on the board of his nonprofit organization in Sacramento, St. HOPE Public Schools. I trusted him immediately. A former NBA star, KJ was an anomaly.

He returned to the community he grew up in to start charter schools. He wasn't about the razzle-dazzle of being a former pro athlete. He worked harder than anyone else in his organization. I got used to getting emails from him at two o'clock in the morning. In fact, he was so different from what people expected from KJ the phenom, that I refused to refer to him as that, preferring KMJ (using his middle initial) instead. As a board member at St. HOPE, I was usually the one giving him advice. This time the tables had turned.

"You may know schools," he explained, "but I know black people. We know when someone is phony. You genuinely care about black kids getting a great education. My people will sense this immediately, and that will help you. But in order for them to understand that about you, you need to get out. You need to go to church."

At 8 a.m. Sunday a few weeks later, I went to Bible Way on New Jersey Avenue, N.W., for the morning service. Bible Way, started in 1957 by the Reverend Smallwood Williams, is one of Washington's bedrock black churches. The morning prayers have been broadcast on WOL-AM every Sunday for the past fifty years.

I tried to attend a black church service as often as possible. I bought KMJ's advice that it was critical to build support in the community. If I was going to be closing schools and firing teachers I'd be finished unless I got the community to trust me, to back me.

The pews were full. Rev. Cornelius Showell introduced me. I was the only one in the church who was not African American. He surprised me by asking me to address the congregation and speak to the radio audience. I walked up the stairs and mounted the pulpit.

"The schools in our city have been failing our children for far too long," I said. "The only people who have paid the price for these failing schools have been the kids."

Some clapped.

"I am committed to changing the way we educate our children," I continued. "There is no reason why children in Anacostia can't have the same education and the same opportunities as children in Georgetown."

The congregation rose and cheered.

"It will require tremendous change," I said. "I'm going to need the entire community to help me. It can't happen only within the four walls of the school building. I need to work hand in hand with you.

"I ask for your prayers."

SOME OF MY PRAYERS were answered when a few of the best minds and hearts in education reform responded to my pleas to start an education revolution in Washington, D.C.

There were also some hidden gems within the district schools—people who relished a real opportunity to turn it around, like instructional superintendent Bill Wilhoyte, operations manager Dave Anderson, chief business officer Abdusalam Omer, administrative assistant Joyce McNeil, and finance guru Noah Wepman. I also sweet-talked some TFA alums with whom I'd worked throughout the years—John Davis, Billy Kearney, and Chad Ferguson, and my coworkers from Baltimore, Michele Jacobs and Deonne Medley—into joining me.

But it wasn't enough. Not by a long shot. We needed to bring in an entire senior staff. Kaya and I went to work building a team.

The first target was Richard Nyankori. Richard had worked for me at TNTP. He had been widely known as my favorite in the TNTP ranks. Unbelievably talented and one of the most innovative thinkers I knew, Richard was the ultimate utility player. He could do anything and talk to anyone about anything. Fortunately, he lived in D.C. He agreed to join us. I immediately put him on the toughest assignment in the district: fix special education.

Next was Jason Kamras. Jason was a TFA corps member who had taught in DCPS for ten years and was named the National Teacher of the Year, the first ever to come from the District of Columbia. I had been trying to get him to join TNTP after he finished what I like to call his "Miss America tour" around the country as Teacher of the Year. It didn't take much convincing. He was sick at heart with what he'd seen as a DCPS teacher, and he was convinced that the teachers deserved so much more.

I knew that one of my biggest problems was going to be data. How could we get a handle on the basic information about how students were performing? I also knew the solution: Erin Mc-Goldrick, a bright young woman who, by her own admission, was enamored of data. Years earlier I had convinced her to join the board of St. HOPE. I was incredibly impressed with her skills in measuring student achievement. Taking this job would require her to move across the country from Los Angeles to Washington. "This is a dream come true!" she said and packed her bags.

I put out the word with every education reformer in the country that we were looking for talent. I got an email from Andy Rotherham, a well-known policy wonk and friend. He told me that a TFA alum he knew had heard about me getting the job and was desperate to come work for me. He assured me that I wouldn't regret the decision for a minute. He was right. Margery Yeager proved to be an invaluable asset throughout my tenure, running the Critical Response Team. Their job, to field the calls from all of the unhappy constituents of DCPS, was one of the toughest in the city. She and her team did it masterfully.

In my early days, my office was a mess. At TNTP I never had an assistant because I couldn't stand other people being in charge of my schedule. It became clear very quickly, though, that that would have to change. Liz Peterson, my TFA roommate from

Baltimore, and Amma Aboagye, an intern I hired from Cornell University, were about to leave. I was in trouble. Richard set up an interview with his best friend, Shawn Branch. We met on the stoop outside of my house. It was not love at first sight. We both had strong wills and spoke our minds; I could foresee conflicts. But I was desperate, so I hired him. It was the best decision I'd made. He and Angela Williams-Skelton ran my crazy schedule and made the office run like clockwork. I started to refer to Shawn as "my boss."

I moved Mafara Hobson and Abby Smith over from the mayor's office, Mafara to be press secretary and Abby to run the DCPS "transformation office," which would engineer school consolidation. I hired Peggy O'Brien, a longtime District of Columbia resident and educator, to run our community affairs.

Last but certainly not least, I needed a general counsel. After being told "no!" by my legal team at every turn for several months, I was fed up. So many of the challenges we were facing in the school district were legal ones, and I needed first-class legal talent. Frustrated, I went to speak at a Legal Aid breakfast, and at the end yelled, "If anyone can find me a decent general counsel can you please send him or her my way?" From that came Jim Sandman, the managing partner at Arnold & Porter, one of D.C.'s top law firms, who agreed to take a huge pay cut to come and work for the district because he believed in the work we were doing. He was a godsend.

MY FIRST CHALLENGE AS chancellor of public schools in the nation's capital was to have a smooth opening of schools after summer vacation. Our goal was pretty simple: we wanted to welcome students back with clean schools, teachers in every classroom, class schedules, and ample supplies. Was I setting the bar too high?

Given the district's spotty record for starting class on schedule, it was hardly a given. In years past, schools would greet excited and nervous students with chaos. Classroom assignments were garbled. Hundreds of high schoolers spent weeks without schedules or lockers. Children sat in a classroom for hours without a teacher. Textbooks? Maybe—maybe not.

The first sign that my inaugural opening day might not go smoothly came when I attended my first meeting in the central office to discuss the progress we were making on the opening of schools. When I walked in the door every staff person stopped chatting and stared.

"Ladies and gentlemen, Chancellor Rhee!" exclaimed the high-level staffer running the meeting.

The participants clapped enthusiastically. They were running for their lives. The district had seen six superintendents in ten years. With each new leader came a shuffling in the central office. Everyone was on his or her best behavior.

All eyes were on me.

"No, no," I said. "Please don't mind me. Carry on with your meeting. I simply want to observe."

That wasn't what they expected me to say. People didn't know what to do. After some shuffling about, they continued. The room was packed. There were representatives from every department, and each had prepared a presentation about what his team was doing to get ready for school opening. The PowerPoints were pretty. But I wasn't sold. Far from it. Every department was putting on a dog-and-pony show with graphs and charts, but no one was asking any basic questions: for example, whether there were enough teachers at every school. No one was talking about problems or challenges. According to the presentations, you'd have thought we were in the highest-functioning school district in the nation.

Most important, there was no evidence or data that what

was being presented was an accurate reflection of reality in the schools.

After the meeting I called Jenny Abramson into my office. The mayor's office had hired Jenny, who had agreed to take a leave from her job at the *Washington Post*, to oversee the transition.

"That is the *last* time we'll be having a school opening meeting like that!" I said.

"What happened?" she asked.

"It was everyone sitting around congratulating one another on their beautiful slide presentations, but it gave us absolutely no indication as to whether or not we're ready to open schools."

I asked her to get her team out into the schools with a checklist: Books, supplies, schedules, lockers, teachers, furniture, clean buildings. It wasn't rocket science, just the basics.

"We need to figure out where the hot spots are so we can fix them immediately," I said.

"Got it," she said, and with that she flew out of the office. Jenny was efficient. I knew she'd get the information.

Then I yelled to Liz Peterson, my best friend from the Harlem Park days and beyond. She had come on her summer break as a teacher to help my transition. "Try Lisa Ruda *again*, please," I begged.

Liz popped her head in my office. "I left her three messages yesterday."

"Call again. Keep calling until she answers. Stalk her."

"Okaaay," Liz said skeptically.

A WEEK LATER JENNY ABRAMSON came back from her tour of schools. She had the data. It was ugly. The schools were in disarray. Most had been locked up on the last day of school and not touched since. Air conditioners were broken all over the district. Each school needed a deep cleaning. There were broken lockers and cracked floor tiles everywhere. Furthermore, no one seemed to know what the process was for making sure that every child knew what to expect.

When I was a kid, we'd excitedly run over to the school a few weeks before it started to see our class assignments. They'd be posted on the doors so you knew who your homeroom teacher would be. We would beg our parents to take us school shopping with the supply list clutched in our hands.

Here in D.C., there were no class assignments. No supply lists. No books.

On August 4, two weeks before the start of school, Mayor Fenty joined me in a search for missing books. First stop was the DCPS central warehouse, a three-story brick building in an industrial district along railroad tracks on the city's far eastern corner.

We found the missing books—not just for opening day 2007 but for prior years, too. We walked across floors piled high with boxes upon boxes of unopened books. By the time I reached the second floor, I was ready to throw up. Some rooms were stacked with new desks and chairs. Those missing notebooks that teachers had to pay for with their own money? Pencils, glue, rulers, binders? All there, but never sent to students.

The press showed up.

"I toured all three floors of this warehouse," I said. "What I found was shocking."

What I didn't find were the shipments of new science and social studies textbooks we had ordered. "A lot of them did get out to the schools," I said, "but not every classroom is complete—again."

Fenty, dressed in a dark suit and tie on a sweltering day, was cool and calm. "We knew we had a huge uphill climb in turning around our school district. Every day we find something worse than we had imagined."

I despaired that I, too, would not open the schools in perfect shape.

. . . .

I HAD ASKED JENNY to put together a presentation showing how bad things were and how much work we had to do in order to be ready to open the schools. At the next scheduled school-opening meeting, I was in the room at the head of the table as people filed in. They smiled and waved at me. I didn't smile back. We were in serious trouble, and I wanted them to know it.

"Good morning," I began. "Since I attended the meeting last week, I sent a team out to the schools to determine our readiness. The bottom line is we're not ready. Not even close. Jenny?"

I handed the meeting over to Jenny and her deputy, Anthony deGuzman, who walked through a slide deck that showed in painstaking detail how ill-prepared we were. When they were done, the lights went up in the room.

"Needless to say," I said, "we're going to have to be working every waking hour between now and August twenty-fourth to get ready. Any questions?"

I could hear some murmurings and saw uncomfortable shifts in the room.

"What's the problem?" I asked.

"Well, Chancellor," someone piped up hesitantly, "a number of us are slated to take our vacation days over the next few weeks."

"You know," another one said sheepishly, "get rested up before school starts."

I stood up and left the room.

I WENT BACK INTO my office. I laid my throbbing head on the desk.

Liz interrupted the ache: "Lisa Ruda is on the line!"

Salvation!

During my years at The New Teacher Project we worked with

most of the large, urban school districts in the country. Great talent was hard to come by. When Kaya and I tried to think of any administrators who had district experience that we wanted to hire, we both immediately thought of Lisa Ruda.

She had served as the chief of staff of the Cleveland Municipal School District. Tough and no-nonsense, she got things done. I wanted her on the team.

"Lisa Ruda!" I said excitedly into the phone.

"Congratulations," she said. "I heard the news."

"Let me cut to the chase. I need you here. Yesterday. This place is a mess," I said.

"What's going on?" she asked.

"For starters, I just got out of a school-opening meeting, and we're totally jacked. The buildings are a wreck, no supplies and books. This is going to be a disaster."

"That's how it was when I got to Cleveland," she said. "Don't worry. It'll get better. It's bumpy at first but you just have to put the right systems in place. Now I can open schools with my eyes closed."

"That's why I need you," I said.

"Yeah, I'm flattered, but I can't," she said. She explained that after serving as chief of staff for years, she was made interim CEO for a stretch, which put her out of her element. She was a behind-the-scenes type, not an out-in-front one, and she was burned-out.

"I've decided to go back into private practice and accepted a job with a white-shoe law firm," she said.

"*Please,*" I pleaded. "This world doesn't need any more lawyers. We do need great schools, though. This is a once-in-a-lifetime opportunity. This mayor is unbelievable. He's given me full authority to do whatever I need to fix the district. At least come out and visit."

Two days later she was in D.C. I sicced the mayor on her to put on the hard sell. On her way back to the airport, I was scheduled to meet with her. I was trying to figure out how to seal the deal.

She walked into my office.

"I'm in," she said.

We were lucky that Lisa brought Sherry Ulery and Tracy Martin with her from Cleveland to work on schools and curriculum and instruction.

"The first order of business," Lisa said, "is that we put a moratorium on vacations for all central office employees. No one goes anywhere until these schools are ready to open!"

WHAT WE SET IN motion that first summer before schools opened, and the talented team that we established, would help organize and propel us for the next three years. The people attracted to our cause and goals were equally committed and decisive.

Fewer roofs were leaky as we got closer to August 27, the day schools were scheduled to open. Mayor Fenty had appointed Allen Lew to manage school facilities. Lew had overseen the development of D.C.'s new convention center and baseball stadium. He was the perfect person to repair all the schools, renovate some, and build new ones from scratch. During the summer of 2007, Lew and his contractors completed thousands of work orders that had been piling up for years. They fixed toilets, refurbished heating systems, patched roofs, and painted walls.

Still, as we got closer to August 27, I was not convinced every school would be ready to welcome students with supplies and books and teachers.

In mid-August we gathered all five thousand teachers at the Washington Convention Center. They didn't know much about me. I would imagine they were as apprehensive as the parents at Angela Copeland's house. I took the stage, looked across the room, and smiled.

"I am Michelle Rhee. I'm the new chancellor of the D.C. public schools," I said. "Just in case there was any confusion, I am, in fact, Korean. I am thirty-seven years old. And, no, I have never run a school district before."

I thought I saw a few smiles out there. After telling them a bit about my years as a teacher in Baltimore, I set out the challenges we faced.

"All the eyes of the country are now on Washington, D.C.," I told them. "I believe what we are embarking upon is a fight for the lives of children. And we can accomplish it, together."

A week or so later, students from one end of D.C. to the other started class on schedule. All 144 schools were clean, staffed, and ready. Not every one of those new books we had ordered was in the hands of the teachers—it was not a perfect opening day—but we notched a success and passed the first test of the year.

EVERY NOW AND THEN I would stroll the halls of the school system's bureaucracy. The central administrators worked out of an office building on North Capitol Street, across from the U.S. Government Printing Office. We could walk outside and see the U.S. Capitol dome a few blocks away.

One day I ducked into an office, introduced myself, and asked the woman behind the desk, "What do you do?"

She gave me her title.

"I see that," I said, "but what do you do every day? What are your tasks? What do you do for the schools? The students?"

She said, "Well, I do whatever Mrs. Johnson tells me to do."

That's a fine response in a bureaucracy that exists to perpetuate itself, but I knew D.C. schools needed workers downtown who were focused on tasks that had a direct impact on children and who understood that everything they did or didn't do would impact kids. That wasn't everyone that I found when I first started.

In his four terms as mayor, Marion Barry had grown the city

bureaucracy to more than forty thousand employees, and even though he had no direct control over the schools, his culture of using the D.C. government as an engine of employment had seeped into the school system. It had grown to nearly a thousand employees, and I was not convinced that all of them were needed or doing essential tasks for students.

The "Central-Office Hydra" is what Colbert King, a *Washington Post* columnist who covered the city, called the DCPS administration in an essay the summer I arrived. "It is a large and powerful creature," he wrote. "It has kept schools from opening on time, swallowed repair orders by the thousands, made teachers' paychecks disappear, consumed tax dollars by the millions without producing any discernible results and, ultimately, acquired a well-deserved reputation for treating schoolchildren as if they are nuisances."

I knew there were many downtown workers who were committed to quality education, and I was determined to find them, keep them, and reward them. The ones who were using the school system for a paycheck would have to go.

From experience I knew that things could get done. I got a call one morning from Susan Schaeffler, head of the DC KIPP charter schools and an old friend from TFA Baltimore. She was running summer school in one of our buildings.

"The kids are supposed to show up tomorrow and the air-conditioning doesn't work. I know this is so petty to bring to you but anything you could do would be great," she said.

I called maintenance and told them to fix it.

A few hours later Susan called back.

"I don't know what you did but two trucks just rolled up in front of the school. They fixed the air conditioners. I don't know how to thank you. Wow! If this is any indication of how things will change, I'm in!" she said.

It was sad to me, though. Susan had been calling the central office for weeks for help, to no avail. She wasn't alone. I had gotten an email from a teacher who said that for the entire year he had deductions taken from his paycheck for health care for him and his wife. His wife had been in an accident and taken to the hospital but was told that she had been rejected by the insurance company as not being covered. He was frantic. In a last-ditch effort, he emailed me. It turned out that his wife's paperwork had never been filed, so while we were taking his money, his wife wasn't being covered.

"Totally frustrating," he wrote.

I was able to fix it.

During my first few weeks, I brought the central office staff together.

"As I walk around the halls of the central office," I said, "and I listen to how people operate, listen to the way they answer the phone or the way they deal with people coming into the building, it sounds like they are annoyed. That has to change. This is not a nuisance. This is your job.

"So if you consider answering questions from parents and teachers, fulfilling their requests or giving them information an annoyance, this is not the place for you to work."

Some clapped. I froze hiring.

MAYOR ADRIAN FENTY WAS by my side when I met with the central office staff. In every way, whenever I needed him, he was there. Our connection, our commitment to education, and our capacity to support one another were paramount.

Fenty broke the mold when he was elected mayor in 2006. At thirty-five, he was the youngest to run and win. He was the city's sixth mayor and the second native Washingtonian to hold the office. His mom, Jeanette, came from Italian roots; his father, Phil, grew up in Buffalo, New York, but Phil's parents were originally from Panama and Barbados. Jeanette and Phil came to Washington, D.C., in the late 1960s, became active in civil rights, and then opened Fleet Feet, an athletic-shoe store in the Adams Morgan neighborhood. Adrian, a middle child, grew up in Mount Pleasant, a community with a mix of white, black, and Hispanic working- and middle-class families. He attended D.C. public schools but graduated from Mackin Catholic High School. He attended Oberlin College, where he focused on English and economics, then returned to Washington to get a law degree at Howard University.

Fenty worked on Capitol Hill for a few years, then entered the D.C. political scene as a council aide—with higher ambitions. In 2000 he campaigned door-to-door in Ward 4, home to both the city's African American elite and rough neighborhoods along Georgia Avenue. He knocked off veteran politician Charlene Drew Jarvis and emerged as the highly energetic, fresh face in an ossified legislature. Fenty was restless and impatient on the city council. He focused on constituent services and easily won a second term. Then he shocked the political establishment by taking on council chair Linda Cropp, a stalwart of the old guard, in the decisive Democratic mayoral primary. He walked neighborhoods in all eight wards. Against all odds, he won.

Even before he took office, Fenty started showing signs that he would not be governing within the limits that had become accepted and familiar in D.C. He vowed to apply best practices to running the city. He cast a wide net to staff his government and brought on national leaders as agency heads. He embarked on well-publicized pilgrimages to take pointers from big-city mayors. He visited Los Angeles mayor Antonio Villaraigosa, who was attempting to take control of his city's public schools.

Chicago's Richard M. Daley had taken over his city's schools. Boston mayor Tom Menino encouraged Fenty to be bold and decisive. New York mayor Michael Bloomberg had taken over the school system and advised Fenty to do the same.

In one of his last acts on the council, Fenty engineered passage of a $1 billion commitment to completely refurbish D.C.'s public schools. Then, on his first day as mayor, in January 2007, he introduced legislation to dissolve the board of education and place the D.C. public schools under mayoral control.

If I could distill Fenty's style into three elements, they would be speed, no excuses, and accountability. None of the three had been a feature of local government in the nation's capital, particularly in the school system. Especially accountability.

The flip side of accountability is consequences. I started testing Fenty's backbone on that score, early and often.

In my first months as chancellor, I met with all 144 principals. We had already gathered data on how their students were scoring on achievement tests. We knew which schools were improving, which were in decline. I asked them to set goals and present them when we met. I fired two principals on the spot.

Word was getting out that business as usual was over, and that I would fire people if necessary. It soon got back to Mayor Fenty, through city council members and political operatives, that his new school chancellor might be causing too much trouble, with political costs coming his way.

Fenty called together his top staff, from the attorney general to the city administrator to the chief of staff.

"I want everyone in this room to know that Michelle Rhee has my one hundred percent support, at whatever she does," Fenty said. "The number one priority of this government is to improve the schools. There's only one person who's allowed to say no to the chancellor and that's me. Anyone else who does will be looking for a new job."

. . . .

MAYOR FENTY'S RESOLVE WAS about to be tested: we needed to close dozens of public schools.

In the mid-1960s, DCPS schools topped out at 146,000 students. The number of students had been in steady decline since. Middle-class families had moved to the suburbs. The city's population had been falling, new residents were not starting families, and many who remained were elderly. Charter schools were attracting students from the public schools. By 2001, there were 66,000 students in the public schools and 11,000 in charters. When I became chancellor, the total number of students in both public and charter schools was around 70,000—half of the number in 1967. More than 20,000 were in charter schools, which had opened 70 new campuses. Yet DCPS had closed fewer than 10 schools.

The result was that many schools east of Rock Creek Park and the Anacostia River were half full. We couldn't staff them with art, music, or language teachers, so the students were getting half an education. Take Slowe Elementary, built for 300 students but currently teaching 90. Keeping every school open was not an option.

Starting in October 2007, I called in three well-respected, local research organizations—the Urban Institute, the Brookings Institution, and the 21st Century School Fund. I asked them to analyze enrollment patterns and neighborhood demographics to provide a foundation for our difficult decisions on which schools to close. I assigned Abby Smith and Eric Lerum the task of distilling the raw data down to neighborhoods and their schools. Which schools could we expand as educational and community hubs? Which were too old and too depopulated to save? Which neighborhoods could live together? They had to advise us on those granular decisions and choreograph the process.

Fenty was involved from the start. He knew that superintendents had attempted to close schools in the past. He had witnessed the way they had been beaten down by opposition in the neighborhoods and the city council. I briefed Fenty early on in the process. I said we might have to close or consolidate as many as forty schools.

"Do it," he said. "Rip the Band-Aid off. Don't peel it."

Much easier said than done.

We considered every aspect of each school that was a candidate for closing: from the condition of the facility to the connection to the community; from the safety and walkability for students to the quality of the teachers; from the pattern of feeder schools to the expectation of population growth. We arrived at twenty-three schools that we wanted to shutter. Then the hard work began.

Race and class immediately became fulcrums of controversy. The facts were that many of the schools in Ward 3, home to the majority of D.C.'s white families, were filled to capacity or bursting at the seams. Take Lafayette Elementary, in the Chevy Chase neighborhood of D.C., adjacent to Chevy Chase, Maryland. It was so stuffed, the District of Columbia had to put trailers on the basketball court to accommodate neighborhood students. All of the schools slated to be closed were in the city's eastern wards. Seven of the twenty-three schools were in Ward 5, a working-class black neighborhood with a sprawling industrial zone. Those folks were not pleased.

Knowing that we would be kicking over hornets' nests—twenty-three of them, to be exact—we planned to break the news to council members and principals before the list went public. We had a carefully conceived plan.

It went awry. The night before we were scheduled to brief the council and district staff, a list of schools was leaked to the *Washington Post* on November 28, 2007—with errors. It was a nightmare. Once again people across town felt betrayed, especially council members.

For the next six weeks I met with students, parents, teachers, principals, and council members. I didn't decline a single request for a meeting. I walked into community meetings with Eric Lerum and Abby Smith or alone and stood my ground as people yelled in my face, because I knew that operating half-empty school buildings was part of the reason our schools felt so poorly resourced.

Immediately, I got a call from Marion Barry's office.

"The councilman would like to meet you to discuss school closings," his office said.

We arranged to meet at Draper Elementary, in his ward; the school that had fewer than a hundred students. I decided to arrive early. We parked at the school and I headed across the street to a housing project where a number of older gentlemen were sitting outside.

"Ma'am," Jimmy, my driver, said, "I don't know if this is a good idea."

"I'll be fine," I said, and hopped across the street.

I approached the group of men.

"Hello," I said. "I'm Michelle Rhee, the new chancellor of the D.C. public schools."

"Oh yeah, I know you. I've seen you on the TV," one of them noted.

"What brings you here?" asked another.

"Well, we're considering closing some schools and this is one of the schools on the list," I said.

"Oh no, you can't close this school," said one of the men. "This here is a great school. The principal has been here for thirty-some years. She's wonderful. The teachers are wonderful. The school is wonderful. You can't close down this school. Look at this neighborhood. Do you think what we need is another boarded-up vacant building?"

He was right. The neighborhood was filled with abandoned buildings. But he was wrong about the school. It wasn't a wonderful school. At the time, only 16 percent of the children at the school were working at grade level in math. Sixteen percent! How could anyone think that was wonderful?

They could because in the midst of the despair in the neighborhood, the school was a beacon. It served as a foundation for the community. The familiarity of the institution, the faculty, and its purpose were stabilizing forces in an otherwise chaotic world. For these men, the value of the school wasn't simply in its reading proficiency rates; it was in the constancy it represented in the community.

I saw Marion Barry's Mercedes pull up. I thanked the gentlemen for their insights and walked back across the street.

"Morning, Chancellor," he said.

"Good morning, Councilman Barry," I responded.

"You don't know Ward Eight, but you have to know Ward Eight. Come with me," he said and opened his car door.

I could see Jimmy's eyes widening.

"We can follow you in our car," I said.

"Nonsense, get in!" he said, and I jumped in. In the rearview mirror I could see Jimmy trailing us.

He drove me around from school to school pointing out different landmarks along the way.

"You can't just close schools. That's not the way things work here," he said. "You need to understand the community. These schools are anchors of the community. Like me. I know the community, I am the community, that's why they love me."

"Marion Barry! Marion Barry!" I heard the screams as if on cue.

A group of kids had spotted Barry's car and were jumping up and down excitedly, waving their arms. One little boy ran up to the car.

"Marion Barry!" he exclaimed. "Will you buy a raffle ticket from me?"

"Nah, I don't want no raffle ticket. Why are you selling those anyways?" he asked.

" 'Cause we need money!" said the kid.

"For what?" Barry asked.

"I need a soda and some chips," said the kid.

Barry reached into his back pocket. He pulled out a twenty-dollar bill.

"Here," he said, "go get you some chips and a soda. And stay out of trouble, hear?"

There was no doubt about it. They loved Marion Barry.

THEY WERE NOT LOVING me, however. It was very clear from looking at the data that we had to close schools. Though we were spending more money per child than nearly every other urban jurisdiction in the nation, we were not educating all our children. As I traveled from school to school I saw a lack of supplies and resources and decaying buildings. Teachers were spending money out of their own pockets for the classroom basics. No one felt that we were one of the richest school districts in the nation.

Part of the problem was that we were running far too many schools. For our 50,000 students, we should have been operating about 70 schools, fewer than half of the 144 in the system. We were paying to light, heat, air-condition, and maintain half-empty buildings. We knew that if we closed the twenty-seven schools and right-sized the district we could ensure that every school in the district had an art, music, and physical education teacher as well as a librarian, nurse, and guidance counselor/social worker. It was what families across the city had told me they wanted. It was just at a price they weren't necessarily willing to pay.

IF I WAS GOING to keep ripping off Band-Aids, my next chore would be to make the DCPS central office staff more responsive and smaller.

We interviewed all staff members and assessed their performance and passion for helping students learn. I met with Mayor Fenty and told him that about a quarter of the staff might have to go. However, I didn't know how we were going to do it. There were rules and regulations in place that made it nearly impossible to fire employees.

"If we don't like the rules of the game," Fenty said, "we need to change the rules."

So he introduced legislation to the city council that would make central office employees "at will" employees, which meant they served at the pleasure of the chancellor, who could replace them at any time. Word got out to the city council that we were looking to fire workers. I was called in for a hearing in early November.

"I am convinced that we must not let the rights, privileges, and priorities of adults take precedence over what is in the best interests of students," I said. "We cannot allow children to languish while we try to remediate adults. We cannot forsake their futures for adult issues in the present."

Fenty introduced the legislation, and the council held more hearings and voted in the spring to give me the power to fire central staff. In March 2008, I handed out ninety-eight pink slips.

The reaction from the city unions was swift and loud. The AFL-CIO and American Federation of State, County and Municipal Employees organized protests on the steps of the Wilson Building. Their placards targeted me as the incarnation of evil.

"This is not reform," one radio spot charged. "This is a dictatorship."

Perhaps, but in my eyes and those of Mayor Adrian Fenty, we had to start off doing the hard things first. Closing schools was painful, but it was done. We could focus on the positive side of building up programs, curricula, and services. Firings in the central office were necessary, too, and better done quickly and early.

They also gave me the freedom to bring in new staff whose clear goal was improving schools.

I had fired thirty-six principals and twenty-two assistant principals.

Tough? Uncompromising? Decisive? Yes to all three. But totally necessary, given the condition of the public schools that I found on my first day.

Now I had to prove that I could create schools that would educate all D.C. children.

This was going to be the hard part.

6

—

In Labor

We were backed into a tight corner.

According to the federal "No Child Left Behind" mandate, we were required to take drastic action in twenty-seven of the District of Columbia's schools that had failed to make adequate yearly progress for five consecutive years. Shortly after taking over the schools, I realized that neither the district nor the schools had been paying attention to the federal law or its potential ramifications. I had to act.

We held countless meetings with each of the twenty-seven schools, trying to put together the required turnaround plans. The school communities were not pleased with the four options. A school could be turned over to a charter management organization; the state could take it over; part or all of the staff would need to be replaced; or an unspecified option could be employed. There was no escaping reform.

After a lot of work and many sleepless nights, we prepared to finalize the plans. Something wasn't sitting right with me. I just couldn't put my finger on it. Finally, I figured it out. All ten of our large comprehensive high schools were identified as failing and headed for drastic change. However, we hadn't yet had the *opportunity to talk to the students and engage them in the process of restructuring their schools.*

"We forgot the students," I told Michael Moody, who had become my chief aide on academics, and Abby Smith. "We can't completely restructure their schools until we hear from them."

"You're right," Abby responded. "We're on a really fast timeline. Let us figure out how to do this; it's going to be a tough one."

The next day they came back to me with an idea. We could pull students from all the schools together for an afternoon—not ideal, but better than nothing. Within hours we asked each of the high school principals to send a contingent of students to the meeting.

When I pulled up to Ballou High School the afternoon of the meeting, I wasn't sure what to expect. As I entered the auditorium, I could see groups of students chatting with one another. I marched up to the front, where they were still working on setting up the microphones. It was taking longer than expected, so I got started.

"Thank you so much for joining us today, especially on such short notice," I began. "As many of you may already know, all ten DCPS high schools must be restructured this year because of failure to make progress according to the U.S. Department of Education."

I told them we had been through a long process to try to write improvement plans, but before we took any formal steps, we wanted to hear from students.

"What do you think can help us improve your schools?" I asked.

Grumbling. The kids were unimpressed.

"Does anyone want to share some beginning thoughts?" I asked. "If you do, please raise your hand and tell us what school you're from."

Deafening silence.

Then one young man stood up.

"I know that you did that Teach For America program," he said. "I'm afraid that you are going to fire all of our teachers and replace them with those young teachers."

He said students need older, experienced teachers who know what they're doing.

"We need people who know us and our neighborhoods," he said, "not a bunch of young, white people from Yale."

There were appreciative snickers rippling through the audience. A young woman stood up.

"I totally disagree with you," she said. "Yes, some of the TFA teachers are clueless when they first get here. But they improve really quickly."

She said they were dedicated, cared about learning, and worked harder than everyone else. She added: "The best teachers I've had have all been Teach For America."

Another student stood up and said, "My best teachers have been veteran teachers."

The dialogue continued. Students from all the schools stood to express their opinions on their best teachers.

Finally a young man stood up and said, "I actually don't think we're disagreeing here. Based on what I've heard, what we all know is that whether you're Teach For America or not, whether you're white or black or new versus old, great teachers care about their students, know their material, and are interesting. We can't make assumptions based on groups; we have to look at the individual teachers. But the bottom line is what we need most is great teachers."

The kids murmured in agreement. They were getting restless, and I had heard what I needed to hear. We adjourned the meeting.

A reporter approached me.

"What did you think?" he asked.

"What did you think?" I asked him back.

"Well, I've been to a lot of these community meetings about

the plans, and I'd have to say that this was both the most civilized and the most thoughtful," he remarked.

"I agree one hundred percent," I said. "Kids have a way of doing that."

I AM NOT A big believer in fate or destiny, and I am not the best at planning or setting career goals. But in many ways it seems that my entire professional life had been preparing me to negotiate a new teachers' contract on the national stage of Washington, D.C.

My family ties and days teaching in the Baltimore classroom had taught me to respect teachers and see what strides students could make with good ones; at TNTP, our research and direct contact with school districts had shown me the destructive impact that some teachers' contracts could have on schools.

The culture in education is what TNTP refers to as the Widget Effect, meaning that teachers are treated as if they are interchangeable widgets, as if they are all the same. Everybody gets tenure. Everybody gets a good evaluation.

That culture does not actually help the profession. It certainly does not help students. The reality is that teachers are not interchangeable widgets, not even close. The differences that highly effective teachers have on kids are massive.

A recent Harvard University study that looked at more than two million students over a twenty-year time period showed that kids who had just one effective teacher in their lifetime had a higher likelihood of graduating from high school, going on to college, and making more money as a professional. They were also less likely to have a teen pregnancy.

If this is the case, it's our obligation to ensure that every student is taught by a highly effective teacher every day.

When I took office in June 2007, I knew that the union contract was about to expire in September. I could not wait to get into the negotiations. This was my wheelhouse. With all of the research we'd done at TNTP, I knew exactly what we needed to change in the new contract.

IN LATE SUMMER, KAYA HENDERSON set up a meeting with George Parker, president of the Washington Teachers' Union. We met one hot weekend in my office. The air-conditioning was off.

Parker pulled out a pad and pen.

"Who are the seven negotiators on your side?" he asked. "We need to determine our negotiating teams."

"George," I said, "I know you're used to conducting negotiations in a certain way, but that's not the way I operate. These are incredibly complex issues and I think they are best discussed mano a mano—just me and you."

I could see Kaya's eyes widen.

George laughed.

"We can't do that!" he said.

"Why not?" I asked. "Nothing that's a real breakthrough is going to be accomplished through group negotiations. I say the two of us work it out on our own and then we can take it to our folks to put it on paper."

He laughed again, nervously this time. Beads of sweat were breaking out on his forehead.

"I have read all of your studies, Chancellor Rhee," he said. "I know what you want."

I had read about George Parker, too. George was a lifer in D.C. schools. He had taught math for years before rising through the union ranks. He had a deep, mellifluous voice that Washingtonians loved when he sang and played keyboards in his band, Special Delivery. He had a reputation as a thoughtful, patient man with a sweet side. He was the opposite of the corrupt union leaders he had replaced.

"If you want to bring stuff like merit pay and tenure to the table," he said, "you had better bring a whole lot of money with you! The last time we did well with a contract was a ten percent raise over three years under Mayor Anthony Williams. And we didn't have to give many concessions to get that."

The Washington Teachers' Union had not been doing very well for years. It was known more for scandal and corruption than for organizing and teaching. Former president Barbara Bullock had pleaded guilty in 2003 to stealing nearly $5 million in union dues. In court, Bullock testified that she and two top union officials had systematically skimmed union dues and blown them on extravagant shopping trips. It's safe to say the WTU would not be dealing from a pristine position.

"So you're saying that in order to be able to negotiate around things like tenure and seniority that I have to give raises larger than that?" I asked.

"A *lot* more," answered Parker.

"What if we offered a twenty percent raise over three years?"

Parker was flummoxed.

"How can you pull that off?" he asked. "Everyone knows the economy is in rough shape and cities will face tighter budgets. The city CFO has already announced that revenues are falling. You can't come up with that kind of money."

"You're right about that. The city doesn't have any money. But I think there's a chance I could raise it externally."

"Doesn't really matter where it comes from as long as it's real," he said, "but there better be a whole lot of it for what you're talking about."

I KNEW EXACTLY WHAT I wanted in the contract: Mutual consent, under which both the teacher and the school had to agree before the teacher got a position. No more forced placements or "the dance of the lemons." Teacher evaluations would be based in large part on student achievement. Layoffs would be based on quality, rather than seniority. I wanted the new contract to establish rewards and consequences, so that we could pay our most highly effective teachers a lot more and move ineffective teachers out of the system. We would develop strong professional development programs to ensure that teachers at every level had the opportunity to improve their practice every year.

I was aware that these kinds of changes to a contract wouldn't come cheap. I had to find a lot of money fast. But where? I hated raising money. As it turns out, though, I didn't really have to ask.

After we published our first report at The New Teacher Project, foundations had offered to help finance additional research and studies. For the most part, I had turned them down, because we had our own resources. As soon as I landed in Washington, D.C., many of the same foundations came to us unsolicited and asked if they could help finance my reforms.

With that in mind, I directed Jason Kamras and Kaya to take the lead in coming up with the proposal that we would eventually refer to as "the Grand Bargain."

Under the plan, all teachers would receive a retroactive pay increase of 5 percent as well as generous raises for the next few years. That was the hook to earn broad-based appeal for the proposal. Here was the revolutionary aspect: teachers had the choice of two paths, red or green. A teacher who chose the red track could expect to continue with similar work conditions and expectations set out in past contracts. Teachers who chose the green track would be eligible for much heftier salary increases and bonuses, based on performance and increases in student achievement. But those choosing green would give up their tenure protections. Seniority would no longer apply for teachers in either track. We offered generous professional development opportunities for all.

Yes, it was the age-old carrot-and-stick approach, but this time with a golden carrot.

If teachers chose the green track, had strong classroom observation ratings, and raised student test scores, they could be making $100,000 after three years, with bonuses of $20,000. After fifteen years, the pay scale reached $146,000 for high-performing teachers.

In our first meeting, when I came on board in the summer of 2007, George Parker told me the prospect of high-dollar raises could help push through my basic goals. We spent the next year researching and writing our proposal and raising funds. George and I met in late spring 2008 to discuss the red-and-green proposal. He was amenable. He requested a few changes. We agreed. In late June he was ready to present the proposal to his rank and file. He and I would spend the rest of the summer meeting with union members, answering their questions, and selling them on the merits of the plan. The WTU would vote in the fall.

We were all set to unveil the plan the first week of July. A union member opposed to Parker and the plan got his hands on the package, leaked it to the *Washington Post*, and trashed it.

RHEE SEEKS TENURE-PAY SWAP FOR TEACHERS, the headline read on July 3. The unidentified union member was quoted as saying, "You may be trading off your future, your tenure, your job security. When you trade that, it seems to me you're not getting much."

Thanks to the leak and the publication of the plan's bare details, we lost the high ground and the chance to make a nuanced pitch. Not only did the red-and-green plan fail, but the American Federation of Teachers was furious at the direction we were taking.

Randi Weingarten, now the president of the AFT, was not pleased.

. . . .

NOT LONG AFTER OUR red-and-green proposal was unveiled prematurely, Randi Weingarten invited me to her office in the national office of the American Federation of Teachers, on New Jersey Avenue, not far from the U.S. Capitol. It didn't look nearly as posh as a K Street lobbying firm from the outside, but Weingarten's suite on the top floor was not too shabby, with lovely wood paneling and high ceilings.

I arrived on time—and waited. And waited. Finally an aide ushered me in to see Weingarten. A petite woman, she flashed her wide, toothy smile and grabbed my hand in a firm grip. We sat in a small room attached to her grand office, just the two of us.

"I have studied your first offer, if you can call it that," she said. "George finally gave me what you describe as the red-and-green proposal. Would you call that an offer?"

"It's not an offer," I said. "It's the agreement that we want to put up for a vote."

The smile was gone.

"Let me tell you what's not going to work," she said. "Teachers at the same school cannot work under two different sets of work rules."

Interesting. She was saying that two schools could have different rules but not two teachers within the same school. Apparently, my plan to give teachers a choice between two tracks with different pay plans was out, at least in Randi Weingarten's mind. I would have expected nothing else.

Weingarten was born in New York, the daughter of a teacher who was active in the union. One of the stories she tells everyone is her early memory of her mother going out on strike and getting docked pay, at the time her father was out of work as an electrical engineer. The family suffered and struggled. She says it seared in her mind the need for a strong union that protected the rights of teachers.

No doubt Weingarten is smart—and committed. She has an undergraduate degree in industrial and labor relations from Cornell and a law degree from Cardozo. Right out of law school she was making big bucks at the Wall Street firm of Stroock & Stroock & Lavan, but she tossed it aside for the union. She became general counsel to Sandra Feldman, head of New York's United Federation of Teachers (UFT), rising through the union ranks to become president of the UFT, which represented an estimated 200,000 members, including 75,000 teachers.

Weingarten was a union powerhouse in Manhattan, but she had bigger ambitions. Political office? Perhaps a run for the U.S. Senate in New York? In the summer of 2008, she was elected president of the American Federation of Teachers, moved to Washington, and set up shop in the union's national headquarters. She also announced she was taking a hand in the local negotiations between DCPS and the city—which is why she had invited me for a chat.

"Here's what else is out," she said. "We are not going to give up tenure. And we cannot have individual pay for performance."

"My turn?" I asked.

She nodded.

"We must be able to pay individual teachers for the work that they're doing and results they attain," I said. "Tenure as a job for life regardless of performance doesn't work for me. And we must have mutual consent. No more forcing ineffective teachers onto schools."

Weingarten was as unsurprised by my reaction as was I by her approach. We knew one another's positions. We were worthy gladiators. We said our cordial good-byes.

Weingarten tried to get to Mayor Fenty. She requested a meeting. No response. She called him directly. He didn't return her call. It must have driven her crazy. In New York, she had Mayor

Michael Bloomberg's ear. When she differed with school chief Joel Klein, she could call Bloomberg, and he would hear her out. Bloomberg was a seasoned, smart politician. He knew Weingarten had a significant power base that could swing elections. Randi knew how to work New York. She was comfortable with the dynamic she had on her home turf.

Now she was in new territory. Fenty ignored her. She was livid.

WHY DID I GO through the painful process of closing twenty-three schools my first year as chancellor?

Certainly, I was justified by the raw numbers, since so many schools were half empty. But there was another reason: I believed that art, music, and physical education were not extras, as they had been for decades at some schools because the number of students could not support teachers.

My goal was to make sure that students at every school could take art, music, and physical education. Each child deserved to attend a school that also had a librarian, a nurse, and a guidance counselor or social worker. On the first day of school in 2008, we delivered. Schools were ready for children; textbooks and supplies awaited them; we had begun to bring in stronger principals and teachers.

Test scores in reading and math began to rise dramatically for the first time in decades, in both D.C. and national tests. Our DC-CAS tests showed that elementary school reading scores rose by 8 points, math by 11. In high schools, reading rose 10 points and math moved up by 9. The numbers of students showing proficiency were still way too low, but we were on the right trajectory.

Why? Did the students get smarter just because I showed up? Hardly.

Achievement levels increased because we set the bar higher and asked principals to show improvement in student learning.

Our critical response teams were one call away. They took many nagging problems off the table. When principals didn't have to worry about leaky roofs, textbooks, or teachers who had lost interest, they could direct their teams to improving academics and the curriculum.

The quality of the principals made a difference, too. I had been scouring the nation for great school leaders and had found a few, in nearby Maryland school districts. I had convinced a few to join us—such as Dwan Jordon at Sousa Middle School, Pete Cahall at Wilson High, and Darrin Slade at Ron Brown Middle School. And they were setting new standards.

People were starting to notice—not just within the city but outside as well. Our actions and the subsequent progress were winning the attention of the national press. Reporters were intrigued by the story of the Korean girl from Toledo, Ohio, who took over the worst school district in the country.

The press was helping me attract fans and detractors by the thousands.

I had never sought the limelight. In choosing education as my life's work, I was not making a media play. As a breed, educators are focused, serious wonks. So I was more than a little taken aback when reporters from national newspapers and magazines started requesting interviews. PBS proposed a yearlong series of videos for its *NewsHour*.

I became what they call good copy. I wasn't savvy enough to say no and manage the press, which a more seasoned professional might have done.

Amanda Ripley, a reporter with *Time* magazine, requested an interview in the early fall of 2008. Ripley had written on education, and I knew her work. I agreed to the interview and let her follow me in action. Her article, in the November 26, 2008, issue, was thorough and fair. It was the photo that wound up sticking in the collective consciousness.

The photographer must have taken a thousand pictures of me, or so it seemed. Most of the shots showed me with a group of students. At the end, however, she took pictures of me holding a variety of rulers, pencils, and teaching tools. I called it quits.

"One more, please," she pleaded. Her assistant grabbed a broom and asked me to stand with it in my hands. "Straight face, please."

The picture with the broom made the cover.

That photo would wind up defining me, for better or worse, in a one-dimensional way. Fans saw me as an agent of necessary change; plenty of future enemies latched on to the image of a tough, brusque dictator bent on change, whatever the cost.

I got my fair share of hate mail after the *Time* cover, but I could find solace in the quiet of private emails.

A teacher in Hawaii wrote: "The students are behind and the expectations are low. I say if you are a good teacher then you should have no problem laying your job on the line. People need to man/woman up and realize this isn't just about holding kids' hands. We can't baby another generation. Keep up the good work."

And from Portland, Oregon: "I would like to be part of a higher mission to try and reform our public school system in America. If you are looking for teachers outside your district, please feel free to contact me."

And a short one from closer to home: "A DC voter, NW. No kids yet but when I have them I want to send them to your schools—so stay tough RHEE!"

Those helped.

IN FEBRUARY 2009, RANDI WEINGARTEN inserted herself into the negotiations and ushered George Parker and the WTU to the sidelines. Her mother had recently passed away, and she spent the first twenty minutes of the first negotiating session talking about growing up the daughter of a teacher, and what it felt like to be an orphan. She was warming us up.

Then she said, "I know you'll be upset when I say this, but I feel like we're more at the beginning of the negotiations at this point than the end."

"You've only gotten involved in the past fifteen days," I said, completely annoyed.

"I know you are very frustrated, Michelle."

Frustrated and not at all interested in starting over. By that point, we had been in talks with the WTU for a year and a half. We had made progress. The union wanted the 20 percent raises and generous professional development we had offered, but it balked at the reforms we were demanding in exchange. Four months before Weingarten stepped in we had reached a stalemate.

We couldn't remain in limbo. The reforms had to move forward.

The federal control board that had taken the city's fiscal reins in 1995 had given DCPS the ability to develop a teacher evaluation system. It needed only to consult with the union, but not reach agreement with it. Lacking movement toward agreement on the contract, I directed my staff to develop a new teacher evaluation system with strong input from our rank-and-file teachers. They did. I called a press conference.

"We must do everything in our power to provide high-quality teachers for every student," I said, with Mayor Fenty by my side.

We unveiled a new performance evaluation system that would essentially bypass tenure. Instead of everyone being rated as satisfactory, we would finally begin to differentiate within the teaching force. Teachers were rated in one of four categories: highly effective, effective, minimally effective, or ineffective. Ineffective teachers would be subject to termination. Minimally effective teachers would have one more year to improve their practice. If they couldn't, they would also be subject to termination.

Our hope was that the union would agree to the contract so that we could also recognize and reward the highly effective teachers who could receive double the pay of the old system. With the leverage of the new evaluation system, we thought that the union would see that there was a lot of downside, but upside only if they agreed to the contract.

GIVEN RANDI'S INSISTENCE ON her nonnegotiables and my equally ardent demands, we could agree on one matter: we needed a mediator. We each proposed and rejected a few candidates. We finally settled on Kurt Schmoke, then dean of Howard University Law School. Schmoke had been mayor of Baltimore when I taught at Harlem Park in the 1990s. It was Schmoke who encouraged reforms at Baltimore's worst schools, so I was encouraged that he would help us reach our goals within the collective bargaining process.

Schmoke made it clear he wanted to come to an agreement in June 2009. We would—a year later—in part because Weingarten did not want to give an inch. She often showed up late to bargaining sessions and left early. She would occasionally look across the table at me and say, "I can tell this is your first serious contract negotiation. This just isn't the way it's done."

She spent a lot of time focused on the evaluation system. Our lawyers instructed us to stay away from the topic. We already were using our authority to unilaterally impose a system. The minute we brought the evaluation system into the contract, our lawyers told us, we would lose that authority, and it would become subject to collective bargaining. Randi knew this, too, so she insisted that we couldn't continue until we addressed it.

I staunchly refused. Teacher input on the evaluation system was critical, but we'd gotten that. We had held scores of focus groups and work sessions with teachers to get their insights on the new evaluation system. We felt good about how we'd engaged with them on its development. But we weren't going to be held captive by the union bosses. That's where we drew the line.

We were also stuck on due process, which described how, when, and why teachers could be fired—and their recourse and review.

I believed in due process and thought it was necessary. I'd seen too many examples of good teachers who had been railroaded by ineffective administrators. Those teachers had to have a structure through which they could appeal evaluations when appropriate. However, due process had come to mean that it was impossible to fire an ineffective teacher because of all the hoops administrators had to jump through. In many other cities, it routinely cost several hundred thousand dollars and several years to fire a teacher because of the process.

In one of the first negotiating sessions with Kurt Schmoke, Randi pulled out the due process procedures she'd negotiated in New York. They set up a cumbersome process for firing teachers, even if they had been accused of assault or sexual abuse. It took years of hearings and reports. It was costing New York millions to pay teachers as they sat idle during their evaluation process. As mentioned earlier, they spent their days in what became known as the rubber room, where teachers who had failed in the classroom had been bounced until their due process had been exhausted— sometimes never. It was the bane of Joel Klein's life as chancellor.

"No way I can agree to that," I said. "None."

An hour into the negotiating session, Weingarten announced that she had to leave to give a speech. All of us were shocked, including Schmoke. After she left, I spoke my mind to the dean.

"The bottom line is we don't need this contract to move forward," I said. "I can evaluate teachers under the new process that we just established to get poor teachers out. When our budgets are cut, we also have the ability to lay teachers off based on quality instead of seniority. Agreeing on a contract would be great, but I have these authorities, regardless.

"However, we don't want to enact these evaluation systems without an upside for effective teachers, too. That's of critical importance. We want to give them bonuses and recognize them for the amazing work they're doing!"

Kurt Schmoke listened. I wasn't sure what he was thinking.

THE 2008-2009 SCHOOL YEAR showed more measurable improvements.

Scores rose again in reading and math, though the increases were not as dramatic as those of the previous year. Still, D.C. was no longer the worst-performing urban school district in the nation. That's a low bar, but we had to come up from the bottom. In our first two years D.C. was the only major city school district to show double-digit growth in both math and reading at the secondary level.

We also started to get a vote of confidence from students and parents. The number of students in D.C. schools had been dropping since 1969. We stabilized enrollments after one year and in 2010, my third year, we reversed a forty-one-year decrease in enrollment and finally grew our student population.

Why?

We could trace the rise in scores and enrollment to specific initiatives. Our D.C. Collaborative paired principals from successful schools with schools that had been struggling. The cross-pollination allowed them to share talent, instructional methods, and professional development. The best example was Scott Cartland. He had been a great success at Janney Elementary in a wealthy, white community, but he requested a transfer to Webb/

Wheatley, a low-performing elementary across town in the troubled Trinidad neighborhood. In one year he had changed the school's teaching and culture.

When I had taught in Harlem Park I used data to track every student. By my second year as chancellor we had started to put in place a similar system to measure every student's progress. If a student was not operating at grade level, what intervention must we put in place? What math intervention? What on reading? And if a student was not performing at grade level, he had to stay after school for what we called an "academic power hour."

For the first time in D.C., we opened schools on the weekends and offered Saturday Academies.

We aggressively added seats for three-year-olds. We increased enrollment at prekindergarten and brought families into the system early. We actively worked to keep students and families in the school system as they entered middle and high school. Parents who might have enrolled their children in private schools or moved out of the city were staying in the public schools.

None of these positive changes came by accident.

Kurt Schmoke was a patient man, but he was becoming impatient with the lack of progress in our contract talks. He could see that Weingarten and I did not work well together. Through the spring, it looked as though we might have to declare an impasse.

So he put us in separate rooms and started holding marathon sessions where he would shuttle back and forth instead of having us battle it out across the table. It turned out to be a more effective strategy, though it was frustrating to us. Jason; Kaya; our general counsel, Jim Sandman; and I would spend hours in the room together often just waiting. We were clear about what we were willing to give on and what we weren't. We'd rather walk away than sign a contract that we felt compromised children. So we often sat, and sat, and sat. . . .

The long hours took their toll. Often both sides were so frustrated that it led to heated discussions. One in particular was when Randi was arguing about a point, noting that teachers would never go for it.

"I disagree," said Jason. "I think there is a big disconnect between what teachers think on this issue and what the union leadership believes."

"What do *you* know, Jason?" Weingarten said, dragging out *Jaayyson* in her most dismissive tone. "Teachers are union, and union is teachers. There is no difference." As she said it, she was clearly questioning Jason's ability to comment on the subject. Never mind that Jason had not only taught successfully for a decade, but that as the National Teacher of the Year, he spent an entire year engaged in conversations with teachers. He certainly had a right to express his thoughts and was a credible voice in the debate, but not to Randi. To her, he was a nuisance.

On June 10, 2009, we met in the AFT offices at five thirty in the afternoon. Schmoke put us in different rooms and refused to let us out until we had made progress, even if it meant staying up all night. He ran back and forth. After midnight the union gave up ground on mutual consent. Both sides agreed that principals could choose to accept or reject teachers who had lost their positions. The union held fast on seniority but showed signs of compromise. We took a break.

At 2 a.m., we came back together and started talking dollars and cents.

"We want across-the-board raises of twenty-four percent," Weingarten said.

"Are you on crack?" I asked.

Weingarten stormed out.

"I'm done negotiating," I said.

George Parker begged me to stay. Schmoke separated us. They came down to 22 percent; I stayed firm at 20. We decided to call it a night.

Parker called the next day at noon and agreed to an across-the-board pay increase of 20 percent, but we left open the question of the performance pay system. Could we reward the best teachers? Weingarten seemed unalterably opposed. We still couldn't close the deal.

A few weeks later I met Weingarten for a drink at Bistro Bis, a fine-dining restaurant down the street from her office. The union had gone back on some of the agreements I thought we had reached. I wasn't seeing a light at the end of the tunnel.

"Let's call it a day," I said. "No one can say we didn't try hard. We both did our part. We just couldn't pull it off. Let's accept that we've reached a point where it's clearly not working."

I felt like I was breaking up with her. She said we were close and spent an hour trying to convince me to attend one more meeting.

"I'm sure we can get there," she said.

"I'm done," I said. "Really done. I am ready to call an impasse."

She asked for a couple of days before I announced anything.

At noon the next day Kurt Schmoke phoned to say the union was willing to agree to the terms I thought we had worked out during our marathon session.

"Fine," I said. "What about performance pay? I'm not doing it unless there's an upside for great teachers."

"I'm working on it," he said. "But I think we can make it happen."

EARLIER IN THE SPRING of 2009, during one of our marathon negotiating sessions, Schmoke had come up with an idea that I thought was a stroke of genius.

"I actually think we can come to resolution on everything

else," he said to both sides at the time. "Having listened to you all for a long time now, I think the major issue is individual performance pay. The problem is that this is a nonstarter for Randi, but Michelle has to have it in the contract. It's a nonnegotiable for her. So here's what I think . . ."

We were all waiting with bated breath.

"We aren't going to come to agreement on this, so my proposal is that we not continue trying," he said.

As I was about to jump up, he gave me the look.

"I think we can give you both what you need, though," he said. I paused, intrigued. He pulled out his pad, where he had written some very carefully crafted language.

"I propose we insert the following language: 'DCPS will implement an individual pay-for-performance program, the details to be shared upon implementation. The union will neither endorse nor block the initiative.' "

It was brilliant. I could implement pay for performance, but because it wasn't going to be defined specifically in the contract, the union was free to rebuke it, since it had not actually agreed to it. No one said a word, but we all knew it would work.

I WAS ELATED AS I headed to California for a long weekend getaway. It seemed as if the end was in sight. I was going to meet Kevin Johnson, my longtime friend and adviser who was becoming much more important to me. When I had to resign from his charter school board in 2007 to take the chancellor job, he came out to testify on my behalf at the city council nomination hearings. In 2008 he decided to run for mayor of Sacramento and asked if I could help him craft his education platform. I worked closely with him. During the campaign our relationship changed from the politics of education to the intricacies of romance.

KMJ and I were driving to Santa Barbara from Los Angeles.

"What's going on? You are excited, I can tell. Spill it!" he said.

Over the course of the drive and a stop at In-N-Out Burger, I laid out where we were and what Schmoke had done.

"That brother is the real deal," he said. "Seriously. Brilliant."

After I finished telling him the story he conceded, "Dang, baby. I think we might actually pull this thing off! We're close! I can feel it. It's going to happen."

AN UNEXPECTED AND UNSETTLING chain of events was about to drive the negotiations either off the rails or toward the final destination.

The Great Recession had depressed revenue in governments across the country, compressed budgets, and forced the firings of teachers from San Francisco to Philadelphia. Washington, D.C., was relatively immune thanks to the federal government as the city's engine of revenue. But D.C.'s 2010 budget was coming up short, and I was forced to cut $43.9 million from the schools.

Cutting budgets is never easy, but in education, where a disproportionately large percentage of expenditures is in personnel, it often means cutting jobs. We would have to balance the budget by cutting teachers. Never a good thing, never easy.

For decades D.C. had followed the path taken by most districts, which was to lay off teachers based on seniority. What few people knew was that we actually had the authority to make the decisions based on quality rather than years in the classroom. I suppose most previous administrations had resisted using this discretion because it would anger the unions. But my priority wasn't to keep the adults happy. I wanted to minimize the impact the cuts had on students. The way to do that was by shedding ineffective teachers when possible. Some schools had just reorganized with a brand-new faculty. In those schools, new, unproven teachers might have to be let go. But in other cases, principals were able to lay off low performers and keep less senior but more effective teachers. There was no doubt that it was the right move if we were focused on kids.

In order to ensure that the process was not arbitrary, we created guidelines that required principals to show evidence of teacher effectiveness to accompany their layoff recommendations. Among the teachers that would be fired were some who had used corporal punishment, had had sexual relations with a student, or had missed seventy-eight or more days of school.

My staff reviewed each recommendation and then approved the final list of 266 teachers to be cut. Seniority would not be the deciding factor.

No more LIFO: last in, first out.

We briefed Mayor Fenty at a senior staff meeting. Fenty's reelection was a year away. His staff members worried that we would get slaughtered in the media, and Fenty would suffer.

"I am okay if you want to rethink this," I told Fenty.

"Are we laying off the people who are adding the least to the classroom?" he asked. "If that's the case, it's the right thing to do."

Some voiced concerns about the political repercussions.

"We haven't made any decisions based on politics yet," he said. "The minute we start doing that, it's a slippery slope. We can't go back."

With the mayor's blessing, we proceeded with the layoffs. Notices went out on October 2. Except for an unfortunate incident at McKinley High, where police had to escort some teachers out, the layoffs went smoothly.

The reaction was not as placid.

A week later the unions rallied on Freedom Plaza, a broad expanse across Pennsylvania Avenue from the Wilson Building. They came in force from across the city and the country. They set up port-a-potties and rented a stage with lights. My favorite sign: "This is not Rheezistan." Another read: "Sweep Her Out."

Richard Trumka, who had just been elected president of the AFL-CIO, accused me of union-busting and said to the crowd: "The labor movement is right here with you. We'll stand shoulder to shoulder with you for as long as it takes."

Randi Weingarten took the microphone to say, "We are not getting any real, valid, truthful information from DCPS."

That was not quite true. We had briefed union leadership.

The day before the rally, the union had taken the city to court to enjoin it from executing the layoffs. The union argued that the layoffs were a deliberate effort to get rid of veteran teachers, since we had hired more than nine hundred new teachers over the summer—before we learned of the budget cuts. The lawyers argued their cases in early November. We prevailed when we showed the data that undeniably proved that we'd laid off teachers of different years of experience, race, and age. The differentiating factor was their effectiveness compared with the others at their school.

On Tuesday, November 24, Superior Court judge Judith Bartnoff denied the union's claims. We received the decision at 10:45 a.m. I knew Kurt Schmoke was meeting with union negotiators at noon. We let him know about the decision.

"You not only lost, but you lost badly," Schmoke told the union.

I took no pleasure in the entire process, from choosing teachers to fire, to seeing people lose their jobs, to being the target of protesters, to being sued. But the rallies didn't affect me. They were noise. I knew Mayor Fenty had my back. I was safe and simply kept pushing ahead.

The effect of the firings surprised me. Teachers suddenly realized we already had the power to lay people off based on performance rather than seniority. I started hearing teachers talk about getting the contract done. If they were vulnerable to getting fired, they at least wanted the raises we were preparing to

deliver. Rank-and-file teachers started pushing the union negotiators to make a deal.

I wish I could say it had been deliberate on my part, but I am
not that smart.

In the midst of the drama, Kevin Johnson came to D.C. for a
visit. On a cool October evening he took me to see a performance
of *A Streetcar Named Desire* at the Kennedy Center. Afterward,
we drove through downtown D.C. We pulled over in front of the
Capitol. He pointed out the window.

"That's where we were sitting during the inauguration, do
you remember?" he asked. He'd been invited to Obama's inauguration, and we had had amazing seats atop the Capitol for the
swearing-in.

I peered up to where he was pointing, but it was dark outside.

"I think so," I said.

"Come on!" he said, and dragged me out of the car.

I wasn't thrilled. It was cold, wet, and rainy outside, but my
man wanted to reminisce, so I went along.

Standing at the fountain at the foot of the West Lawn, he
asked, "Do you love me?"

"Yup," I said.

"Then marry me," he said.

He pulled a wad of toilet paper out of his jacket and unwound
it to produce the ring. It was beautiful.

"Yes," I said.

My life was about to change—in more ways than one.

After the layoffs, a different Randi Weingarten came to the
negotiating table. At first she refused to negotiate or talk to me.
Then, suddenly, she became agreeable. I wondered why.

One reason may have been that the WTU rank and file was hungry for raises. They had not had a salary increase in three years. They knew our contract proposal included healthy raises, going back retroactively and forward for years.

Schmoke ordered another series of marathon sessions. We came to an agreement on the most contentious issues, one at a time. We settled mutual consent and seniority under our terms because the union already had seen us fire people without regard to seniority. We accepted tenure but changed the terms. It was no longer a guarantee of lifetime employment. Under this contract, tenure allowed teachers to use a due process mechanism to guard against what they considered unfair dismissal, but it was quick. And ineffective teachers could swiftly be dismissed from the system.

"If this is tenure," Joel Klein said, "sign me up!"

Kurt Schmoke's solution to performance pay helped make the rest of the contract palatable to Randi Weingarten. The language said we would propose a merit pay system without spelling it out. But the contract began to describe a program where teachers could opt into a pay-for-performance system that could add $20,000 to $30,000 to their salaries if they could show significant improvement in student test scores. A top-performing teacher could be making $147,000.

Finally, the best teachers would be rewarded for their talent and dedication.

In the end, I was under no illusion: money talked. We agreed to pay increases that would raise the average annual salary of our teachers from $67,000 to $81,000, comparable to their counterparts in the suburbs. I remembered what George Parker said when I asked him to go "mano a mano" in 2007.

"If you want to bring stuff like merit pay and tenure to the table," he had said, "you had better bring a whole lot of money with you."

I did. Much of it came from foundations that had agreed to finance my reforms.

We signed a tentative agreement on April 5, 2010.

The agreement in the end was even better for us than the red-green system. In the new contract, no teacher would have "tenure," a permanent job for life. Seniority would no longer be a determining factor of staffing, and our best teachers would be recognized for their work. It wasn't just a choice for those who opted in. It would apply to the entire workforce.

I called my senior staff in to congratulate our team and give "full credit" to the WTU and AFT.

"I am incredibly confident that this contract is going to be a game-changer," I said. "We are paying out the nose for it, but it's going to serve the children well. It could be a model, nationwide. Now we have to produce the results that go with it."

The contract went to the Washington Teachers' Union members in mid-May. On Tuesday, June 2, 2010, they approved the pact, 80 percent to 20 percent.

Randi Weingarten was extremely involved in the details of how we would announce the contract, who would speak at the press conference, and what they would say. I relented to her wishes. There would be no gloating on my part, little grousing from her, and a modicum of backslapping.

"At the end of the day," Weingarten said at the press conference, "this is still one of the industrial model contracts where a lot of the authority is reposed in the chancellor herself."

I didn't feel the need to disagree.

Brad Jupp, a senior adviser to U.S. Secretary of Education Arne Duncan, read the contract and declared it "more revolutionary than the Declaration of Independence."

In the contract, we made some breakthroughs: mutual consent for all placements and no more last in, first out. Tenure and seniority no longer ruled. Teachers would be evaluated on how well they taught rather than how long they had been teaching.

But the contract was good for teachers in many ways, beyond pay. We organized teacher centers for professional development. We established discipline policies that teachers favored. The contract provided better classroom resources.

We worked out a contract that, taken as a whole, could go an incredibly long way in beginning to change the dynamic, to make teaching something that the most talented people aspire to do and a profession they wanted to stay in. That was the most rewarding part for me.

ADRIAN FENTY CHOSE DECEMBER 5, 2009, his birthday, to kick off his campaign for a second term. One of his supporters opened his home to hundreds of friends, family, and supporters.

Outside the lovely home and expansive grounds, union members protested in the streets. As KMJ and I walked in, he put his arm around me protectively. More than a few carried signs saying "Rhee Must Go" and hurled insults as we walked by.

Despite the protesters, at that point I figured Fenty was a lock for another four years. No one had stepped forward to run against him. Crime was falling. City services were running smoothly. Fenty's high standards for accountability had permeated the government. His administration had fixed schools and playgrounds from one corner of D.C. to the other. He had begun to house the city's homeless. Wasn't he unbeatable?

What I didn't know, thanks to my sheltered existence in the education bubble, was that many Washingtonians saw Adrian Fenty as remote, dismissive, and arrogant. In his focus on making the government and schools run well, he neglected to make nice with people, whether they were in business, health care, hospitality, or politics. They complained that he would arrive late to community or business meetings and leave early. He wasn't playing politics at the retail level. To me, it made sense: he was focused on results.

When poet Maya Angelou and African American leader Dorothy Height tried to meet with Fenty about the closing of a tennis center in a black community, he declined. Blacks saw his willingness to dedicate bicycle lanes and build dog parks as favoring white communities. He refused to kiss the rings of the established old guard who traced their roots and contracts back to the days when Marion Barry was mayor. Critics accused him of bestowing city contracts on his friends. The city council investigated and came up empty, but the accusations of cronyism stuck.

Although he came from the city council, or perhaps because of it, Fenty dedicated little time to most of the thirteen legislators. He rarely met with Chairman Vincent Gray. Peeved that Fenty disregarded him and prodded by some members of the city's establishment, Gray declared himself a candidate on March 30, 2010.

FOR THE NEXT FOUR months running up to the September primary, much of the campaign revolved around me and our education reforms. Fenty and I were joined at the hip, for better or worse. I recalled asking Fenty before I took that job what he would be willing to risk to improve D.C. schools. "Everything," he responded.

Now "everything" was on the line.

Closing schools had stung some African American communities, and they supported Gray. Unions threw millions into the race to demonize me for firing teachers. They were able to portray me and the mayor as the enemies of African Americans. Yes, some people lost their jobs, but we were focused on the future of African American children. It was an insane argument, in my mind, to say that we were against blacks, given that our primary focus and deep-seated goals were to ensure that African American students in the city were finally getting a decent education.

But the negative narrative became reality, especially in black wards.

Over the summer, as we neared the decisive Democratic primary on September 14, Fenty's poll numbers started to drop. I wasn't worried. But two Sundays before the election, the *Washington Post* published a poll that showed Fenty behind by double digits.

Joel Klein read the polls and sent an email: "I just read this. We need to have a conversation about your future."

"Nope," I wrote back. "I'm still convinced my boss is going to win. No conversation needed about my future."

New Jersey governor Chris Christie called.

"Michelle," he said, "I just saw the *Washington Post* poll. For the sake of Washington, D.C., and the children of that city, I hope your boss can pull off a win. I say that even though he's a Democrat and I'm a Republican. You all are doing the right things. If the numbers don't improve, though, you have to think about your next step.

"Come to New Jersey!"

I told him I was honored that he called but added: "I'm fully confident that my boss will win reelection, and I'm dedicated to being here for four more years."

"Okay, kid," he replied. "I respect the optimism. Just know that if it goes south, I'm going to be the first person calling you on September fifteenth."

ON SEPTEMBER 14, FENTY lost, by a wide margin, defined by race and class. He won the white wards and lost the black ones. I sent him an email expressing my remorse for not having been able to do anything to help him and, more important, for the fact that our reforms had played a large role in his defeat.

"It has been my honor to work under you for the past 3 years. This country and this city owe you a debt of gratitude for the incredible courage you've shown in fighting for children. I regret that I didn't do a better job to ensure that you won this primary election. I will follow your lead from here, as always. If you feel this is over I will respect that. If you believe that the right thing is to forge ahead on a slightly different tack, I am ready to fight on."

At 2:17 the next morning Fenty replied:

"I can't answer the political question just yet, though those things r usually a long shot. What I do know is that as long as I live I will never do anything as meaningful or important as what our team has been able 2 do in reforming dcps and energizing this city and so it is 2 u that I will b 4ever grateful. No regrets whatsoever."

For the first time since I became chancellor, I cried.

DAVIS GUGGENHEIM, AN AWARD-WINNING documentary film-maker, had interviewed me a few times while he was putting together his film on public education. I hadn't heard much about it. The night after the election, KMJ and I were invited to the film's debut in Washington, at the Newseum on Pennsylvania Avenue.

Guggenheim had titled the film *Waiting for "Superman."* It was a lyrical, truthful, honest portrayal of the dire straits of public education in America. The title's conceit was that the nation was waiting for Superman to swoop in and save the schools; meanwhile, few were actually doing anything to fix schools that were failing kids. Guggenheim portrayed me and my work in D.C. to illustrate the struggle.

After the film, I spoke on a panel that included Randi Weingarten. We didn't have much to say to one another. What went unsaid was that she felt victorious in knocking off Fenty; I felt secure in that we had negotiated a game-changing contract.

Someone asked for my reaction to Vincent Gray's victory.

"Devastating," I responded.

I used the word to describe the reaction from education reformers. I'd fielded calls all day from colleagues who were terrified that Fenty's defeat would dissuade other politicians from taking on the unions. What politician in his or her right mind would try to reform schools as Fenty had?

The media took my "devastating" line to mean that Gray would be devastating for the schools. That's not at all what I meant, but "devastating" set the tone for the debate about whether I might remain in D.C. and serve as chancellor under Gray.

I knew very firmly that I could not finish the job if Vincent Gray was my boss. No way. He never got over the way Fenty presented me to him as chancellor. As city council chair, he had kept me at arm's length, played politics with schools and students, and berated me in public hearings. I flat-out didn't trust him. In my mind, he couldn't hold a candle to Fenty.

Gray and I circled one another. We met for an absurd discussion in which he lectured me about higher education and other random topics instead of talking about whether it made sense for us to work together. For me it was a foregone conclusion that it was the end of my time as chancellor. I wouldn't be able to continue without Fenty's solid, uncompromising support.

I had one move to make before I stepped down. We had assembled a terrific team of talented people. I had broken the china. Who could keep the team together and continue to the next stage of reform?

The answer was Kaya Henderson, my deputy. She had been working with DCPS since our days with The New Teacher Project. She had been by my side for the past three years. She had been the lead negotiator on the contract. I had a strong sense that Vincent Gray would keep her on as chancellor.

But was she up for the task? I asked if she would take over as acting chancellor.

"I need to think on it," she said. "I'm not sure I'm up for being number one."

"The city council would support you," I said. "Vincent Gray and you get along. You know this system better than anyone. You can make sure our work continues."

The next day Kaya agreed to take over if I could get Gray to agree.

On October 13, I announced my resignation, and that Kaya Henderson would take my place. I believed in my heart that it was better for students to have Kaya leading the schools rather than have me stay and be at constant odds with the new mayor. That dynamic wouldn't be good for the city. I was at peace.

A few weeks later KMJ and I attended "A Standing Ovation for DC Teachers" at the Kennedy Center. It was the first annual gala by the D.C. Education Fund to recognize highly effective teachers, based on our IMPACT evaluation system. The first class had 663. The concert hall was all decked out. "Looks like we're ready for the Oscars," Kaya said.

Among the presenters were *New York Times* columnist Thomas Friedman, NBC *Meet the Press* moderator David Gregory, and former Washington Redskins star Darrell Green. Arne Duncan took the stage and said, "When I think of all the legendary people who've performed on this stage, I don't think there have ever been more important people than those who are here tonight."

In a few words, I said that some children come to school with problems that might seem insurmountable, "but all of those obstacles can be overcome if you have an amazing teacher in the classroom."

It was a lovely, uplifting celebration and the perfect reward for the turmoil of the layoffs and the contract negotiations.

Driving home KMJ asked, "Tomorrow will be your first day not being chancellor. How does it feel?"

"Lousy," I said. "In my ideal world, I would be the chancellor for four more years. I have loved this job. I can't imagine having a better one for as long as I live."

7

Students First

The day after the screening of Waiting for "Superman," *KMJ and I flew to Hawaii. We had planned the trip months before. It was originally supposed to be our honeymoon, but we had postponed the wedding because it was turning into a media circus. Instead the trip was now supposed to be a time to celebrate Adrian Fenty's primary victory. I figured I would want to relax and recharge for the next four years as chancellor. As it turned out, I needed the recharging, but for very different reasons.*

I felt like a zombie, but I could neither sleep nor turn off my mind.

On the flight west I closed my eyes and kept replaying the calls and conversations the day after Fenty lost. Dozens came in from my friends and allies in the education reform movement. They went like this:

"Wow, I can't believe your boss lost. What are you going to do now?"

Or: "What a surprise! We didn't even know Fenty was in trouble. I feel so bad, I didn't even help!"

And: "Fenty was the most important politician in the country for education reform. I can't believe this happened."

I sat up straight next to KMJ: "That's why we're losers," I said.

"What?" he asked.

The unions knew Fenty's primary was crucial. They took polls and surveyed D.C. politics and realized Fenty was vulnerable. They figured they had a chance to take him out and sideline me at the same time. The Teamsters and public employee unions from up and down the East Coast brought in members with vans to get people to the polls. The teachers unions threw in $1 million.

"They knew what was at stake," I said. "They were focused. And they got what they wanted. We have no such equivalent on the education reform side. All I got were these sad condolence calls. Where was the reform movement's political muscle?"

"The bottom line," said KMJ, "is that we education reformers don't know how to play the game. They do. You're right. We are losers. But it doesn't have to continue to be that way. We can beat them. We're smarter than they are, and we have right on our side."

I was angry. Then I was tired. Then I slept. I didn't like being a loser.

WHEN WE SETTLED INTO our hotel, KMJ set the tone and gave a few clear orders: no BlackBerry, no phone, no work.

"It's time to turn it off," he said. "We are going to relax."

Relaxing was also something we weren't very good at. But this time was different. We snorkeled; we swam; we kayaked. We rode zip lines and flew over the islands in a helicopter. Our vacations in the past had been a mix of work and play. These three days were pure play. It was the first time either of us had ever completely stopped working before.

On day four, sensing my angst, he gave in. "Okay. I know you're dying. You can check," he said.

"Michelle, this is Rahm Emanuel."

"Michelle, Chris Christie. I told you I'd be calling, and I'm good for my word!"

Meg Whitman had called. She was in the midst of a race against Jerry Brown to be governor of California.

Eli Broad, head of the Broad Foundation, left a message. There must have been fifty more.

More opportunities and calls would come my way over the next few weeks.

Leaders from a large, well-known for-profit company offered me an executive position on strategic change. I couldn't quite figure out what that meant, but they were talking about a ridiculous salary, in the range of $1 million a year.

A number of think tanks and academic organizations, including the Aspen Institute and the Hoover Institution, invited me to join them for a year. That sounded appealing.

Los Angeles mayor Antonio Villaraigosa called KMJ to talk about education reform and insisted on speaking with me. He had just seen *Waiting for "Superman."* He was almost screaming into the phone: "This film has changed my life and my approach to education. We have to lead this charge!" He kept me on the phone for half an hour talking about changes he intended to make in his school system.

"Enough," KMJ said at some point. "Turn them off. We're not going to jump into the next venture. I know how you are. You want to just pick the next thing and start running. That's not how we're going to play this. I think it's a good idea for you to hear everyone out and for you to consider all of the options first. Let's wait a few weeks and see where we are."

We devoted ourselves to the task of vacationing. I returned to D.C. with batteries fully recharged.

. . . .

IN THE MIDST OF arranging my exit from D.C., I flew to Aspen, Colorado, to participate in Ted Forstmann's annual visionary conference for the smart, the wealthy, and the well connected. I certainly wasn't wealthy or well connected, and I wasn't feeling overly smart in the wake of the political defeat we had just been handed. Forstmann, a financier who had made billions as a pioneer in the leveraged-buyout industry, created his annual gathering to generate intellectual debate and give birth to new ideas. He also gave generously to a few favorite causes, among them school reform.

It was my first chance to sound off after Adrian Fenty's defeat at the polls. Forstmann asked me to take the stage one day with Charlie Rose, who interviewed me about my thoughts on D.C. I vented. I talked about how the unions were aware of the opportunity to defeat Fenty and neutralize me at the same time. I aired my disgust with the frailty of the reform movement. My rage returned, and it felt good to articulate it.

At one point I turned to face the audience.

"People like you like to think big thoughts and come up with great ideas," I said, "but we're not playing to win. We need something different to happen. We need to connect ideas with action. Something has to change."

I didn't know what that might be, but my thoughts were starting to come together.

Eli Broad was in the Aspen audience. Funds from his organization had helped finance reforms in D.C. schools. He took me aside after my Charlie Rose rant.

"We really need to talk. I think everything you said today made sense," he said. "I still want you to consider having a role with the foundation."

"I don't think I can," I said, "but I know I have to do something about this political dynamic. I'm just not sure what."

"Whatever it is, I'll help you," he said. "I've been doing this a long time now and I'm fed up. The change is too slow in coming. I want to see major change while I'm alive and I'm willing to invest in it."

After Aspen I flew to Sacramento on September 24 to spend time with KMJ and his mom, Mother Rose. During the entire flight my head was spinning with ideas and questions. Why not join the Broad Foundation and give money to good causes? Something was bothering me. I was feeling unsettled—"angsty" as KMJ would say.

As soon as I walked into Mulvaney's restaurant, KMJ took one look at me and asked, "What is it? You're contemplating something. I can tell."

I told him about my comments in Aspen and the thoughts that filled my head on the flight.

"Whatever we do has to be something big," I said.

KMJ had been pondering the politics of Fenty's loss, as well. Late in the game, he had campaigned for Fenty in African American neighborhoods in Wards 7 and 8, where KMJ was big because of his days in the NBA. He had talked to Washingtonians who were angry with Fenty and prepared to toss me out with him.

"Why," he wondered, "in a city with the worst public schools in the nation, would people turn against a mayor and a chancellor who were actually starting to improve their schools? Why reject them?"

Clearly, he said, we failed to build a grassroots following.

"You can't make change from the top alone," he said. "That was our problem in D.C. We had the right policies but not the right politics. We didn't make sure that the very people who would benefit most from the reforms were driving and fighting for the changes."

My frustration came from the perspective of an education reformer—from the top. I figured that the right superintendent who was willing to make changes and had political backing could accomplish bold reforms. I was proved wrong, because I didn't figure in the power of the unions.

KMJ was plotting and jotting notes.

"If we are going to make a difference, we need to start a movement. A movement of everyday people who are fed up with their kids getting a subpar education. We need to create a vehicle through which they can take action and drive change," he said.

He was right. It's what was missing in D.C. I recalled how when I walked up and down the streets people often came to me, encouraging me to "keep going!" Yet those were not the voices that were heard in the debate. The opposition was loud and organized. The people who supported me didn't know what they could do to help.

It clicked. "How many people would it take?" I asked.

"One million, at least," he said.

He asked how much money we would need. I said, "A billion, at least."

KMJ kept jotting. We kept talking. Finally, he turned over his notes for Mother Rose and me to see. He had sketched out our new organization.

We settled on a plan to create a national advocacy group that would raise money and build membership with the goal of providing political muscle to leaders who stood for change.

We had no name, no staff, no business plan, no location. All we knew was that it was going to be big.

A million people and a billion dollars. That was big.

COULD WE RAISE THE money? I set out to start answering the question.

First stop was Jim Blew, the education head of the Walton Family Foundation. Jim was one of the most thoughtful minds in education reform and understood the political dynamics in a way most of us did not. I had just taken my daughters to see a screening of *Waiting for "Superman."* He called on our drive home. I offered my take on why and how we lost in Washington, what we had accomplished, and how we could take the reforms nationwide.

"I'm tired of us reformers getting our butts handed to us time and time again," I said. "We run good programs, great schools, and get results. Then we naively believe that we can take those results to the powers that be, and that they'll want more. Wrong."

I explained that the teachers union is on the other line telling politicians that they'll finance their next campaign if they support them. And who wins out in the end? Self-interests. Adults. I said we had to give politicians who were willing to take courageous stands the same backing that the unions did. *And* we had to play their game. It had to be both with dollars and boots on the ground. We needed our own power base.

"I'm thinking about starting it," I said. "With a million members and one billion dollars."

"Terrific plan," Jim said. "Very exciting. I absolutely think this is the right next step for you."

"But I will need money," I said.

"How much?"

"I was hoping I could count on the foundation for one hundred million," I said.

He didn't hesitate.

"I can't guarantee it," he said. "But I'll take a request to the family."

Ted Forstmann called. "It was hard to take some of your tongue-lashing at the conference," he said, "but what are you going to do about it? What's your next move?"

I told him I had a plan; he invited me to New York to discuss it face-to-face. I flew up and described it much as I had to Jim Blew, but I found myself refining the concept with each encounter and homing in on the unions.

"I am a Democrat and I support unions," I said. "The teachers unions have millions of dollars and millions of members to bring to bear in political and legislative battles. They are very effective. Good for them. They do a great job of representing the special interests of their members.

"But who is standing up for the special interests of students and parents?" I asked. "No one. They have no way to balance the union's clout, no way to compete at the state and national level.

"I want to establish an organization that will seed a movement nationwide to give voice to students and parents," I said. "What do you think?"

"I'm in," he said.

"I need one hundred million dollars from you," I said.

"Fifty," he said.

"But I need one hundred," I replied.

"Fifty," he answered.

My next stop was John and Laura Arnold. They had virtually come out of nowhere in the last few years as education reform philanthropists. A very young couple from Texas who made their fortune through an energy hedge fund, they had become supporters of my teachers union contract in D.C. They were the dream funders. No bureaucracy, no crazy staff, no ridiculous hoops to jump through—just the two of them asking incredibly thoughtful questions and then making quick decisions. I knew they had to be in.

The Fishers at the Doris and Donald Fisher Fund had become bedrock supporters since TNTP. Don Fisher, who had founded the Gap clothing stores, had been generous with both money and wisdom. Shortly before he passed away he called to say, "If you can manage to get a revolutionary contract there in D.C., I know you can raise the money to support it!" He was right.

This time, it was his son John who provided the wisdom. He listened to my pitch and said he would try to help out on the money end. "But be forewarned," he said. "You are taking on powerful institutions in a very direct way. Not everyone will understand. Even some of your friends in the education reform movement might be either nervous or jealous.

"In the end, they might become some of the biggest impediments."

In September, Oprah Winfrey had invited me to appear on her show to discuss *Waiting for "Superman."* I'd held in check my sadness at Fenty's loss.

"People say, 'Chancellor Rhee, you are so mean,'" I said, "and 'Chancellor Rhee, you are so harsh.'"

"'We should give ineffective teachers more time,' they tell me.

"I look at this from the vantage point of being a mother," I said. "I can tell you that if I showed up on the first day of school with Olivia, and the principal said, 'Here's your teacher. Guess what? She's not so good.' He explains that the school system is giving her one more year to improve, and he says: 'Olivia and her classmates might not learn how to read this year, but we think this is the right thing to do for this adult.' There is no way I would ever accept that for my child. So why should we accept that for anyone's child?"

The audience cheered.

Mark Zuckerberg later appeared on *Oprah* with Governor Chris Christie and Newark, New Jersey, mayor Cory Booker. The creator of Facebook was contributing $100 million to launch reforms in Booker's public schools. Oprah gave them a forum and brought her audience of seven million to focus on public education.

Thinking about it, KMJ saw an opportunity. Though our organization was still in the birthing stages—no name, no staff and all—KMJ wanted to announce it on *Oprah*.

"You're crazy," I said. "There's no way that's going to happen."

"It will," he replied. KMJ has a self-assuredness about him the likes of which I've never seen. It's not cocky or immodest, though. It's just matter-of-fact.

"I've already been on the show once; there's no way they'd have me on again!" I said.

"Let me take care of that part," he responded. "It will be good for us, because it'll give us both a deadline and a powerful launch. Green?"

As in, green light.

"Green," I said.

He called Oprah.

"Michelle is going to start a new advocacy group," he said. "It's going to change education as we know it. We need your help. We want to announce it on your show."

"I get it," she said.

They booked me for December 6. Great, I thought—we had a launch date for an organization that existed only in our minds.

WE BROUGHT TOGETHER A group of longtime advisers—my brain trust—to meet in New York and put some flesh on the bones of an idea.

Along with me, KMJ, and Joel Klein, the group took shape. First was Anita Dunn, who had been on Barack Obama's communications team for his 2008 campaign. Living in D.C. and having seen the media struggles that I had endured in my early years as chancellor, she began to help me on the PR front in my last year with DCPS. She had masterfully guided us through the announcement of the new teachers union contract. Next was Bradley Tusk, founder of Tusk Strategies, who had served on Michael Bloomberg's 2009 reelection campaign. Bradley was known as a keen political strategist who was very familiar with the politics of education reform. As I started to conceive of StudentsFirst, Anita suggested I meet with him. After the first meeting, he whipped out an impressive plan of the next steps that would be necessary to launch a major national organization.

Then came Joe Rospars, with Blue State Digital, the company that took online grassroots mobilization to a new level with Obama's 2008 presidential campaign. Anita connected us, and we immediately hit it off. Also in the room was Byron Auguste, with McKinsey & Company. Byron was the lead McKinsey person working with DCPS when Mayor Fenty first took control of the schools, and he remained a trusted adviser throughout my tenure. Joe Williams, with Democrats for Education Reform, was a friend and fellow reformer with whom I had had a long-standing relationship. The groundwork that DFER laid in the education reform landscape was critical to future advocacy efforts. Next was Dmitri Mehlhorn, who Byron thought could be a valuable member of the team. Dmitri would become one of my top executives at StudentsFirst. David Coleman also joined us. David is one of my dearest friends and also one of the smartest people I know. He had masterminded the strategy and messaging around my entry into DCPS and was a natural to aid this second transition. Adam Mendelsohn, head of Mercury consulting in Sacramento, a strong adviser to KMJ, and an activist in Republican politics, was also in attendance. Rounding out the group, my brother Erik served as our legal counsel.

Bradley Tusk hosted us in his conference room, high in an office building on Broadway. For the better part of the day, we barely left the room.

On the high-concept level, we had to decide how the new organization would present itself: as one that was somewhat faceless, defined by an idea rather than a person? Or would it be stronger if it were associated with one person?

"That's an easy one," Joel Klein said. "Michelle is the face of StudentsFirst. She will help define it, get press, convince governors and state legislators to back our reforms. It's got to be led by her, at least initially. That's what makes it noteworthy. Otherwise, it's nothing."

"Let's be honest," KMJ said. "We're creating an organization to build out your vision. You're our biggest asset. So what is your vision?"

I explained the basic premise. KMJ listened and looked around the room.

"There's no diversity in this room," he said. "We can't make all these decisions from the thirtieth floor of an office building in New York City.

"What did we learn in D.C.?" KMJ asked. "We can't make the same mistakes. Why are we here? To build a group that appeals only to white, male Republicans? Is that what we're doing?"

Silence. There was no easy answer.

What we all knew was that money alone would not be the solution. KMJ knew best that we had to build a real and sustainable grassroots organization that was demanding change from the bottom up.

KMJ had put down a marker and set a goal to build a real movement. As it turned out, he would be instrumental in getting us there.

We ended the meeting with more definition behind the concept. We knew that I would need to build a strong staff to execute our plans. We knew we could expect to have the funds necessary to hire staff and rent space. We already knew there was demand for our reforms in a number of states, but we needed everyday people to drive those changes. And we still needed a name.

For a few weeks we batted names back and forth in emails and texts. I pitched "Save Our Schools." Then "Fix Our Schools." Among the comments were "Too bland," and "There's one in every city, including D.C.," and "Way too generic."

I was a minority of one.

We tossed around more names. Nothing worked.

"It has to be about kids," Dmitri Mehlhorn argued. "I think we should go with StudentsFirst."

I ran it by KMJ.

"Name says it all," he said. "I like it."

I did, too. StudentsFirst it would be.

EVEN BEFORE I WAS officially finished in D.C. at the end of October, politicians at the state level started to call. I had declined Florida governor Rick Scott's offer to move to Florida, but I had agreed to serve on his transition team. Governors and legislators from both parties in states like Nevada, New Mexico, Tennessee, and Ohio had said they would welcome our reforms. Governor Paul LePage asked me if I'd consider coming to Maine.

"I'm not going to work in just one state," I responded. "I'm thinking about something broader. But I promise that with this new idea, we are going to be able to help you."

Were a name, a promise of funding, a concept, and invitations from a number of states enough to launch StudentsFirst on *Oprah*? It would have to suffice. The show was two weeks away. We designed a logo. We created a website and prepared to go live.

Oprah's audience tuning in on December 6 saw me in a serious tweed dress. Oprah wore pink. I described StudentsFirst and said we were launching today.

"I love that title," Oprah said, and added that I hoped to attract a million members.

"We have ten million people watching today," she said. "Will one million of y'all please go sign up?"

The address Studentsfirst.org flashed on the screen.

I quickly laid out our goals: highly effective teachers in every classroom, excellent options for parents, taking money from the bureaucracy to the classroom. Oprah said she had been using her show as a platform for fixing education; now was the chance.

"Somebody needs to fix it!" she said. "You can do it! I am behind you! We are behind you!"

She turned to the camera.

"This is an urgent call to action," she said. "America, hear me now. This is a seminal moment for us."

She said students in the United States ranked very low among thirty industrialized nations in reading and math.

"We're either going to fall further behind or move forward," she said. "It's in our hands. Get yourself fired up! Stop complaining. Log in and sign up!"

She wrapped me in a big, pink hug.

The StudentsFirst website went live. By the end of the day we had more than one hundred thousand members, on our way to a million—and more.

I ALREADY HAD A small office and staff in Washington, but that didn't feel right as a permanent home. Kevin Huffman, my ex-husband, had been offered the job of commissioner of education for the state of Tennessee. He would be moving to Nashville. KMJ pointed out that Kevin had agreed to move to D.C. so I could take the chancellor's job. It was our turn to return the favor. I started making plans to set up a house in Nashville with my parents, and I would be there half-time, but it wasn't the right place for StudentsFirst. KMJ and I had postponed our wedding, but it was inevitable that I would marry the mayor of Sacramento. Would his hometown make a good base for StudentsFirst?

"You have to come to the belly of the beast," he said.

California was the most populous state, and its teachers union was arguably the strongest in the nation. Its legislature, run by Democrats, was in the union's thrall. It would be the hardest state to reform.

A few days later I knew for sure: Sacramento would be our home base.

My first hire was Shawn Branch, the native Baltimorean who had run my schedule and my life in D.C. He was integral to my sanity and agreed to pull up stakes and make the move to Sacramento in January. My second hire was an eighteen-year-old named Julian Nagler, who had interned for KMJ the summer before. He was taking a gap year before college and handled every problem, small or large. He was a great utility player when I needed one.

In addition to fielding calls from governors, we spent December writing a business plan and a policy agenda. Bain and Company, under the leadership of senior partner Chris Bierly, helped with the business side of the plan. Dmitri Mehlhorn came on as COO. Kathleen deLaski, an executive who had worked at places as varied as the Pentagon and AOL, agreed to manage all facets of the political operation. I was able to convince Eric Lerum, who was essential to reforming the D.C. schools in the deputy mayor's office, and his fiancée, Rebecca Sibilia, to move to Sacramento, too.

I swept up as many Fenty administration folks as I could. Kate Gottfredson, Ximena Hartsock, Mafara Hobson, and Bridget Davis rounded out our original team.

We pounded out a twenty-five-page policy agenda. It would serve as a road map that states could follow, including specific laws that they would need to adopt if they wanted to match our reforms in D.C.

Our blueprint suggested that states establish teacher evaluation systems based on student achievement and classroom observations. "State law should give districts the autonomy to develop teacher evaluation systems apart from the collective bargaining process," we wrote. We also recommended that states evaluate principals on their success with student achievement and their ability to manage their schools.

One of the most promising developments in public education

that I witnessed, from our years at The New Teacher Project through the time in D.C., was that professionals were willing to make midlife career changes to become teachers. However, the process was often cumbersome.

To address that, we wrote: "States must reduce legal barriers to entry in the teaching profession." We suggested that states break down complicated credentialing and certification schemes. As in D.C., states should be able to reward excellent teachers with individual performance pay, and they should take tenure off the table. We recommended that states adopt mutual consent and end "last in, first out" policies.

We also wanted to empower parents. Our first recommendation sounded simple and easy: state laws should "ensure that parents receive meaningful information about their schools and teachers." In most states and districts, parents have to demand and dig for basic information on the quality of teaching and teachers. Teachers' track records on student achievement should be disclosed to parents, and parents should have access to alternative, more effective classrooms.

Why not grade the schools? We suggested a law for that.

I have always believed that students should be able to attend the best schools, whether public schools, charters, or private schools. Our policy paper recommended that states remove arbitrary caps on charter schools. Many charters, which are supported with public funds but managed independently of the public schools, have been enormously successful in raising achievement for students in rough circumstances. Students in charters in New Orleans and Washington, D.C., have excelled, which supports my contention that great teachers at focused schools can improve achievement.

We also recommended that states create a mechanism to close low-performing schools. Parents should not have to see their children stuck at bad schools. If parents join together and come to the conclusion that their local school is not helping their kids learn, they should be able to employ a trigger petition to force fundamental changes: from removing the principal and teachers to turning it into a charter school. State legislators could pass laws to give them that power.

On the finance and governance side, we recommended that states move toward leaner and more efficient ways of running schools. That meant that we supported mayoral control of city schools. And if school districts were failing to provide a quality education, we were in favor of the state taking over the schools.

Parents often struggle to get information about not only their individual schools and teachers but also system-wide budgets. Our recommendation: "A school district's budget should give an average member of the public a clear sense of where the money goes and what the district's priorities are."

Why not?

And why not make sure that central offices serve the direct interests of students? I found in D.C. and school districts nationwide that school bureaucracies existed in part to perpetuate themselves rather than to promote learning in the classroom. Our recommendation: "Bloated central offices should be pared down to eliminate redundancies in a way that connects every member of the central team with a goal of driving student outcomes."

WE CIRCULATED OUR POLICY agenda to a number of trusted veteran education reform leaders. It received mixed reviews.

Many colleagues argued that our goals were not broad enough. If we wanted to put students first, why not address curricula? What about nutrition? Why not recommend that states offer a variety of social services within the public schools?

I could see why reformers would suggest that we cover all aspects of public education. But I wanted to stay on the ground, focused very tightly on teaching and teacher quality, all directed to improving student outcomes. Curricula and nutrition are certainly important, but neither would be our focus nor our strength.

At the same time, we heard from political leaders in many states who wanted to translate and transplant everything we did in D.C. to their systems. They welcomed us into their states. We wanted to create an aggressive approach to making these reforms happen.

We completed our policy statement by Christmas, just in time to work with state legislatures that began meeting in January. On January 2, 2011, we fanned out and started hitting state capitals.

EARLY IN JANUARY I flew to Tallahassee, Florida, to meet with newly elected governor Rick Scott and state legislators in the first days of the legislative session.

Florida was friendly territory for our reforms. Former governor Jeb Bush had paved the way. He started overhauling the state's public education system as soon as he took office in 1999. He passed laws to grade each school. He pushed through laws to increase student testing and demand accountability. He ended social promotion, where schools allow students to move up a grade with their peers, even if they have not mastered the material required for promotion. He favored vouchers. And as a result, the state was leading the way in improvements nationwide.

Governor Scott was eager to bring D.C.'s reforms to his state. Republicans had a two-thirds majority in the Florida House and Senate, so support for his agenda was there. I had high hopes.

Before I arrived in Tallahassee, legislators were invited to see a screening of *Waiting for "Superman."* By the time I showed up to speak at a luncheon for all, they were beyond excited to see me and hear what I had to say.

In a short speech, I waved a copy of our policy agenda in the air and said, "If you want to do what we did in D.C., pass this agenda." It's safe to say that legislators and their aides mobbed me after lunch.

That afternoon Governor Scott took me on a tour of schools, starting with one that was under renovation. He stopped to chat with every construction worker on the site. More than one thanked him for keeping his focus on school reform.

Scott and I had met at the Republican Governors Association meeting in November 2010. My sense was that Scott didn't care whether he was well liked or would be reelected. He wanted to do what he believed was right, especially in focusing Florida schools on students. Frankly, he reminded me of Adrian Fenty.

We had the support of Scott and many legislators, but passing our agenda was far from assured. The legislature had passed Senate Bill 6 the year before. It was a vibrant reform package that embraced many of our goals, including merit pay and a curtailing of tenure. Then-governor Charlie Crist vetoed the bill in exchange for support from the teachers unions for his run for the U.S. Senate. Crist lost, but legislators remembered the union's clout. Teachers called in sick. The union rallied outside the Florida Capitol and vilified pro-reform legislators.

So I was not surprised when many Florida House and Senate members were on the fence in the days and weeks after Governor Scott introduced his reform package. The union was working them hard.

What to do?

Even by January 2011, little more than a month after we had launched StudentsFirst, we already had thousands of members in Florida. Many were teachers. When committees held hearings on the education bill, we brought in teachers to testify in favor of the reforms. There were more teachers from StudentsFirst than from the unions. Our members testified in simple terms: the reform package was good for teachers, good for kids, good for schools.

We took the wind out of the unions' sails.

Governor Scott and the state legislature passed virtually every piece of the educator quality strand of our policy agenda. It was a big win for StudentsFirst, the students of Florida—and the teachers. I figured it would take ten years to accomplish that level of reform in California.

AMONG THE MANY CALLS and invitations we fielded in our first few months, some of the most persistent came from Michigan.

"You have to go to Lansing," Kathleen deLaski told me. She had been working in education reform for decades and knew the national landscape. We had met in D.C. when she was working as senior program director on education for the Walton Foundation. I trusted Kathleen.

But I was not eager. Michigan had a reputation for being one of the worst states for education reform. Teach For America had pulled out of Detroit. When I was running The New Teacher Project, I had met with Detroit school officials. I came away so discouraged that I declined to get involved.

"Things have changed," deLaski said. "The governor and legislators want you to come in."

Governor Rick Snyder had taken office and promised education reform.

I relented and flew to Lansing.

State representative Paul Scott greeted me there. Scott was a young legislator from the suburbs of Flint. He was appointed chair of the House Education Committee, with the goal of moving quickly to adopt the basic elements of our policy agenda. He set up meetings with the Speaker of the House, the chair of the Senate Education Committee, and Governor Snyder's political director.

I wanted to make sure these Michigan leaders understood the stakes and the obstacles. Were they ready for the battle?

"This is our first year, and we have only limited resources to work with in our partner states this year," I explained. "When we commit, we go all in and support you across the board.

"But I know what you are up against in Michigan," I said. "As soon as you introduce the reforms we're talking about, the unions will strike back. They will call you evil, say you hate kids and are against teachers."

They looked at one another and nodded.

"What we do is give you air cover," I said. "We will go on the offensive in the media. Instead of waiting for you to get attacked, we'll talk about the importance of the reforms and your courage in leading the way if you choose to take on the fight."

The legislators huddled for a few minutes. I took a break and returned.

"We have a real opportunity to do something meaningful here," Paul Scott said.

They said they were committed to passing our policy agenda, but something was missing. I didn't want to launch our state legislative agendas with the support of Republicans alone. I approached Tim Melton, a veteran Democrat serving in the Michigan House. He had chaired the House Education Committee and helped establish Democrats for Education Reform in Michigan. Would Melton help bring Democrats to the table?

"We are on the same page on most of our issues," I said at our first meeting. "You can support merit pay and closing failing schools. You favor teacher evaluations based on student data. You want to remove caps on successful charter schools. We should work together on this."

Melton agreed to get as many Democrats as possible to support the reform agenda.

Still, many Michigan legislators started to wilt under the unions' pressure. We found ourselves losing votes. We mobilized our members. Some wrote emails to their representatives. Some showed up at their doors. Many called.

It was effective. So much so that one House member called StudentsFirst and said, "Please stop the emails. I get it already! I am going to vote for the reform."

With pressure from our members and the help of Tim Melton, Michigan passed a slate of strong reform laws on bipartisan votes.

The teachers unions were not pleased. The Michigan Education Association and its allies sought retribution. Their target was Paul Scott. They gathered enough signatures for a recall. StudentsFirst joined the fight on Scott's side. At the start of the campaign, our polls showed Scott was down by 20 points. With an aggressive campaign in support of Scott, we helped narrow the polls to almost even. In the end, Paul Scott lost, but by fewer than 250 votes.

We passed all of our laws, but we lost Paul Scott. I mourned the defeat of one our staunchest supporters. But the education reformers in the Michigan legislature were undeterred. They were angry at Scott's demise, and our defense of their colleague built trust between StudentsFirst and many legislators.

WE WANTED TO ENSURE that we passed laws with bipartisan support. If we were affiliated with a specific party, it would compromise our ability to appeal to our broad base of members. We wanted the membership of StudentsFirst to reflect the diverse America we hoped to serve. People were flocking to StudentsFirst. Membership rose steadily, from one hundred thousand when we launched with Oprah to nearly a million by the end of our first year. But who were they? Did they comprise a diverse group?

"How do we go about building a broad-based organization?" KMJ always asked. "If we don't have Democrats, Latinos, and African Americans represented, we're going to fail, just as we did in D.C."

I agreed.

It made intrinsic sense. As a Democrat, I believe that access to a high-quality education is not only essential for the health of our democracy and economy, but a civil right fundamental to fulfilling the American creed. I believe civil rights delayed are civil rights denied. And the right to a high-quality education was being denied to too many of our children—especially those of color and in low-income communities.

"I am one of the kids you're trying to help, just forty-six years older," KMJ said. "I came up here in Sacramento with lousy schools defined by my zip code. That was my reality."

"What do you propose?" I asked.

"We have to reach out to Latino and African American communities. We must be driving the reforms for our own kids," he said. "Let me take that on."

KMJ knew the terrain. Remember that he and I had met because he created St. HOPE Public Schools to give poor kids in Sacramento a better choice for public schools. So he knew about the challenges to improving schools in poor neighborhoods. In 2009, he had launched STAND UP, an organization to support high-quality schools in Sacramento.

KMJ introduced our StudentsFirst policy agenda to the Urban League and NAACP in California. He brought it before the National Conference of Black Mayors and convinced the group to adopt our policies. At the U.S. Conference of Mayors, he chaired the education task force and aligned the conference with our agenda as part of its goals. The feedback was incredibly encouraging. These groups were clear with us that they had always wanted to make a difference on these issues, but hadn't always been engaged by the reform community before. We were reaching out to them in the hopes of building the movement together.

At the same time, more high-profile Democrats joined our small band. Tali Stein, a veteran Democratic fund-raiser for Hillary Clinton, among others, came on to help us raise money. Hari

Sevugan, a former teacher and then the spokesperson for the Democratic National Committee, came on to take over our communications shop. Like me, our staff had always been predominantly young Democrats, but we were adding more credibility to our bipartisan nature with these new hires.

Critics have tried to paint us into a corner populated by only white Republicans. If they check our supporters and our membership, they would be surprised to find teachers, police officers, lawyers, doctors, carpenters, stay-at-home moms, and farmers—in all colors, races, and income levels.

The only absolute that our members have in common is a willingness to act on behalf of students.

IN THE SPRING OF 2011, soon after I left DCPS, *USA Today* published an investigative story on standardized testing procedures in the District of Columbia. It revealed an unusual number of erasure marks on the local standardized tests of our students between 2008 and 2010. It caused quite a ruckus because it implied that the gains that our students had demonstrated weren't real.

I reacted as someone who had seen firsthand how much hard work the teachers, parents, and students of D.C. had put in over the past three years. I knew how much real change we had accomplished. I was resentful that anyone would question the ability of kids raised in challenging circumstances to succeed.

Our impulse was to attack the messenger. "How dare they question the success of our students?" "There will always be cynics that can't see—or maybe don't want to see—our kids succeed with the right support."

We were misguided.

There will always be doubters. Journalists will scrutinize school systems. It's their role. But our reaction shouldn't be to push back at every cynic or negative article. We have to welcome scrutiny. We don't want any doubt about the success of our students. If that means we audit every test, so be it. Journalists and investigators are critical to showing us what we are doing well and where we need work. If audits and investigations expose cheating on tests, we are cheating our kids.

Well before *USA Today* raised questions, we ordered a comprehensive review of allegations of wrongdoing on the part of the some teachers and administrators in D.C. For the first time in the history of DCPS, we brought in an outside expert to examine and audit our system. Caveon Test Security—the leading expert in the field at the time—assessed our tests, results, and security measures. Their investigators interviewed teachers, principals, and administrators.

Caveon found no evidence of systematic cheating. None. Moreover, the District of Columbia inspector general conducted a seventeen-month examination of testing procedures and results. It found problems in only one school. The report concluded there was "insufficient evidence on which to conclude that there was widespread cheating" on tests across the city from 2008 to 2010.

D.C. students are proving the doubters wrong with their continued progress. Since the initial tests that the *USA Today* story focused on, DCPS has released six sets of standardized test scores for public school students. Each of these exams has been administered under greater scrutiny and increased testing security. Some tests have included greater numbers of special education and students not yet proficient in the English language. If there had been rampant systematic cheating, as some allege, you would expect to see dramatic drop-offs in these scores after new security measures were implemented. We saw the opposite. As a whole, D.C. students have either held steady or made significant gains.

The *Washington Post* noted these results in a series of editorials under the headlines "CHEATING ALLEGATIONS CAN'T MASK REAL GAINS IN D.C.'S SCHOOLS" and "MORE EVIDENCE THAT D.C. EDUCATION REFORMS ARE WORKING."

Investigations into testing procedures are ongoing. Test scores keep rising. The best response to allegations of cheating is more transparency and higher achievement.

OUR FIRST YEAR WASN'T easy. We had ambitious goals but didn't yet have the infrastructure in place to always support our efforts the way we wanted to. We were flying the plane as we were building it. In many ways, we were a typical start-up.

But the dedication of our staff and our members was remarkable. By the end of year one, we had met our goals and exceeded some. We had helped change more than sixty policies in seven states. We had attracted more than a million members. We were making headway with our fund-raising goals. Given that we had started from scratch in January, we engineered an encouraging start.

I came away with a new understanding of our potential.

The power of StudentsFirst is not in playing the inside game. The teachers unions have a thirty-year head start on walking the halls of state capitols, bonding legislators to their causes and meting out retribution to those who cross them. We are not going to beat them at that game.

We have to play and win in the outside game. We have to bring pressure on legislators through our members. In Florida, we brought in teachers to testify for our agenda. We mobilized so many members in Michigan that legislators begged for mercy.

In the long term, if we are going to be successful, it will take focused and concerted action by our members. We will have to put pressure on legislators they have never felt from anyone other than unions. We will need to counterbalance the unions' money with our members.

PART II

The Movement

8

Honoring Teachers

I met Wanda Smith midway through my third year as chancellor of District of Columbia Public Schools. Little did I know that we would leave a lasting imprint on each other.

Wanda taught kindergarten at Kimball Elementary School, in a predominantly African American neighborhood east of the Anacostia River, at the foot of Fort Dupont Park. For two years the school had done a solid job of raising student achievement.

When I talked to the principal about it, she said, "Great! Can you come out and meet my teachers? They were afraid you'd be disappointed!"

A few weeks later I ordered lunch for the staff. We broke bread, and I congratulated them for taking their students to new levels in both math and reading. Many of their students came to school every morning from difficult circumstances. The staff, such as fifth-grade teacher William Taylor, whose gains with students were among the best in the city, set high expectations, and the students met them.

As I was leaving, one of the teachers approached me. She was older and had that knowing look behind her bright eyes and broad smile. "My name is Wanda Smith," she said. "I want you to come to my classroom."

Wanda had been at Kimball for about fifteen years. She had been a dependable teacher of young kindergartners. When I visited, her classroom was orderly, her kids were attentive, and her lessons were sound. I could tell that she sent her students to the first grade with the tools to continue their progress.

Wanda and I started up an email correspondence. We talked about her classroom and the latest in pedagogy. And we gossiped about our lives.

"What are you doing with that fine man you have?" she asked when she heard I was dating Kevin Johnson. When she learned we had gotten engaged, she wrote, "I want to plan your wedding." The next week she brought a wedding planning book to my office. "I know you're too busy to do this stuff, so I thought I'd give you some assistance," she joked.

What I didn't realize at the time is that I had been giving some assistance to Wanda Smith, too. True, she had been a good teacher before I became chancellor. But she took my challenge that "we can't keep making excuses in DCPS" and "every child can learn, and every child will learn" to heart.

Wanda Smith had upped her game.

At the end of the year, we invited teachers who had been rated "highly effective" in the IMPACT evaluations to a reception at Union Station. Since this was our first group of highly effective teachers, we wanted to celebrate them in a resounding way. We announced that each of them would be receiving a check ranging from $3,000 to $25,000 and that we would be holding a black-tie gala in their honor at the Kennedy Center in a few weeks. The teachers were thrilled.

Wanda Smith ran up to me. Of course she had made it.

"I want you to know you made me highly effective," she said.

"That's not true," I said. "I had nothing to do with it! You have been a great teacher for years before I showed up."

"Not the case," she said. "I've been teaching for fifteen years, and I was an okay teacher, but I didn't know how to be really good until you laid it out for me. You established the expectations for being an excellent teacher. I haven't always been as good as I was this year.

"You made that happen."

Several weeks later, Wanda was one of the 662 teachers honored at the Kennedy Center in the first "Standing Ovation for DC Teachers." It was the last night of my tenure as chancellor, and it might also have been the best night.

THE CONFLICTS AND CONTROVERSIES of my three years made headlines and dominated coverage: the layoffs, the union protests, the school closings.

What got lost were the stories of the great teachers who took the new culture we brought to DCPS and ran with it. Wanda Smith was not alone.

Holding people to a high standard is a way of showing respect. I hold students to a high standard because I am pro-student. I hold teachers to a high standard because I am pro-teacher.

So it is with utter dismay that I find some people portraying me as anti-teacher. This couldn't be further from the truth.

How can I be against teachers when I come from teachers? Teachers made me who I am. My father's father was a principal in Korea. My mother's mother taught kindergarten. Inspired by their example, I spent the first three years of my career after college as a full-time teacher in a classroom in Baltimore that served primarily disadvantaged students. Many of my aunts were teachers and came to the United States to help make supplies for me when

I taught in Baltimore. My best friend and sister-in-law are both teachers. After graduate school, I launched a nonprofit focused on recruiting and placing teachers.

But more than that: how can I be anti-teacher when I believe, and research has repeatedly shown, that it's teachers—high-quality teachers—who hold the key to improving student achievement?

To paint me as anti-teacher is simply inaccurate, a caricature to fit a political agenda. It is neither honest nor real.

This myth was especially clear during my time as chancellor of DCPS. The reality in DCPS was that, for the first time, we finally raised our expectations and appreciated the potential of great teachers like Wanda Smith.

Consider the case of Eric Bethel, a fifth-grade teacher who had been teaching for seven years at DCPS before IMPACT was rolled out. When StudentsFirst launched in 2010, he wrote on our blog: "It was extremely enriching to finally receive feedback that could help move my teaching forward. In the seven years prior, I never received feedback from an evaluation that allowed me to grow specific areas of instruction." Eric Bethel wanted feedback that would help him grow as a professional. At StudentsFirst, we have conducted many surveys of teachers, and significant majorities of teachers want what Eric Bethel and Wanda Smith wanted: high expectations and clear feedback that will help them develop.

Crucially, at DCPS and StudentsFirst, we also paired high expectations with high compensation. It's not all about the money, but significant compensation rewards for excellent teachers are a way of signaling appreciation, raising the status of the profession, and retaining great teachers.

As Eric wrote in that same blog post: "Lastly, but certainly not least, especially if you ask my wife who has been dreaming of us owning our first home for years now, is the compensation connected with being a highly effective teacher. In the next few weeks, I am set to receive a highly effective bonus that is about half of my entire teacher's salary from last year. This bonus will greatly contribute to our dream. It is incredible that my district has moved beyond the lip service that teachers have become accustomed to hearing and has actually decided to show that they get how meaningful yet challenging teaching is. They are showing that they get it by appropriately compensating teachers who can do a great job at this extremely meaningful and incredibly challenging work."

STORIES LIKE THOSE OF Wanda and Eric too often get lost in a more negative narrative. Consider the media stories about the District of Columbia's IMPACT evaluation system in July 2011, nearly a year after I had resigned from DCPS. At that time, 227 teachers were asked to leave the system for poor performance: 65 who received "ineffective" ratings that year, and another 141 who were "minimally effective" for the second year in a row. These headlines were reported in many newspapers. But you had to read deep into the stories, and sometimes search through several newspapers, to find out that 663 teachers—three times as many teachers as were let go—were rated as highly effective, making them eligible for bonuses of up to $25,000. And another 2,765—more than thirteen times as many as were let go—were rated as "effective," meeting the raised standards that we placed on them.

But it's not just about evaluations. It's also about listening. One of the major unreported stories of school reform is that it is the reformers who are actually listening to teachers, while the status quo is demanding silence and conformity.

During my time in D.C., we held teacher listening sessions a few times a month. I would choose a school and show up for a meeting after class. There was no agenda. Administrators were not allowed to attend. It was simply an opportunity for teachers to ask questions, express concerns, share ideas, and tell me whether our reforms were working for them. These sessions were a great way for me to keep my finger on the pulse of classroom teachers. They were not always easy or positive. Teachers were honest. They trusted me enough to air their concerns. We were able to oftentimes establish strong, true bonds.

THERE'S A MISCONCEPTION THAT because teachers unions are against certain reforms, then teachers must be against those reforms. That's anything but true.

In D.C., while the national teachers union opposed the changes we wanted to make in the union contract, 80 percent of the membership ended up voting for it. My staff at StudentsFirst is full of former teachers, and tens of thousands of our members are teachers. When I speak in other cities, teachers often come up to me afterward to tell me how much they appreciate my approach. They stop me in airports to show their support.

What people do not know are the many sacrifices some teachers have made to fight the status quo and come out strongly to advocate for policies that put kids first.

Rhonda Lochiatto, a seasoned teacher in Florida, is a great example. She drove four hours each way to testify in Tallahassee in support of teacher quality reform policies. For her brave stance, Rhonda was harassed by the opposition, but she remained strong and fought to put kids first. Rhonda still emails me with a message I have come to find invaluable: "I need you to stay strong so I can stay strong."

In Michigan, Todd Beard helped lead the fight for reform against the strong opposition of his local union leader. Not only did he testify before the House Education Committee, but he recruited and ferried other teachers to Lansing to do the same.

On July 4, 2012, KMJ and I—as Sacramento's first lady—were walking the Independence Day parade route down the California capital's Cottage Way when a young woman rushed up to us. I expected her to want to take her picture with my husband, as had happened all morning. As I looked for her camera so I could snap the picture, she looked me straight in the eye. She was a teacher at Jedediah Smith Elementary. "I just want you to know that I love what you are trying to do, and I want you to know I am with you," she said in stride.

There are countless teachers across the country who have been fighting side by side with me to establish policies that put kids first. Their message is consistent: keep up the fight. Perhaps they are the silent majority of teachers. But they know that the public school teaching system is broken, and they want to see it fixed.

The question is, How?

FINLAND HAD AN OPPORTUNITY to re-create itself after World War II. The Nordic nation had survived decades under the control of either Sweden or Russia. As an infant nation, experimenting with independence, it struggled to figure out how to establish a successful economy and compete in the global marketplace. It chose to build on a foundation of public education. It exalted teachers.

In 1963, the Finnish parliament voted to focus the small nation's civic energy and financial resources on public education. "It was simply the idea that every child would have a good public school," writes educator Pasi Sahlberg in his book *Finnish Lessons*. "If we want to be competitive, we need to educate everybody. It all came out of a need to survive."

The Finns did more than survive. They put their teachers on a par with doctors and lawyers—in training, expertise, status, and job satisfaction. Teaching became a very attractive career, respected and desired across the country. In 2010, Sahlberg says, about 6,600 applicants competed for 660 primary school training slots.

Now Finland ranks top among nations in students' abilities in reading and math.

We cannot compare ourselves to a small, Nordic country, of course. We are a huge, diverse nation with two hundred years of devotion to public education. But I do believe we can take a lesson from Finland's approach to elevating teachers in its society.

Why not devote our entire nation, as Finland did, to putting teachers first among professionals? Why not make teaching an endeavor that will attract our best and brightest? Why not treat teachers as professionals to whom we entrust the academic development and future success of our children, for generations to come, literally, for the future of the United States?

My goal is to help create an environment where teachers can thrive as they do in Finland. But that will take time and some wrenching changes.

IN FINLAND, TEACHERS ARE expected to take the child who comes to their classroom and teach him to read and write, to add and multiply, to reason and understand. No excuses. Every child gets to learn.

Not so in some quarters of the United States.

There is an odd and somewhat unhealthy debate going on today in education reform circles that can serve to compromise a teacher's standing in the community. Unfortunately, I find myself in the middle of that debate. It has to do with the role of teachers, how much teachers can actually influence student achievement, and to what extent we can hold teachers accountable for that growth.

On one end of the spectrum you find the people who believe that teachers can have little impact on kids when environmental circumstances are tough. They argue that the trials and tribulations of poverty, uninvolved parents, violence in the community, a lack of health care, and inadequate nutrition present insurmountable hurdles that schools cannot overcome. They believe that we cannot hold teachers accountable for student academic growth in the face of these tremendous obstacles.

Others argue that none of those environment factors matters, and that good teachers and good schools can educate students and raise achievement despite problems of poverty and family dysfunction. This side believes that we should hold teachers and schools accountable for everything that happens to kids.

The debate is taking place on those extremes: either we cannot expect teachers to make a dent with poor kids, or poverty doesn't matter. That's not how the vast majority of Americans see the situation, though. And it's certainly not how I view it. Having been a teacher in a low-performing urban school, I know firsthand how difficult it is to teach students who face a multitude of challenges before they even set foot in the schoolhouse door. These challenges are real and severe and have dire consequences.

I don't believe that educators and schools can fix all of society's ills.

That said, I do believe that schools and teachers can make a tremendous difference in the lives of kids who face these challenges every day. Do our children face significant obstacles that impact their ability to learn? Absolutely. Can we, as educators, still make an enormous difference in their lives, if we're doing our jobs well? Absolutely. Those are *not* two mutually exclusive notions.

The research is very clear: teachers make a real difference. In fact, of all in-school factors, the quality of the teacher in front of the students every day has far and away the greatest influence on student achievement.

According to a 2011 report prepared by the Center for American Progress and the Education Trust, "Students who have three or four strong teachers in a row will soar academically regardless of their racial or economic background while those who have a sequence of weak teachers will fall further behind. . . ."

Many argue back, "But that's a measure of *in-school* factors. Compared to the factors outside the school, teachers don't play as large a role."

I would ask, "What is our job as educators?" I would argue that we, as educators, cannot be focused on the external factors. There are social service agencies and programs that exist to help families deal with problems beyond the schoolhouse. Educators should, while acknowledging those circumstances, focus relentlessly on what can happen when we have the children in the classroom.

If we believe that the external factors are simply too difficult to overcome, then why do we have schools? In a city such as Washington, D.C., if we believe schools can't make a difference, shouldn't we have just shut down the school system and used the $1 billion annual budget to enhance social services and fix poverty?

Therein lies the problem. While some contend that you can't have great schools in every community until you solve the problem of poverty, I would argue the opposite. In the words of my mentor, Joel Klein, "You cannot solve the problem of poverty until you fix the public education system." If you look at any country through any period of time, you will see that the single most effective strategy for combating generational poverty is education.

WHEN I FIRST BECAME chancellor, schools knew when I was scheduled for a visit. They prepared. After I'd seen my fair share of pep rallies, musical performances, and dance routines for my benefit, I decided to move toward unannounced visits. I wanted to see what was happening in the schools every day, when I *wasn't* there.

One day I decided to visit a school in Trinidad, one of the toughest and most dangerous parts of Washington. I pulled up to the front of the school. I stepped on the sidewalk and looked across the street to see a liquor store and a nightclub. Approaching the front door, I stepped over broken beer bottles and cigarette butts strewn across the open walkway. It was the picture of urban blight.

When I visited schools I didn't stop by the main office. That created too much of a scene. Instead I just walked around. On this particular day, I chose a random hallway and entered the first classroom I saw. What was happening in this particular fourth-grade class was amazing.

Thirty pairs of eyes were transfixed on the teacher, a woman of boundless energy bouncing around the classroom. She had the kids' rapt attention. It was clear from listening to the dialogue for a short time that the class was in the midst of a unit on Greek mythology. They were reading a chapter book together about a group of children who had traveled back in time (to the mythological time of Greek gods) and had an adventure. They were at the part of the book where they wanted to go back home.

"Okaaaaaaayyyyy," said the teacher. "Please look up at the posters I've put on the walls." She'd created a variety of posters, each with the name of a Greek god and their kingdom. "And tell me," she continued, "if you were one of these kids and needed help returning home, and you could choose one Greek god to help you, which would it be and why?"

I scanned the posters on the wall and chose my answer.

The first child raised his hand. "I would choose Zeus," he said emphatically, "because Zeus is the god of gods! He's the boss of everyone else. If he tells you to do something, you have to do it. So I figure, just cut out the middleman and go straight to the big guy!" He smiled broadly.

"Great answer!" I thought.

The next little girl raised her hand. "I would definitely pick Aphrodite," she said confidently. "She is the goddess of women, children, and families. These are kids we're talking about. These are her peeps! She's gotta take care of them!" The other kids snickered in agreement with her logic. One of her table mates gave her a high-five.

"Another really solid answer," I thought.

A pudgy boy raised his hand next. "I would choose Apollo," he said. I looked up at the Apollo poster. "The god of art, music, and literature," it read.

"Okay, kid, that's a total misfire," I thought.

Then he went on to explain his answer. "As you'll remember from the book, the way the kids traveled back in time is they dug up an old Greek lyre. When they strummed the strings of the lyre, they were transported back in time. I figure if they have to go back, it has something to do with the lyre, so they should call on the god of music."

"Huh," I thought. "That was pretty darn good."

The students in the room gave five or six really thoughtful answers before someone came up with my answer, which by that time seemed pretty lame and boring, of Hermes, the god of travel.

The classroom was amazing. It was exactly what you want to see happening in a classroom every day—the kind of place where you'd want your own kid to be. All of the children were engaged. They were learning critical thinking and analytical skills. The room was alive with learning. I was thrilled.

AND THEN I WENT across the hall.

As I opened the door I nearly knocked over the teacher, who was standing in the opening. She was screaming at the top of her lungs.

"Everybody be QUIEEEETTTTTT!" she belted. "I just don't understand what's wrong. I've been telling you all morning to close your mouths and stop the yapping. But you're just not listening.

I'm going to give you one more chance. I'm going to count down from ten and by the time I get to one, everybody's mouth should be closed."

"Ten . . . nine . . . eight . . . I'm waiting," she said as she started to turn the light switch on and off.

"seven . . ." Flick, flick, flick went the light switch.

"six . . ." Flick.

"five . . . I'm waiting . . ." Flick.

"We're waiting too," you could tell the kids were thinking, "for something to *happen*!"

I was in each of those classrooms for no more than ten to fifteen minutes, and I could tell you that those two groups of children, both from the same troubled community, who came to the same dilapidated building every day, with rainwater leaking through the roof and ceiling tiles falling on their heads, were getting two wildly different educational experiences because of the adults who were in front of them.

I SIMPLY REFUSE TO believe that what we do in schools can't make a difference. It can. A big one. The research bears this out. According to Eric Hanushek, an economist from Stanford, if the United States were to raise its PISA scores—which evaluate student achievement across the globe—to the level of Finland, we would raise our gross national product by more than $100 trillion over the lifetime of a child born in 2010. How do we do that? Hanushek presents data showing that replacing the bottom 5–8 percent of teachers with average ones would have us performing near the top in PISA scores.

We know having the right teachers in the classroom can make a big difference for kids—a life-changing difference. What I've found fascinating is that when I go out and talk about these facts, I'm accused of being anti-teacher.

That mystifies me—and teachers like Jennifer Miller.

Miller had been teaching second grade at Janney Elementary in D.C. for years. She was a great success. Her students in the largely white neighborhood adored her. But she wanted a new challenge. So she wrote to me: "I am thrilled to work in a public school system where we are expected to raise achievement levels and have our results measured. I just found out that you've asked our principal, Scott Cartland, to take on a more difficult assignment in a failing school. I've decided I'm going to go too!"

Cartland and Miller were heading to Webb-Wheatley, an elementary school in the troubled Trinidad neighborhood. Jennifer struggled through her first year but was able to use her skills to connect with the students and improve their academic achievement.

Teachers like Jennifer Miller can have a significant impact on students. We should do everything we can to make sure that every child has an effective teacher in front of her every single day. How is that viewpoint anti-teacher? If anything, it's incredibly *pro*-teacher. It's saying teachers matter. It's saying how you do your job makes a big difference. I think that acknowledging how difficult it is to be an effective teacher in a challenged environment honors teachers.

IN ORDER TO ENSURE that every kid has a highly effective teacher, we have to differentiate among teachers. We have to have a rigorous evaluation system that determines which teachers have the greatest success with kids and which do not. And it also necessitates that we intervene with those who are not performing. We either quickly improve their skills and capabilities or we move them out of the system, because our kids can't afford to be taught by an ineffective educator.

Some people cast that as anti-teacher because it means that some people will lose their jobs. I disagree. I think it does two important things: first, it elevates the teaching profession; second, it ensures that we're putting students and their interests first—above job security and tenure for teachers. That's not anti-teacher; it's pro-kid.

It's fascinating, though, to watch how conversations about this seemingly innocuous topic of teacher evaluation unfold. I say "seemingly innocuous" because you would assume that everyone, including teachers unions, would think that the current evaluation system, which relies on principal evaluations alone, is overly subjective, unfair, inconsistent, and prone to politics and corruption.

The question then is "How do we change this?" Some would argue that it's impossible to truly capture the effectiveness of a teacher. And while I would agree that it may be impossible for a tool to capture every last essence of a teacher, I also believe that we can measure a teacher's effectiveness with as much accuracy as we can that of a doctor, lawyer, or management consultant.

Does simply looking at a doctor's mortality rate capture his true effectiveness as a physician? No, because it doesn't give you any indication of their bedside manner. But if we were choosing an open-heart surgeon for our child, would bedside manner be the first thing we looked at? Of course not. We'd want to know how many of the doctor's patients survived to see another day. You could have the best bedside manner in the world, but if all your patients died on the operating table, it wouldn't matter one iota.

So should surgeons be evaluated solely on the basis of their mortality rate? Absolutely not. Should it be a major factor? Definitely.

The same is true of teachers. People don't like the notion of teachers being evaluated partly on the basis of how their students perform on standardized tests. In fact, I had a conversation with a legislator that went something like this:

"I don't believe we can make judgments about the effectiveness of a teacher based only on test scores," he said.

"I don't believe we should, either," I responded. "We should look at teacher effectiveness through a variety of lenses. However, I think it's critical that student achievement growth is a significant one of those factors."

He looked at me skeptically. So I continued:

"When I came to Washington, D.C., public schools, eight percent of the eighth graders in the city's schools were on grade level in mathematics. Eight percent! That means ninety-two percent of our kids did not have the skills and knowledge necessary to be productive members of society."

I told him that when I looked at the evaluations of the adults in the system at the same time, it turned out that 98 percent of teachers were being rated as doing a good job. How can you possibly have that kind of a disconnect? And I asked, "How can you have a functional organization in which all of your employees believe they're doing a great job, but what they're producing is 8 percent success?"

"Well, that's not the teacher's fault," the legislator said.

"Exactly," I said. "The teachers weren't the ones who created this broken and bureaucratic system. They know the evaluation system isn't good. They also know it needs to change."

"But I still don't think we should look at test scores," the legislator continued. "It just isn't fair."

"Let me ask you a question," I said. "Do you have children?"

"Yes," he said. "I have a daughter who is going into the fourth grade."

"Okay," I said. "Let's say that there are two fourth-grade teachers in your daughter's school. You find out that for the last five years, students in one of the classes have consistently scored in the bottom five percent of the state on standardized test score. The other's students have consistently scored in the top five percent of the state on the same test. What would you do?"

"I'd make sure she was in the classroom of the person who had the high test scores," he answered—without a hint of irony to his response.

"What?" I responded. "But how could you do that? You made that decision solely on the basis of test scores! You didn't even go into their classrooms!"

He stared at me for a moment, confused. Then he smiled and said, "Okay, you got me."

"My point is that student academic achievement does matter," I said. "It shouldn't be everything. I think it's important to consider a broad range of factors in a teacher's evaluation. But how much students learn has to be a major piece of it."

I had this same conversation dozens of times. I found that people seem to be all too willing to make decisions for other people's kids that they would never make for their own children.

An evaluation system like D.C.'s IMPACT that measures growth in student achievement as well as using observations of classroom practice and school contributions addresses all of the problems with the current system—it's objective, fair, consistent, and not overly prone to politics.

TREATING TEACHERS WITH RESPECT means that we acknowledge how difficult it is to be a teacher, we remove people who cannot do the job well from the profession, and more important, we recognize those who are highly effective.

This means that we should significantly change the way that teachers are compensated. I see this happening on two fronts. First, the most highly effective teachers should be paid a lot more money than their peers, in acknowledgment of their skills and value. Second, effective teachers should be paid in a way that recognizes their worth to society.

Sometimes when I talk about paying teachers more money, people tell me that money doesn't matter, and that educators don't go into the profession for money. While I agree that the vast majority of teachers haven't made their career choice based on financial reward, you can't tell me that money doesn't matter. If we stopped paying teachers tomorrow, how many people would show up for work? If we capped teacher salaries at $20,000 per year, there would be an uprising, and rightfully so. Money matters, so let's not pretend that it doesn't.

The merit pay system that we put in place in Washington, D.C., is seeing benefits in the retention and satisfaction of the best teachers in the district. I'll give you two examples of teachers whose stories made the *New York Times* in 2012.

Mark LaLonde, thirty-two, was getting high marks teaching social studies in a D.C. high school. He and his wife were living in Baltimore. Why make the commute? He could have found a teaching job in Baltimore. He stuck with D.C. after he was rated "highly effective" twice. His salary increased from about $58,000 to $87,000 last year. Under the contract we negotiated, LaLonde also brought home a bonus of $10,000 for two consecutive years. The union pay scale in Baltimore sets his salary in the low $50,000s.

Take Jimmie Roberts. His job was to tutor slow readers. He was good—highly effective. At twenty-eight, he saw his salary increase from $53,000 in 2010 to about $75,000 in 2011–2012. He also received $30,000 in bonuses over two years. The money helped him pay off college loans. The recognition, according to the *Times*, helped keep him in the classroom.

Teachers like LaLonde and Roberts are not motivated solely by dollars, but there's no doubt that healthier compensation can make a positive difference in their lives and their views on the profession. Given that, let's pay effective educators in a manner that recognizes the incredibly important work that they do. Let's pay them on par with the best lawyers, doctors, and investment bankers out there.

That will ensure that our society takes a first step in respecting teachers for the incredible professionals that they are.

It should also dispel the notion that I am not on their side.

Wanda Smith still keeps me close.

"You taught me to make no excuses," she wrote in an email long after I had left D.C., "because excuses are totally unacceptable. We have to keep in touch."

And we will.

9

Listening to Students

L ate one night in the winter of my first year as chancellor in D.C., I was about to turn off the lights when I checked my email one more time. My BlackBerry pinged with a note from Brandon, a senior at Anacostia High School. Brandon wrote to me because he thought there might be too many people giving me too many ideas about how the school district needed to change.

"I think you should hear straight from students," he wrote.

That sounded like a fine idea to me, I responded.

I arranged to visit Anacostia High, where Brandon promised to pull together a group of students.

It was neither my first nor hardly my last conversation with students.

Throughout my years as chancellor of the D.C. public schools and now CEO of StudentsFirst, one thing I know for sure is that children are quite capable and willing to articulate what needs to happen in order to fix our public education system. Time and time again, through my tenure in D.C., students confirmed that fact to me. And they're often very reasonable in their solutions, unlike a lot of us adults!

As chancellor, I was committed to being very responsive. I believed that the entire school system had an obligation to serve our children, their families, and our school staff well, and to be customer service oriented. Word got out very quickly that I read and responded to my emails, which meant that I got a whole lot more of them!

So Brandon's email in the wee hours of that winter night was no surprise. I welcomed it and arranged to visit Anacostia High.

LONG BEFORE I CONSIDERED venturing into the teaching profession, I had an affinity for children and students. In Toledo I earned cash as a babysitter—and looked forward to caring for little ones. As an upperclassman in high school, I mentored younger students. When I volunteered to help Mary Weiss teach her classes in downtown Toledo, my favorite time was working directly with her students in small groups.

Did I love my students at first in Harlem Park? Not on your life. But things did improve. Tameka Tagg, the one who tormented me my first year, warmed up to me once I gained control of the classroom. Her buddies would become my supporters during my second and third years. We connected over time.

I will never forget Quantray Adams. She came to Harlem Park every day ready to learn. She lived with her grandmother; her mother was not in the picture. She had to navigate a gauntlet of drug dealers and troublemakers just to get to class. Through the poverty and chaos, she was able to focus—and learn, once she had the opportunity and expectations of success, rather than failure.

When Quantray read about my work as D.C. chancellor, she sent an email: "I am about to graduate from college!"

Denise Hall and I have never lost a closeness that started in Harlem Park as well. I taught her in second and third grade. She was tentative, especially at math. When I instructed her how to do long division, she said, "Hey, I'm not supposed to learn that yet." But when I showed her and told her she could handle it, she did.

Denise turned out to be the student who has kept me in contact with many of my students from Harlem Park. They ask about me on Facebook; Denise forwards their questions and lets them know I'm still in the game.

Denise Hall is headed to nursing school. I was elated but not surprised when she gave me the news. When we give children the chance to succeed, they can.

And when we give them a chance to lead and guide, they can do that, too.

Once I settled into the chancellor job in D.C., I formed a Student Cabinet. We invited representatives from all of the high schools to meet with me at least once a month. We knew that we were implementing reforms at a fast and furious pace. I wanted to make sure we kept in touch with the people most affected: parents, teachers, and students. I met parents in their homes and conducted listening tours for the teachers in schools. But I often learned the most from the Student Cabinet meetings.

I always looked forward to these sessions. The kids didn't put on a show for my benefit. They weren't worried about trying to impress me, and they weren't afraid of hurting my feelings. They gave me their opinions, no holds barred, and I loved it. It became our practice that before we rolled out a major initiative, we tried to meet with the Student Cabinet members.

They never ceased to impress me and drive our reforms, especially when it came to evaluating teachers.

When I arrived at Anacostia High, I was led to the library, where Brandon and his group were seated. They pulled out a three-page, single-spaced typed list.

On it were complaints about the cafeteria food, the lack of

working computers, the fact that they didn't have the books they needed for their classes, and more.

"There are a lot of things that need to be improved in our school," Brandon said. They proceeded to read their list, providing thoughtful explanations along the way. An hour later, they were winding down.

"Well!" I exclaimed. "That was very comprehensive. And pretty much on the mark. I'm going to be honest with you, though. I just got here. There's clearly a whole lot broken and a whole lot of work yet to be done. You guys are seniors and realistically, there's no way I can address and fix all of those problems before you graduate from high school."

Groans all the way around.

"If you could pick one thing that you think I could do that would have the most impact on the quality of schooling you got for your senior year, what would that be?" I asked.

They didn't skip a beat.

"Bring us more great teachers," a student said.

Not pizza in the cafeteria, early dismissal on Friday, or relaxing the dress code. They wanted more great teachers.

"Bring us more teachers, like Mr. Wallace," Brandon said. "That guy is the greatest! He works us hard, but he works right along with us."

"He sets up camp at the McDonald's down the street after school," another student said. "The kids all come by to get help. If you're hungry, he buys you a hamburger, but he won't let you leave until he's answered all of your questions, and he knows you're prepared for the next day. If you bring us more teachers like him, we're set. We don't need anything else on the list."

I was intrigued. Who was this Mr. Wallace? I summarized the meeting, thanked the kids for coming, and said I was committed to working hard to change things at their school—not just for them, but for all the kids who would come to Anacostia in the future.

Then I set off to find Mr. Wallace. After walking up and down several hallways I came across a door with a ragged sign reading, "Mr. Wallace." I pushed the wooden door in and walked through.

I found a twenty-four-year-old man who looked like he'd aged about eight years in two years' time. He was a mess. He had chalk dust in his hair and pit stains in his shirt.

"Mr. Wallace?" I asked.

"Yes, I'm Craig Wallace," he replied.

"I just wanted to meet you," I said. "I was just having a conversation with a group of students about what they think needs to change in the school. It was a very enlightening discussion, and there were a lot of things on their list."

"Yeah," he answered back cautiously.

"But the one thing they said they wanted most was more teachers like you. They raved about you. Each one of them had incredible things to say about your dedication and effectiveness. You should be proud. You've really made an impression on those kids."

"Yeah," he said again.

"So, are you going to stay?" I asked.

I surmised pretty quickly that he was a Teach For America teacher. Right about this time of the year was when the corps members were determining whether to stay or apply for graduate school.

"I-I don't know," Mr. Wallace stammered.

"Dang!" I thought. Unlike some TFA corps members, it was clear that this guy had seen tremendous success in his classroom. Other than the fact that he was a twenty-four-year-old who probably spent half his paycheck at McDonald's, I was wondering what he was thinking.

"I just don't know. I work hard, the kids work hard, but I don't know how much I'm really making a difference. And frankly the other teachers don't like me. 'Wallace,' they say to me, 'stop coming in so early and staying late! And don't do that McDonald's thing or the kids will start expecting it from all of us!' I'm just not sure it makes sense for me to stay."

"This is exactly the kind of teacher that we need in the classroom," I thought, "but he's beyond discouraged. We have to figure this out."

Mr. Wallace didn't know what he was going to do with his life. And I knew I couldn't make changes fast enough to satisfy all of the students' demands. But the students made one thing very clear: they wanted more Mr. Wallaces.

Was I able to fix Anacostia for Brandon and his seniors? I couldn't snap my fingers and magically pull a shiny new school with energetic teachers out of a hat. But we did start to turn Anacostia around. We reconstituted it, making all of the teachers reapply for their jobs. We brought on Friendship Public Charter to take over academic instruction. The District of Columbia began renovating the school building.

We improved the teaching corps at Anacostia High, as Brandon and his friends requested, and test scores began to rise.

BRANDON AND MR. WALLACE made an impression on me because the kids defied expectations. As adults, we assume what students care about in school is the cafeteria food or more recess. We don't expect them to be able to articulate their desires for a great education. But students know how to improve their classroom experiences, and given the chance, they can describe what works. I always tried to give them that opportunity.

Nothing showed this more powerfully than the experience at John Philip Sousa Middle School in Southeast D.C. Sousa was once famously referred to in the *Washington Post* as "an academic sink hole."

During my round of principal interviews in the summer of

2008, one of the clear standout candidates was Dwan Jordon. Dwan was the kind of guy who was going to rub some people the wrong way. He spoke his mind, even if his words inflicted pain. I could also tell that he cared deeply about kids and that he was going to get things done. I thought he had the wherewithal to oversee the turnaround of Sousa.

Early in Dwan Jordon's first year, I started hearing positive things about his work. Bill Wilhoyte, a veteran instructional superintendent whose insights I trusted, said he was doing a remarkable job. I heard similar reports from teachers and parents. Kaya Henderson told me that the paperwork and attention to detail on his teacher evaluations were second to none.

When the test scores came out after his first year, Sousa was leading the pack on academic gains. The school saw a 16 percent increase in reading and a whopping 25 percent gain in math. In fact, the gains were so large that they were a little hard to believe. So I wanted to see for myself.

I made a trip to the school. This was not my first time at Sousa. I had visited during my first year as chancellor, and it had been tough to make it through my time there. Kids had been running through the hallways, screaming in classrooms, swearing at teachers, and causing general mayhem. There wasn't a whole lot of learning going on.

This visit was very different. When I walked in, the school was silent and sparkling clean. Class was in session, and there were no children in the hallways. As I walked past the classrooms, I saw kids and teachers hard at work. Everyone was disciplined and focused. There was not a hood on a head or an earphone in an ear. Every student was in uniform with his or her shirt tucked in neatly. It was inspiring.

I wanted to not only congratulate the staff but also hear a bit about how they did it. I scheduled a teacher listening session at the school. The following week at about 3:15 p.m., I pulled up to the school just as the students were being dismissed. I started walking toward the front door and was mobbed by a group of kids.

"Chancellor Rhee! Chancellor Rhee!" I heard them yelling.

"Can I give you a hug?" one girl asked.

"Can I get my picture taken with you?" another asked.

"I want a hug, too, Chancellor Rhee!" said another little boy.

Now, you have to realize that usually when I went to visit schools the kids would look at me and ask, "Who's the crazy Chinese lady and why is she here?" So this was a bit of a surprise.

I asked them how they liked their school and what subjects they preferred. I asked about their teachers. Rave reviews all around.

One boy said it was his first year in middle school and he loved it. "What elementary school did you go to?" I asked.

"Davis," he said. Davis was not too far away.

"How is this school, the same or different?" I asked.

"Well," he said, "the teachers here really teach us. They push us hard to think outside of the box."

"Outside the box"? From a sixth grader?

I said good-bye to the children and made my way into the library. Because I had been holding listening sessions for some time, I could pretty quickly get the vibe on a group of teachers. I knew if they were a happy bunch, a bitter one, angry, and so on. This group was anxious. I could feel it.

I went out of my way to praise them for everything that I'd seen. The academic achievement growth was astounding, but more impressive was the culture that they had instilled in the school. To ease the anxiety a bit, I said, "Look, you all saw huge academic gains last year. That was great, but please don't think we expect that kind of growth year in and year out. That would be nearly impossible. From this point forward if we saw three- to five-point gains a year that would be a real feat."

It didn't work. They were unmoved.

"I don't think you get it," one teacher explained after a lull in the conversation. "The horse is out of the barn with the children in this school. They're obsessed. Three- to five-point gains might be good enough for you, but they're shooting for twenty again. And they're serious."

She said her students kept track of their progress every week. The kids who were blue—advanced—were celebrated. For kids not doing as well, there was peer pressure for them to work harder. She said her students wouldn't accept worksheets anymore. They rejected them. The expectation on their end was that they had to have an interesting, engaging lesson every single day.

"If you really want to help us," she said, "then give us more access to lesson and unit plans!"

Fascinating. For all the talk of my being the "Dragon Lady" and worrying that these teachers were afraid of me, the pressure was not coming from above. The teachers were feeling the heat to perform all right, but it was coming from the kids. The children had gotten a taste of what it meant to be in a great school environment every day, and they were demanding more.

The students were driving the reform at Sousa just as they were from the Student Cabinet.

THE STUDENT CABINET WEIGHED in on everything from school security issues to challenges with food services—even media and communications. But we spent a significant amount of time on our "Teaching and Learning Framework" and the teacher evaluation system. I remember the meeting where we introduced IMPACT, our new teacher evaluation process. The kids listened very carefully. We asked them to read some materials to prepare for the meeting. When it came time to give feedback, their thoughts were very specific.

"This is great," said Ally. "I absolutely think it makes sense for teachers to know what is expected of them."

"*But*," Thomas chimed in, "you're missing something major. *Us*. No one knows better what's going on in the classroom than students. We're there every minute of every day. You need to hear from us."

"Yeah," said Max, "he's right. We know that when our principals come in the room or the outsiders show up to observe, sometimes the teachers start doing things they *never* do! It's like 'who are you and what did you do with our teacher?' "

The other kids laughed.

"It can happen the other way, too," said Sarai. "You can have a great teacher who is fabulous but just gets really nervous when the evaluator walks in. We have a much better sense of how that teacher performs every day."

"So what are you suggesting?" I asked. "Should we make student feedback part of how a teacher is evaluated?"

"*Yes!*" shouted a group of kids.

"Hmmm . . . I'm not so sure," Kara said. "We have some real knuckleheads in our school. Kids who just make it hard for teachers to teach and kids to learn."

She said these kids would probably give the good teachers bad ratings just because the best teachers are hard! They give tons of homework and don't let kids slack. If those kids are giving the good teachers poor evaluations for those reasons, it wouldn't be fair.

Some kids nodded in agreement.

"Yeah, but there are more good kids than bad kids, so I think it would even out," said Isaiah.

"Well, let's give it a try!" I said.

I proposed that the cabinet take on a project where they researched the prospect of students evaluating teachers. Peggy O'Brien, our head of Family and Public Engagement, and Kaitlin McKee, a communications specialist who was a former teacher, led the charge. They worked with the kids to develop potential questions for a survey. The students would then field-test it and make recommendations based on what they found. The kids loved the idea and spent a significant amount of time over the next few months doing the work. They split up into groups, each of which was responsible for putting together a presentation for me and my senior staff. They did a great job.

"We were worried," they said, "that the boneheaded kids might skew the evaluations and rank the easier teachers high, just because they're easier, not better, but we found that that was not the case."

They found that they had underestimated their peers. People did a pretty good job of putting aside their personal feelings, and they rated teachers very consistently.

"What was interesting," said Ally, "was that I think the best teachers were the most open to getting feedback. Obviously, we didn't want to do this without teachers' permission."

She said that her group found that the good teachers really were excited about implementing the survey, but the weaker teachers were less open to it. The students did such a good job and made such a strong case that as I was leaving DCPS, the school system considered a pilot project the following year to gather student feedback on teachers.

Our students were ahead of the curve. Evidence from a recent study of teaching by the Bill & Melinda Gates Foundation showed that students know a great teacher when they see one. The foundation's "Measures of Effective Teaching" (MET) project studied student feedback through surveys on teacher evaluations. The study found that there is a very strong correlation between how students rate their teachers and how well those teachers do at attaining gains in student achievement. Students can tell us with pretty good accuracy whether their teachers are effective. Many who underestimate students would guess that kids would dislike teachers who might be good ones, but were strict or gave a lot of homework. As it turns out, children can effectively synthesize information about their teachers without a lot of bias, and on the whole, they can identify great teachers.

The MET study recommended that states and districts consider adding student input to teacher evaluations.

WHAT DOES THIS MEAN on a practical level? Well, it doesn't mean that children should be running schools or districts. But it does mean that we should be very serious about engaging them in the process of improving our schools.

As we debate the need to revamp teacher evaluation systems across the country, I would advocate for a portion of the evaluation to be based on the views of students and parents. For younger children, parents might offer valuable assessments. As students gain age and maturity, they could add value to evaluations of teacher performance.

Radical? Why not?

In many ways I think that's what it's going to take to change the dynamic in our country. The children who are in our schools every day, who know how critical it is to their experience to have a great teacher, who are the subjects of the various reforms we put in place—*they* should have a much greater voice in what happens in school reform.

If my experience with students from Harlem Park to Anacostia to Sousa is any indication, the children will be much more reasonable, respectful, and right about what needs to be done.

It's time we adults listened.

10

Empowering Parents

T wo Moms Desperate for Your Help" read the subject line of the email that came my way in September 2010. How could I not open it? The few weeks directly following the defeat of my boss, Adrian Fenty, in his reelection bid for mayor, had been a whirlwind. I was trying to figure out the next step in my career. My work in education reform was far from done. In fact, I felt like it was just starting. I just didn't know how to proceed. I opened the email with great curiosity.

"We read that you may be leaving Washington, D.C.," it said. "Whatever you decide to do, you have to stay in the fight!" It was from two mothers who lived in Naples, Florida. They had grown frustrated with the poor quality of schools in their community and decided to do something about it. Both moms had young children, but their biggest concern was Lely High School, their neighborhood school. Lely was rated a "D" on the state report card enacted by Governor Jeb Bush in 2005. Only 22 percent of tenth graders were at grade-level proficiency in reading in 2009, and there was no sign that anything was going to change.

Their plea was familiar to me. Parents from tough neighborhoods in D.C. had appealed to me to come up with ways to get their kids into schools that would give them a better chance at success in life. Here were parents from a thriving town on Florida's Gulf Coast presenting me with the same conundrum. Clearly, parents beyond D.C.'s borders were yearning for change, too.

Jane Watt and Jody Barrett knew that their kids might struggle to compete in college if they went to Lely. And that was if they were lucky enough to get into college. So the moms decided to start a charter high school. They had recruited hundreds of volunteers, found a campus for the new school on Marco Island, written the school's charter and budget, and developed the curriculum for the school's focus on math, science, technology, and environmental studies. They had followed all of the rules and regulations required to open Marco Island's first charter high school.

The school district was not pleased. Fearing the new charter school might have a negative impact on enrollment at Lely, school and state officials started trying to squelch Marco Island Academy. First, they asked for cumbersome additional details that went beyond what was required in the application process. Next, the district refused to cooperate in providing information so that the academy could start recruiting students. When those issues were cleared up, the district's concerns focused on a bird's nest that was seen on the potential site and the need to protect the environment, despite the fact that environmentalists said the birds and kids could coexist.

But what could I do for them? Honestly, I didn't have any idea. But they seemed so desperate and just wanted to do right by their kids, so I called them.

"I read your email and very much admire what you're trying to do." I said. "I also know that the district is going to continue to do everything it can to stop you from starting this school. It's the way most districts operate."

"But what they're doing is wrong," said Jane. "And some of it is against the policy of how they're supposed to be operating."

"I know," I said, "but there's no accountability. Trust me, their goal is to make this so hard for you that you give up."

"I can't believe this," Jody said. "We've worked so hard. And all we want is a high-performing school for our children. Is that too much to ask?"

"It isn't," I said, "but unfortunately, it's how things work. I'm really sorry. I hate to be the bearer of bad tidings. I just don't think there's anything I can do to help."

"But what if you came here and created a ruckus?" Jody asked. "What if you were the accountability? If you came out here, the media would be all over it. You could show how crazy this is and how the district is blocking us. That would be embarrassing to them. It's the only thing that might get them to do the right thing. Shame them into it."

That conversation and the predicament those mothers faced stuck in my mind.

"Create a ruckus"? "Shame them into it"? Bring attention to a clear example of how adults—in this case school district officials—were working to close off an opportunity for students?

No, I could not swoop in and persuade that school district to clear the way for one particular charter school. But what if there were potential parent activists across the country who were frustrated with local laws and policies that favored adults over children? What if we could ignite a movement that would allow me to "create a ruckus" for reform, but backed by hundreds of thousands of parents?

Jane and Jody persevered. They started Marco Island Academy, and after its first year, it's showing promise. The academic achievement levels are already above state and district averages. It is outperforming Lely by nearly 20 percentage points in reading. Though there's still a long way to go, they're off to a strong start. Through their courage, these two moms created better learning outcomes for the kids.

Even before the idea to create StudentsFirst came into being, parents such as Jane and Jody helped sow the seeds of a movement.

DURING MY LAST WEEKS as chancellor in D.C. and in the time soon after my resignation, I was inundated with emails and pleas from all across the country just like the one from Jane and Jody. I heard from parents who were focused on ensuring that their kids were getting the education they deserved. Others were frustrated with their system's inability, or disinterest, in helping their children. They were reaching out to me in hopes of finding a solution. "What should I do?" was usually how the emails ended.

It struck me that there were so many parents in every corner of the country who were ready to confront the difficulties their children were facing in the public schools. The emails came from parents in urban communities and rural ones. From Democrats and Republicans. From hyperengaged parents in the PTA and those who were just getting involved. But what they all had in common was anger that public schools, funded by their tax dollars, were denying opportunities for their children and their neighbors' kids, too. They were furious that many officials in charge were at best ignoring them and at worst working against them to maintain the status quo. And they were looking for somewhere to turn.

I had an email exchange with one father from Southern California that perfectly illustrated the dilemma. The dad wrote to me about his son, a second grader who the dad admitted was a bit of a handful. They'd faced many challenges throughout his short schooling life. However, his son was fortunate enough to have a wonderful second-grade teacher.

"This teacher changed my son's life," the dad wrote. "She challenges him, engages him, and is extraordinarily patient with him, as well. Now my son wakes up every day excited about going to school."

This dad went on to express his bewilderment that when the school had to lay off teachers, his son's teacher was handed a pink slip because she was a relatively new teacher. "How does this make any sense?" he asked. "There's another teacher that has been at this school for more than a decade who is awful. All of us parents work hard to navigate around her and make sure our kids are in other classes. If we have to lose someone, why can't it be her?"

When I asked this father what he planned to do, his ideas were as follows: (1) go to the principal and fight to get his son put in another class; (2) apply to one of the charter schools in the area and hope they might gain admission; (3) explore private schools; and (4) move to a different neighborhood with a better school.

It was very clear to me in talking with this father that he was very engaged in his child's education and also really wanted to keep sending his kid to the neighborhood public school. When faced with this unfortunate situation, though, his thinking about the solutions was parochial. He was 100 percent focused on fixing the situation for his child, which is very understandable. However, what parents need to understand is that if they concentrate only on fixing the problem for their own child, the problem will arise again for their next child, and their neighbor's child, and then one who lives a few doors down.

Parents must begin to see their role in changing the laws and policies at the district and state level so that they can solve the problem once and for all. For all kids.

What parents lack has been a way to organize, to find others to effect change alongside them. I began to realize that parents from one city and county to the next, from one state to another, didn't realize that they had common problems. They were fighting tiny skirmishes to improve their own kids' situations. What if they had a way to communicate, to join forces and lobby for broader changes, and to realize that their desire for better public schools was shared by parents from the Atlantic to the Pacific?

The power of a million parents could be an awesome force for change. When joined by concerned teachers and members of the community, that kind of movement would be unstoppable. That's why we started StudentsFirst.

FOR MANY PARENTS, THIS isn't an abstract question. Their children are in dire situations. So these parents are mobilizing for change, fighting for the lives and futures of their children and their communities. Their voices and actions have led to legislative changes throughout the country that would have been unfathomable just five years ago.

Take LaQueta Worley, Sharon Irby, and Cheryl Mays, from Cleveland. Cleveland's schools are the worst in the state and among the worst in the nation. According to the last National Assessment for Education Progress (NAEP) tests, only 12 percent of Cleveland's fourth graders were able to do math at grade level. In the last six years, Cleveland schools have made little progress. Parents, community leaders, and some politicians said, "Enough!" Mayor Frank Jackson began a dialogue in the community about what needed to change. Parents fed up with the poor results and lack of options for their kids began to rally.

Mayor Jackson, a liberal Democrat, and Ohio governor John Kasich, a conservative Republican, began to work with legislators to craft a bold plan to give the mayor more authority over the city's ailing schools. The proposal called for the mayor to have the ability to hire and fire teachers and to evaluate them based largely on student achievement growth. The teachers unions balked and began a massive campaign to defeat the legislation.

Advocates on both side of the issue began to mobilize. Many Cleveland moms, like LaQueta, Sharon, and Cheryl, became heavily involved in the advocacy efforts to pass the Cleveland plan. They engaged other parents in their communities and were relentless in their lobbying efforts, including visits to the legislature in Columbus to support the bill. Other moms, like Jessica Nelson, Erin Randel, and Tearra Smith, hosted events in Cleveland to educate fellow parents. At those events they highlighted how the reforms in the Cleveland plan would benefit their children, and they encouraged others to participate.

StudentsFirst joined the battle for reform. We were uncertain whether we would have the votes to pass Jackson's plan. Parents and students from all corners of Cleveland flocked to Columbus, but the opposition turned out its forces as well. These parents, however, would not take no for an answer. During the last hearing and the deciding votes on the reform, many of these parents made the trip to Columbus once more. After a two-and-a-half-hour bus ride and more hours of sitting in committee hearings, they made their way to the House chamber to listen to the debate. Representative Bill Patmon, whose district includes Cleveland, rose to speak.

"I tried to pray over it and do what's right. And I spent time praying about this and couldn't even find the answers to voting in committee this morning, still thinking about, 'Is it a good vote, or is it not?' And you sleep with what you do down here. As a movie said, 'What you do echoes down through time, whether you like it or not.'

"So I stand today with some explanation, because my last prayers I believe were answered. I left this chamber a few minutes ago thinking about 525. And lo and behold just outside the lavatory, I run into who? Cleveland parents, and we had a short discussion. We're down here for the vote, not for the party, but for the vote. And these are parents, and they're down here for the kids. They're down here to see something done for the children of the city of Cleveland. . . . Today, I am going to be guided by that short meeting and support the bill."

The audience cheered. LaQueta, Sharon, and Cheryl were

stunned. They were the ones who had caught Representative Patmon on his way out from the washroom. Not only were they recognized on the floor of the House, but Patmon's vote helped the bill pass with strong bipartisan support. They knew that what they'd done was about to change the game for Cleveland's children.

POLITICIANS INVITED US TO Michigan to help lobby for reform, but parents pushed the reforms over the victory line.

Parents like Nancy Damoose. In sending their children to the public schools, she and her husband had had experiences with scores of teachers. "Many of those experiences," Nancy testified to the Michigan legislature, "have been extremely positive and extremely rewarding. Many, however, have not."

She talked about Ms. Angot, who had taught English composition at Birmingham's Seaholm High School during the 1980s and '90s. Angot was one of those teachers, according to Nancy, who seemed to have been around forever. She was nearing retirement when Nancy's two eldest children were in her class. She was financially secure and did not need to teach, but she loved her students, and she wanted them to become not just good, but great writers. "Today, my two grown children are both accomplished writers. My son became a published author at the age of twenty-six; today he writes and produces television documentaries. My daughter is now a high school teacher who desires for her students to learn as she learned under the guidance of Ms. Angot," said Nancy.

She wanted all kids to have a teacher like Ms. Angot.

Then she heard about StudentsFirst and the initiative we had started in Michigan to put in place a new teacher evaluation system. It sounded simple and made a lot of sense. Based on the evaluation, the best teachers would be recognized, and the ineffective ones would be moved out of the classroom. It sounded perfect to Nancy. She figured that a system such as the one we were proposing would allow Ms. Angot to be rewarded for being an effective teacher. It would also ensure that the other teachers would either receive more training or move on to a different career.

StudentsFirst was mobilizing parents and other members to support the bill. Nancy joined the fray. Along with other parents and teachers, she spent countless hours emailing, calling, and visiting legislators. One of the parents' state representatives was on the fence. It was important to show him how much his constituents wanted the policy in place. We were looking for mothers who would be willing to be featured in an advertisement asking members to vote yes on the bill. Having the face of a constituent making the plea to other community members would be a powerful testament. We warned potential participants that it could mean being targeted for harassment by the teachers union.

"Harassment?" Nancy and the others asked. "Why? This seems basic. We want to keep the best teachers and pay them more money. We want to move the ineffective ones out of the classroom. Who could argue with that?" She and the others agreed to be a part of the effort.

Overnight, it seemed, parents like Nancy Damoose became the face of the movement. She, Div Buegeleisen, Shannon Mayo, and other parents were featured on thousands of mailers that were sent to friends and neighbors asking them to contact their legislators about supporting the law. For Nancy, it was a unique experience. People whom she knew started asking her about the legislation. She told them very simply that as a mom, she wanted to make sure that her kids had the best teachers, and that as a member of the community, she wanted the same thing for all kids in Michigan.

House Bill 4627 passed. It was one of the most sweeping educator quality bills in the country. And it happened because of moms, like Nancy Damoose, who decided to take a stand.

. . . .

ONE OF THE MOST common critiques you hear when you talk to union leaders about accountability is that teachers can't be held solely responsible for the achievement of their students. According to them, poverty and parental engagement are the key factors in whether a student can succeed in school. Notwithstanding that this argument presupposes that we should have no accountability to teach poor children, the parent argument is especially specious.

A perfect example of this is the new parent-trigger laws that are growing in popularity across the country. The first such law was passed in California and allows parents in failing schools to trigger, or force, the turnaround of that school if more than 50 percent of the parents sign a petition. The parents can then choose from a range of intervention options, which include replacing the staff, closing the school, or allowing a charter management organization to run the school.

In 2010, parents at McKinley Elementary in Compton, California, became the first in the country to "pull the trigger." They worked for months to organize and collect the signatures necessary. Parent Revolution, a nonprofit group led by another Democrat, Ben Austin, helped to mobilize the parents and the community. At their request, I visited Compton and met with the parents.

I walked into Ismenia Guzman's house, where a group of about twelve parents had gathered. They had been working for some time to gather signatures and were close to meeting the 50 percent threshold. I was there to encourage them as they were crossing the finish line.

As I listened to them talk, the stories sounded familiar to me. One mother in particular struck me. Shamika Murphy said that as her daughter was going through McKinley, she received very good grades. When she spoke with her daughter's teachers, they were always very positive and complimentary. Then, when it came time for her daughter to go to middle school, Shamika realized something was amiss. Some of the schools pointed out how poorly her daughter was performing on standardized tests. They noted that she would have to start middle school far behind her classmates.

"I was shocked," she said. "Here I was thinking everything was fine. But it wasn't. My daughter hadn't learned what she was supposed to in elementary school. Heading into middle school everyone was telling me she was far behind. How is this possible? How could McKinley have done that? I feel like they pulled the wool over my eyes!"

As the parents shared their stories about how McKinley had failed their children, the determination in the room grew. By the end of the meeting, the parents left, ready to continue their battle to take over the school and ensure a different future for McKinley.

In December 2010, the parents turned in their petition. By then the process had become controversial and contentious. Parents were divided. The petition campaign was hampered by charges of harassment, lies, and deceit. Some parents were threatened regarding their immigration status. The Compton school board ultimately rejected the petition on technicalities, and the parents' drive to take control of the school failed.

The teachers union and the district worked extraordinarily hard to thwart the first parent trigger campaign. But what were they protecting? McKinley had been a failing school for decades. In fact, it was one of the lowest-performing schools in the entire state of California. If you were a child attending McKinley for elementary school, your chances of graduating from high school and going to college were abysmal.

It amazes me that union leaders and school administrators who point to a lack of parental involvement as a culprit in defending their teachers from accountability would then turn around and fight tooth and nail against parents who are taking true owner-ship of their children's education.

How can anyone in good conscience fight to protect a status quo that subjects kids to such dismal outcomes?

WE PARENTS ARE ADVOCATES for our children every day.

From defusing a fight on the playground to making sure our kids get some playing time in the soccer game to preparing them for the new school year with the right supplies, we parents fight for our children and their interests. Parents know what's at stake with their children's education. That's why they must mobilize around education reform. Whether it's demanding a better option because their child is stuck at a failing school or understanding the need to fight for the rights of *all* children, parents have to become the powerful special interest group that demands we put students first.

Jane and Jody, with their email about starting a charter school in Florida, helped me realize that parents across the country were poised to take action to improve public education. They and other parents encouraged me to create StudentsFirst. Once we founded our organization and gave parents the opportunity to join a movement, I was surprised and elated at the response. Within months of announcing StudentsFirst, we had more than a hundred thousand members. In six months the organization had grown past five hundred thousand. In a year, we topped a million members, and we're close to hitting the two million mark today.

Parents are the backbone of this movement.

11

Challenging Politicians

For most of my life, I've considered myself a lefty liberal. At Cornell, I used to have two buttons affixed to my backpack, which became somewhat of a calling card for me. The first read, "Bush, Stay Out of Mine," making clear my disdain for the first Bush administration's policies on reproductive rights. The second one was as a phrase popularized by Gloria Steinem: "A Woman Without a Man Is Like a Fish Without a Bicycle." It's hard to get more liberal than Gloria Steinem.

I voted for a Democratic president, worked for one Democratic big-city mayor, and married another.

My identity as a Democrat is central to my beliefs about public education. I believe that children of all backgrounds and races have both the innate ability and the right as Americans to a high-quality education. I believe that public schools—government institutions—have the ability to make America more prosperous and just. The idea that the government can work to help overcome poverty and racism is a key element of the Democratic Party's ideals—right?

So you can imagine my surprise of late that people have begun to skewer me for linking arms with Republican leaders. How did that happen? Simple. My positions on education reform promote civil rights—and a civil right that was being denied mainly to children of color and in low-income communities. I have sought to make government a more effective tool for change. But some of my proposals threaten institutional power within the Democratic Party. I've always thought that we are a party that stands up to special interests when they are disenfranchising communities without power. We are a party that fights for commonsense policies that help people, not a party that stands behind abstract ideologies that help no one in particular.

But that is definitely not always the case.

As soon as I left teaching and started The New Teacher Project, I discovered that the primary motivation for too many Democratic politicians was to ensure their prospects for being elected again, rather than to bring about the social change they promised. The essentials that children need to thrive, especially a great education, are not always in line with what politicians need to survive. Special interests often hold the keys to their reelection. They come with great access and experience. They are well organized and well funded. They are vested in the status quo.

Here's my unfortunate conclusion: When it comes to making laws and policies in the best interests of educating children, our political system is too often stuck, paralyzed, and dysfunctional. The political parties are locked in opposing positions. There's little compromise. Republicans are often slavishly devoted to free market principles and their ideals around policies like gun laws. Democrats are often captive to the dogma of the leaders of the teachers unions. Neither consistently puts students first. We have to show politicians and their constituents that there's an alternative to the current gridlock.

Democrats, especially, believe they cannot take on education reform because they know they are in for a headache, perhaps defeat, at the hands of the teachers unions. This is something the education reform movement first realized many years ago when people like Joe Williams (a former newspaper reporter from New York and Milwaukee) joined forces with finance gurus like Whitney Tilson, Boykin Curry, Charles Ledley, John Petry, and David Einhorn to form Democrats for Education Reform.

As Democrats, they wanted to create space within the party to discuss real reform. Tilson knew that in order for that to happen, they'd have to have money. Without real support for Democratic candidates, he argued, their pleas would go unheard. With StudentsFirst, we are building on the foundation that DFER and other advocacy organizations like Stand for Children and 50CAN have laid. We are showing elected officials that there's an alternative, that they are not alone. We will use our resources and our nearly two million members to support them, give them cover, and level the playing field for kids.

Let me give you an example. We have seen instances of Democrats deciding to lead the charge to reform education laws at the state level. The special interest opponents of reform have paid for billboards accusing the state rep of being against teachers, or harming students. That sets a narrative that the politician can rarely recover from. So at StudentsFirst we know we have to engage in the same type of tactics. After major reform was passed in Connecticut, we paid for advertisements thanking reformers for working on behalf of the state's children.

When opponents of reform mobilized their canvassers, we mobilized our members who were from the community. The voices of local parents and teachers carried our message of reform to their neighbors and to their representatives in the statehouse.

When the special interests pledged to defeat supporters of reform and started making contributions to opponents of reform, we readied a campaign plan and made contributions to political leaders who now saw that there would be a well-funded, mobilized effort on their side, if they did the right thing for kids.

A well-organized, well-funded grassroots organization will give Democrats cover with media, contributions, and constituent support. We will give officials willing to back our reforms a fighting chance.

WHEN I BEGAN MY stint with the D.C. public schools, I had strong ideas about what education reform should look like and what it shouldn't look like. I believed wholeheartedly that we had to have a very strong focus on teacher quality. I was also a believer in charter schools. I had seen their value when I served for a couple of years on the board of the St. HOPE Public Schools. I guess that was my first break with Democratic dogma. I knew that charter schools were anathema to teachers unions. I also knew the best ones could serve children extraordinarily well.

But I drew a very deep line in the sand when it came to vouchers. As a lifelong Democrat I was adamantly against vouchers. Vouchers provide public funds to parents who need help in paying tuition for private or parochial schools. Proponents, mostly Republicans, see vouchers as leveling the field and broadening choice for families. Detractors, usually Democrats, decry the use of public funds to pay for private education. I had bought into the arguments that Democrats and others use in opposition to vouchers: vouchers are a way of taking money away from public school systems and putting them into private schools; vouchers help only a handful of the kids; and vouchers take children and resources away from the schools and districts that need those resources the most.

For all of those reasons, my view on vouchers was set. But soon after I arrived in Washington, D.C., I was in a pickle. The District of Columbia had Opportunity Scholarships, a federally funded voucher program that helped poor families attend private schools. The program was up for reauthorization, and there was a heated debate going on in the city.

"You're the most high-profile education official in the city," a *Washington Post* reporter asked. "Do *you* think the Opportunity Scholarship program should be re-upped?"

My inclination was to say no. As a good Democrat, I should have responded, "I don't support vouchers, because they are not a systemic solution to the problems we face." No one would have been surprised or upset with that answer.

However, I wanted to have my facts straight. So I decided to meet with families across the city and spend some time better understanding the Opportunity Scholarships initiative. It's amazing what one can learn from talking to parents.

The outreach I did about the Opportunity Scholarships was part of a countless number of meetings I had with parents over the course of my time in D.C. Many of those parents were young mothers who came to me looking for answers. Although they were different in many ways, they often came with the same goal: better schooling opportunities for their children. Usually mothers would request meetings with me during the school selection process that takes place each January and February.

The typical mom would come to the meeting armed with data and talking points. For example:

"I currently live in Southeast," she would say. "Our house is zoned to the local elementary school. I have done quite a bit of research into the school and was shocked to find that only twenty percent of the children are operating at grade-level proficiency. That means my child has an eighty percent likelihood of failure. That's simply not acceptable for me and my family."

"Absolutely right," I would think.

Then the mother would tell me she had gone online and researched all the best schools in the district. She had read about Mann and Key elementary schools, in Northwest D.C. She told me either would give her child a better education, even though it would mean two hours of commuting a day. She had applied to those schools and a number of others through a lottery process that allowed out-of-boundary students to attend certain schools.

I knew what was coming next.

"But we didn't get in. I was devastated. So now I don't know what to do. I went to DCPS. My parents went to DCPS. I believe in public schools, but I simply can't send my child to the local school. Can you help me?"

It was a painful experience for me, each and every time. My instinct was always to tell the mother that I'd let her kid into Mann or Key and make the school make room for one more child. But honestly, it just wasn't doable. Or fair. There were so many parents who visited me with these requests and so many more who were on waiting lists for those schools who had followed all of the rules.

Oh, I could have found a spot for them at another D.C. public school, perhaps marginally better than their home school. But that wasn't what they wanted. They were looking for the exact same thing that I wanted for my two girls: the best school possible.

"Who am I," I thought, "to deny this mom and her child an opportunity for a better school, even if that meant help with a seventy-five-hundred-dollar voucher? If they got a voucher, and her child could attend a really good Catholic school, perhaps, why would I stand in the way—especially since I don't have a high-quality DCPS alternative?"

I just couldn't look mother after mother in the eye and deny their children the opportunity I wanted for my own children. It would have required me to say, "Gee, I'm sorry, you're just going to have to suck it up. I know your elementary school is a failing school, and your child will probably not learn how to read, but I really need five more years to fix the system. And while I'm fixing the system, I need you and your neighbors to be really patient. Hang in there with me. Things will get better. I promise."

If someone said that to me, I'd have said, "You may need more time to fix the system but my kid doesn't have time. She has only one chance to attend first grade, and if she can't learn to read by the end of first grade, her chances for success in life will be compromised. So with all due respect—heck no!"

After my listening tour of families, and hearing so many parents plead for an immediate solution to their desire for a quality education, I came out in favor of the voucher program. People went nuts. Democrats chastised me for going against the party, but the most vocal detractors were my biggest supporters.

"Michelle, what are you doing?" one education reformer asked. "You are the first opportunity this city has had to fix the system. We believe in you and what you're trying to do. But you have to give yourself a fighting chance! You need time and money to make your plan work. If during that time children continue fleeing the system on these vouchers, you'll have less money to implement your reforms. You can't do this to yourself!"

"Here's the problem with your thinking," I'd answer. "My job is not to preserve and defend a system that has been doing wrong by children and families. My job is to make sure that every child in this city attends an excellent school. I don't care if it's a charter school, a private school, or a traditional district school. As long as it's serving kids well, I'm happy. And you should be, too."

Here's the question we Democrats need to ask ourselves: Are we beholden to the public school system at any cost, or are we beholden to the public school *child* at any cost? My loyalty and my duty will always be to the children.

NOT EVERYONE BOUGHT IT. In fact, most of my Democrat friends remained adamantly opposed to vouchers. It was interesting, though: they were always opposed to the broad policy, but they could never reconcile their logic when thinking at the individual-kid level.

I was having a heated discussion one day with one of my closest friends, a public school teacher. She was deriding voucher policy. My public policy wonkiness was not serving me well, so I decided to change tactics.

"You watched *Waiting for 'Superman'*?" I asked.

"Of course," she answered. "One of my best friends was featured in the movie." She chuckled.

"Do you remember that scene with Bianca?" I asked.

Waiting for "Superman" director Davis Guggenheim did a brilliant job of distilling pretty complicated education policies into easy and understandable terms. But more important, he humanized the problems by following five families in their quest to find a high-quality public school for their children to attend.

One of the most poignant stories was about a little girl named Bianca. Her mother had had a negative experience in the public schools herself. So she was committed to giving her child a better chance. When Bianca was in kindergarten her mother enrolled her in the Catholic school across the street from their apartment, and she worked extra jobs to be able to pay the tuition.

Unfortunately, with the economic downturn, her hours were cut back, and she fell behind on her tuition payments. There is an emotional scene in the movie when Bianca is gazing longingly out the window. It is the day of her kindergarten graduation. She's watching all of her friends and their families file in for the graduation ceremony, but she's not allowed to attend. Tears are streaming down her face.

"Remember," I pleaded, "her mom owed the school money so they didn't let her go to her kindergarten graduation? How did that make you feel?"

"Ugh, that was awful," my friend said. "It was totally wrong of the school. It was absolutely heart-wrenching! I mean seriously, I wanted to write the five-hundred-dollar check myself!"

"Right," I said, "that would be a *voucher*."

. . . .

MOST PEOPLE IN THIS country do not favor vouchers in education, because they don't want public dollars going to private institutions or businesses. But the logic holds absolutely no water.

We have federal Pell grants that low-income students use all the time to attend private colleges. Pell grants aren't limited to use at public universities. We have food stamps that low-income families redeem at nongovernment grocery stores. And let's not forget about Medicare and Medicaid.

Think about it this way. Say your elderly mother had to be hospitalized for life-threatening cancer. The best doctor in the region is at Sacred Heart, a Catholic, private hospital. Could you ever imagine saying this? "Well, I don't think our taxpayer dollars should subsidize this private institution that has religious roots, so we're going to take her to County General, where she'll get inferior care. 'Cause that's just the right thing to do!"

No. You'd want to make sure that your tax dollars got your mom the best care. Period. Our approach should be no different for our children. Their lives are at stake when we're talking about the quality of education they are receiving. The quality of care standard should certainly be no lower.

FIVE YEARS AGO I could not have imagined winding up working with Republican governors such as Chris Christie and Mitch Daniels. As conservatives, they hold many views that contrast with mine, especially on other civil rights issues including LGBT and women's rights. It surprised me when I started to find common ground with them on matters of education and public schools.

But working through the voucher issue, I realized that Republicans as well as Democrats can be blinded by ideology and interest groups.

When I launched StudentsFirst in late 2010, with school vouchers as one of our signature issues, a number of conservative Republicans embraced me. "That's wonderful!" one told me. "Just wonderful! It will do so much for the movement to have a Democrat like you advocating for vouchers."

But for some, the honeymoon ended quickly. At the end of the day, I have a very different perspective on the issue of vouchers than many conservative Republicans have. I don't believe that an unregulated, publicly funded marketplace will work miracles for children. And I am not in favor of choice for choice's sake. The only reason I care about vouchers is that they can be used to help students get a great education. I'm about choice only if it results in better outcomes and opportunities for a child who is being denied that chance by his or her parents' socioeconomic circumstances. To that end, I believe that voucher programs should be strongly regulated—especially to ensure accountability.

My disagreement with many pro-voucher Republicans manifests itself the most around accountability. In my view, publicly funded vouchers should go only to schools that demonstrably improve student achievement. Any private school that wants public funds should administer similar tests as public schools and should be held accountable for the same student achievement growth metrics to which we hold public schools. We should hold charter schools accountable in the same way.

This point of view gives some ultraconservatives fits. I remember a conversation with two wealthy Republican men in a fancy office building, in which I said that private schools needed to administer public tests and meet the same standards as public schools. "But parents are the best judges of what's right for their kids," said one. "You don't need the industry to be regulated. Parents will pull their kids out of any school that's not good. The market will address the issue."

To me, the argument that we should wait for the market to fix the problem is just as unsatisfactory as telling parents to wait for the government to fix the problem. Government sometimes fails, and markets sometimes fail. We cannot put ideology ahead of students. We have to be ruthlessly focused on students, and promote both policies and markets that will drive student results.

In addition to accountability, another argument I have with hard-line Republicans relates to so-called universal vouchers. Some on the political right argue that every family in the country should have immediate access to a voucher program. This strikes me as unrealistic. At a time when state and local budgets are slammed and huge numbers of children are trapped in failing schools, I am not convinced at all of the urgency of spending taxpayer dollars subsidizing the private school education of a Fortune 500 CEO. Sorry.

I explained all that to the two Republican men in that fancy office.

"Look," I concluded, "we don't let any nut job with a propeller run an airline. That's because it's dangerous and people's lives are at stake. The same is true in education. Kids' lives are at stake, so the market has to be carefully structured."

After several rounds of back and forth, I realized I wasn't going to convince these folks of anything. I think they felt the same way—and so have many other hard-right conservatives along the way. For some, it is about ideology. They can't countenance an argument that doesn't slavishly worship the power of the market. For others, it is political. They are loyal to private school operators who don't want to administer public school tests, perhaps because they are not confident that they will deliver results. Either way, just like union-beholden Democrats, they have priorities other than the interests of students.

My beliefs about vouchers didn't allow me to fit nicely into a Democratic box, but my conversations with Republicans convinced me that neither party always puts students first. This made me a political agnostic on matters of public education.

. . . .

THE TÊTE-À-TÊTE WITH ULTRACONSERVATIVES didn't reflect the
thinking of all Republicans. I have come to believe that many Republicans in education reform are concerned with quality schooling, better outcomes for all children, and elevating the teaching
profession. I believe that Democrats are on that course as well, but
it's much harder for some of them to embrace reform.

For decades, the teachers unions have been a powerful political force. In the words of Joel Klein, they are as effective as they
are at influencing policy and policy makers "because they have
millions of dollars and millions of people." They use those dollars
and those people to elect politicians who support their positions.
The laws they favor pass, and the laws that they don't want fail.

It's important to understand that both the people and the money
matter. In elections, you need to be able to run TV and radio ads,
but having boots on the ground—people knocking on doors and
running the phones—is equally important. The teachers unions
have typically provided both in overwhelming numbers.

In fact, the teachers unions' influence on the Democratic Party
is staggering. At least 10 percent of delegates to the Democratic
National Convention are teachers union members. The two national teachers unions together contribute more money politically
than the top seven defense contractors combined. In the past ten
years, they have spent more than $330 million on political cam-
paigns and candidates. The National Education Association was
the top combined contributor to state and federal races in 2008,
contributing $45 million, more than 90 percent of which went to
Democratic campaigns.

In many cities, teachers union presidents fancy themselves
kingmakers in Democratic politics. We see the impact across
the country. I've been in far too many meetings with Democrats
who've essentially said to me, "Look, I actually agree with you

philosophically. But I am not going to do you or anyone else any good if I'm not in office. If I took on these issues, the union would skewer me. I just can't go there."

The frustration that the reform community has felt with the lack of support from the vast majority of Democrats is palpable, particularly because most of us are Democrats. The ideal that we are fighting for—that all kids have a fundamental civil right to access to an excellent education—is a Democratic ideal, after all.

This reasoning led me to the uncomfortable conclusion that the lack of Democratic support was owed to cowardice. It wasn't until recently that I understood that it's actually much more complex. When I started StudentsFirst, my staff and I often talked about how it would be a game-changer if we could get a high-profile Democrat as an endorser. We've spent hours brainstorming names. Time and time again, we returned to one person who would, in fact, change the game: Bill Clinton.

BILL CLINTON IS CLEARLY the standard bearer for the Democratic Party and its ideals. There is no more gifted a politician and advocate than Clinton. Getting him out there talking about our issues would completely shift the political landscape. I have several staffers at StudentsFirst who used to work for Clinton, and they still have strong ties to the Democratic Party. After several conversations, we devised a plan. The key, they told me, was Douglas Band.

Doug Band is President Clinton's gatekeeper and confidant. If Clinton is going to take a meeting with anyone, it's only going to be because Band recommends it. So one crisp winter morning, I went to meet with the infamous Doug Band. We met for breakfast in a New York hotel.

"First of all," he began, "let me start off by saying that there is no more important work than what you're doing. Education is the most important issue this country faces. If we don't fix it, our country is screwed, plain and simple."

Sounded promising.

"That said . . . ," he continued.

I could almost hear the tires bring the promise to a screeching halt.

"My job is to create and protect the president's legacy. And that is much easier done in other realms than education. For example, if we can negotiate a seventy percent increase on AIDS medication from a pharmaceutical company to distribute in Africa, we can quantify exactly how many lives we've saved. If we raise three million dollars to bring clean drinking water to a Nigerian community, we know exactly how many diseases we've avoided."

I liked the way he thought.

"The problem with education," he said, "is that there is no clear path to victory. You can't list the three, four, or five things that need to happen that will improve student outcomes by eighty percent. So, when you're talking to a politician, the lack of a clear payoff makes it a very difficult sell. 'Hey, come take on this powerful interest group that will work to unseat you. Take a chance on these policies that we can't guarantee are even going to work.'

"What person in their right mind would take you up on that?" he asked.

He was right. Why would Clinton, or any other Democratic politician with his wits about him, for that matter, take on the issue of school reform given how much pushback they'd get with no guarantee of results? Honestly, I couldn't even ask him to do it. I came to the realization that in order for Democratic politicians to tackle the issue, we'd have to guide them on a path to victory.

The path will never be as direct as Doug Band would like. But as a foreshadowing of the fact that it is possible, Doug threw caution to the wind and joined the board of StudentsFirst, New York. We now both know that neither the solutions nor the payoffs will be easy to describe and quantify. The journey will be long, the route circuitous, the finish line forever ahead.

And winning will require resolute leadership the likes of which we've rarely seen in American politics.

ADRIAN FENTY UNDERSTOOD THAT. I was fortunate enough to serve under a leader who put his personal and political interests aside to pursue the lofty goal of reforming public schools. Fenty was willing to back our radical reforms, though he knew his support might cause his downfall. For Fenty, educating children was more important than saving his own political skin.

Despite the fact that many predicted that Fenty's political demise would dissuade any mayor from addressing school reform with the same zeal, others are beginning to take up the mantle.

Frank Jackson, the Democratic mayor of Cleveland, Ohio, is collaborating with Republican governor John Kasich to exert more authority over the Cleveland schools. At great risk to his political base, Jackson proposed encouraging new charter schools by allowing them to benefit from local property taxes. He also advocated using teacher evaluations rather than seniority to determine transfers and layoffs. Improving schools for students, for Jackson, was worth the risk.

Antonio Villaraigosa, mayor of Los Angeles, used to be a teachers union organizer. Recently, however, he has chosen to take over a subset of the worst-performing schools in the city. Along the way, he has called out the unions as "a major impediment to reform."

Under KMJ's leadership, the U.S. Conference of Mayors and the National Conference of Black Mayors both passed resolutions asking for the end of LIFO, the adoption of rigorous teacher evaluation systems, and the ability for parents to force the restructuring of failing schools through a "parent trigger."

While small numbers of brave leaders are beginning to step forward, it's not enough. A courageous leader in Cleveland or Los Angeles or Sacramento is not enough to turn the tide for the nation. We need throngs of mayors, governors, and legislators taking up the charge.

It's still sad to me that Democrats are not up in arms trying to fix this situation. Every Democratic Party ideal is being compromised by the poor quality of our public education system.

The reality, however, is that nothing will change without everyday people getting involved in the political process. When you look at national polls, it's easy to see that the vast majority of Americans think the public education system is broken, and they also agree with the commonsense reforms that StudentsFirst advocates. The problem isn't winning over the public. The problem is that there's a significant disconnect between what the public wants and what our elected officials are doing.

State legislators can get away with passing and maintaining laws that are bad for students because *we* aren't holding them accountable. We aren't demanding that they change. We're not voting for someone else if they don't. But that's precisely what we need to do if we are going to succeed in changing public education.

To my great surprise and appreciation, President Barack Obama has proved himself to be a positive force for education reform—nationally and in California, where reform is stuck in reverse.

Given my experiences over time with Democratic politicians, I was not particularly optimistic about what would happen if we elected a Democratic president. However, I certainly didn't have any reason to question Barack Obama himself; in fact, I counted myself as a big fan. I was skeptical of the party in general when it came to the willingness to take on education reform.

In September 2008, I was watching a debate between John McCain and Obama, but I had had a tough day and dozed off. Suddenly my BlackBerry and phone were going nuts. KMJ was calling, so I answered. "They just talked about you!" he said. "Huh?" I replied, still confused. "The debate! McCain and Obama just talked about you. They were arguing about whether or not you support charters or vouchers."

I could not imagine a scenario in which a presidential debate would lead to a conversation about the District of Columbia's schools, but I thought it was a good thing that education at least had come up as a topic. It was depressing to see how little school reform was discussed in the campaign. It worried me.

KMJ, however, was a staunch Obama supporter. He was not only absolutely convinced that Obama was the right person to become president, but also confident that Obama would be strong on education reform. Based on those conversations, I voted for the president. He hasn't disappointed. I did not think that I'd live to see the day when a prominent Democrat would say the kinds of things Obama has declared about education. He's been clear and consistent since day one. His willingness to support charter schools and the fact that he has said that we need to reward highly effective teachers and move the ineffective ones out of the profession has moved the needle. It has absolutely made it more acceptable to talk about the critical issue of tenure.

And there is no doubt that Obama's key education initiative, Race to the Top, has catalyzed legislative changes the likes of which we've never seen. Race to the Top has set up an incentive for states to adopt reform-minded policies. Not only has it allowed states to take on issues they otherwise wouldn't have been able to; the administration has also used it to force change in states that have resisted reform, such as New York and California.

Take the tortuous course of Assembly Bill 5 in California.

. . . .

WHEN KMJ TOLD ME I should headquarter StudentsFirst in Sacramento because it was the "belly of the beast," he wasn't kidding. The California Teachers Association (CTA) has a stranglehold on the legislature. Assemblyman Felipe Fuentes introduced a bill on teacher evaluation in December 2010 and stated: "I believe the time has come for the state to ensure that all students, regardless of race, ethnicity or ZIP code, have a fundamental right to be taught by an effective, qualified teacher." While the bill was very modest, and not one that StudentsFirst endorsed, what happened to the bill was a clear lesson in California politics.

The CTA opposed the bill initially because it took a small step in the direction of using student performance as one measure in a teacher's evaluation. Not surprisingly, the bill was put on ice.

Meanwhile, in Los Angeles, a group of parents was suing the school district over a little-known 1970s statute called the Stull Act. The act required the district to put in place new systems to measure student progress and evaluate teachers, but neither had been implemented nor enforced. The judge ruled that student achievement be a part of the district's evaluation, though the extent to which that was the case and the means by which it would be measured had to be collectively bargained.

Seeing the writing on the wall, the CTA tried its next maneuver: to resurrect Assembly Bill 5 and modify it to nullify the Stull Act.

So while Race to the Top has inspired thirty-eight states to follow the lead that we set in D.C. to require that student achievement play a large role in teacher evaluation, California, at the behest of the CTA, was poised to move in the opposite direction. That's where the Obama administration and StudentsFirst came in. We worked with our members and reform organization partners across the state to educate the opinion makers, legislators, and general public about how poor the bill was and how it would be a step backward for California. Our members emailed and called legislative offices for days leading up to the vote. And a spokesman for the U.S. Department of Education issued a statement saying that the bill would not necessarily help California win the much-coveted waiver from some requirements in the No Child Left Behind Act.

We were successful in setting the narrative, with the media weighing in heavily on why the bill was not good policy. However, while we were successful in scuttling this bad piece of legislation, the lesson is stark. Not only are we nowhere close to trying to craft meaningful evaluation policy in California, but we're having to pull out all the stops to try to defend against legislation that would move the state *in the wrong direction.* Had StudentsFirst and the reform community failed to mobilize quickly, in all likelihood this bill would have swept through the legislature, moving the state's public education system backward, without any pushback or opposition.

This is the dynamic that we're up against in California and the reason why it will take a massive grassroots movement to achieve education reform in the Golden State.

IN STATES ACROSS THE country, everyday people have already begun to find success. Last year, in Florida and Connecticut, we saw a significant shift in education reform because parents and teachers demanded change. In Florida a Republican governor spearheaded change. In Connecticut a Democrat led the charge. StudentsFirst members encouraged politicians in both states to introduce legislation that would significantly alter tenure and seniority provisions so that teacher effectiveness would be the predominant factor in staffing decisions. The teachers union reacted with vigorous opposition. In Connecticut the union even aired ads attacking a Democratic governor. The man they helped elect!

But we didn't allow that opposition to drive the narrative. We mobilized teachers and parents from throughout the two states to descend upon Tallahassee and Hartford. The numbers of concerned StudentsFirst members even outnumbered the union opposition in some cases. Our members spoke compellingly in front of the legislatures about the need to put student interests ahead of adult interests.

It worked. The legislatures in both states, hearing directly from parents and teachers, voted the bills into law.

It was a powerful example of how dedicated citizens can enact significant reforms on behalf of children. But this is just the beginning. The fight to reform the country's education system will be long and hard. We are taking the fight to the difficult terrain of New York and California, the strongholds of Democrats and teachers unions. To prevail will require significant commitment and courage from all of us. But nothing is more worth fighting for than the future of our children and the integrity of the country that we love.

The bottom line is that if we continue to allow partisan politics to dictate how our schools are run, we'll continue to suffer as a nation. The answer is quite simple: as citizens, we must hold our elected officials accountable for making decisions based on the interests of kids, not special interests.

If we were to do that, we would end up with an agenda and a public education system that are neither Republican nor Democratic. It would create a student-centered society that has the ability to put our country's education system back on top, so we can continue to lead and prosper.

PART III

The Promise

12

A Radical's Vision

I am rarely at a loss for words or action. I don't feel overwhelmed very often. But on this particular day, I was both. I'd been asked to speak at a naturalization ceremony, where the country recognizes and honors our newest Americans.

I was in the atrium of the National Archives. The marble floors and pillars make for a beautiful setting. I was sitting at the front of the room by the dignitaries who were presiding over the event. All of a sudden, I was overcome with emotion. I imagined my parents sitting through their own naturalization ceremony at the courthouse in Toledo, Ohio, forty years before. I know for a fact that at that time, they never could have imagined that one day, their own daughter would grow up to run the public schools in our nation's capital. That she would be the keynote speaker at a naturalization ceremony in the hallowed halls of one of America's most important landmarks. This is what makes America great. Anything is possible.

I looked to my right. There were about fifty new citizens hoping to build prosperous, fulfilling lives, just like Inza and Shang. To see their kids achieve things they couldn't even fathom. Suddenly, my emotions shifted. "Do their kids stand a chance to do that?"

If their children attend the D.C. public schools, are they going to be prepared to attain the American Dream? The judge presiding over the ceremony introduced me. I hadn't thought about what I would say, so I told the story of my parents' journey to America. Their struggles. Their sacrifices. Their hopes and dreams.

"I imagine my parents sitting where you are today forty years ago, with limitless dreams about what would be possible for their children by becoming American citizens," I said. "And here I am. A first-generation Korean American, running the education system in the nation's capital. What other country could that possible happen in? None. Only America. In America anything and everything is possible."

The new citizens applauded in appreciation. They smiled broadly.

"But . . . ," I said. I could see their eyes narrow. "It won't come easy. You can't assume that now that you're here, everything will fall into place. We have a significant problem in our public education system today. It's not what it once was. It's not the institution that serves to equalize the playing field. Your children are guaranteed an education, but they're not guaranteed a good one. That's your job. You have to fight for it. You have to demand it. It is your responsibility to fight to make this nation what it is supposed to be. Demand the best for your kids and for everyone's children. It's your duty to your new country."

WHY AM I A radical?

Because in order to live up to our promise as a nation, we cannot rest until we provide a quality education for *all* of our children. If America is truly going to be the land of equal opportunity, we have to provide that opportunity to every single child, regardless of where they live, what color they are, and what their parents do.

Right now, that's not happening. Right now, our public school system isn't working for every child. It isn't working for our economy. And it isn't working for our democracy. As a result, individuals cannot live up to their potential, cycles of poverty repeat, and the nation is falling behind its international competitors.

A generation of children—too often children of color and from poor communities—is being denied its civil rights to a high-quality education, and just as important, being denied its promise of equality and opportunity by its nation. And at the same time, our nation is being denied an educated workforce and a new generation of innovators and leaders.

But let's not kid ourselves. The troubles in public education spread far beyond minorities and urban areas. They mirror our culture, and it will take a cultural shift to change the trajectory of the American public education system. We've gone soft as a nation. We have to find a way to reclaim our American competitive spirit. This pertains to many aspects of our society, but particularly to the way we're raising our children and the culture that exists in our schools.

Today, we are so busy making kids feel good about themselves that we've lost sight of the time and effort it takes to make them actually good at anything. I see this with my own two children every day. Starr and Olivia are thirteen and ten years old. They play soccer. They suck at soccer. Unfortunately they've inherited their mother's athletic prowess, or lack thereof.

And yet—if you were to go into their rooms today, you'd see trophies and medals and ribbons. If you came from another country, and you didn't know any better, you'd think, "Michelle Rhee is raising the next Mia Hamm!" I assure you, I am not.

And it's not just me.

"What the heck is happening to this country, Michelle?" a well-known philanthropist in Texas asked me one day. "This past summer, I had to attend the summer camp awards ceremony for my great-grandchild."

He said it lasted nearly three hours.

"It was so bad that by the end of the ceremony it sounded like this," he said. " 'The next award goes to the best ten-year-old, blond-haired, blue-eyed boy named Bobby who has red shorts on today.' Bobby's parents are snapping pictures of him with his arms raised triumphantly over his head.

"Why do we have to spend three hours telling all of them that they're the best when they're *not*?" he asked. "Not everyone can be the best."

Other countries operate very differently. I vividly recall the school year I spent in Seoul, where every one of the seventy children in the classroom was given a rank, from one to seventy depending on academic achievement. Being the KSL (Korean as a second language) student, I was number seventy. Every child and his or her family knew exactly where they stood. If you were number eighteen, your mother pushed you to get to at least number fifteen by the end of the semester. If you were number eight, the expectation was that you needed to get to six. There should have been only one happy kid in the classroom: student number one. But that wasn't the case. The top student was always looking over her shoulder. "Oh crap," she'd think. "Here comes number three!" Or, "Number two is gunning for me on this test." Number one turned out to be the most terrified of them all.

I'm not advocating for our society to become like Korea. The constant competition creates too much stress in many students and strains within the families. But it's important to know what we're up against. Children in other nations are fiercely competitive. We are not doing our kids any favors by teaching them to celebrate mediocrity, to revel in the average, and to delight in merely participating.

IN THE WORLD OF education, we don't want anyone to feel bad, so we tell everyone that they're great. Teachers are teaching well;

students are getting promoted, even if they can't read or add. We are creating a skewed and unhealthy dynamic. It's a dynamic that would never be accepted in other realms.

One way that we do this in public education is by treating teachers as if they are all interchangeable widgets that we can move from school to school, class to class with no impact on the children. We don't want to tell great teachers they're great and ineffective teachers that they're not, so we essentially tell all of them that they're doing well. In rating teachers nationwide, fewer than 1 percent are given an unsatisfactory rating on their performance evaluation.

The unfortunate result is that we don't celebrate greatness, because we're not differentiating at all. And it leads to some very negative policies.

This line of reasoning would never be acceptable in other endeavors. Take sports. When StudentsFirst recently lobbied to change "last in, first out" policies in Minnesota, we found an unlikely ally. Fran Tarkenton, famed Minnesota Vikings quarterback, weighed in.

"Today," he wrote in an op-ed essay, "the only factor that goes into teacher layoff decisions in most districts in Minnesota is how long a teacher has been on the job. And while experience matters, it clearly shouldn't trump everything else. By that absurd standard, I should probably still be the starting quarterback for the Vikings. For the record, I recently turned 72."

If we make those basic calculations in professional sports, it ought to be even easier to make them in public education. For whatever reason, we have a standard in education where just trying is good enough. If a kid participates today, she gets a medal! When a teacher shows up, he gets tenure, which equates to having a job for life, regardless of performance. With all due respect to professional athletes and my husband's past career, athletics are not a do-or-die enterprise. Educating our children is.

There's nothing more important we can do as a country than to ensure that our children have the skills and knowledge necessary to compete in the twenty-first century. It's a matter of grave importance to the entire nation.

I don't think you can overstate the importance of shifting our cultural mind-set on education. We have to make America competitive again. The best place to start is in the public schools.

Teachers should compete to create the most engaging classrooms and achieve the best outcomes for their students, and they should be rewarded for their success.

Students should be expected to achieve, and we should reward them when they do well, too.

Schools should compete for students and dollars.

No more mediocrity. It's killing us. The acceptance and celebration of mediocrity is just one aspect of the crisis in our public schools.

The question shouldn't be "Why is Michelle Rhee radical?" The question needs to be "Why aren't we all radicals?"

RESTORING THE COMPETITIVE SPIRIT in America will require a massive cultural shift, but I believe moving our public schools toward the interests of students is more attainable. The problems and the solutions are within our grasp. For too long we approached education policy decisions by pitting the interests of the adults in the system—the school boards, the union leaders, the textbook manufacturers, the charter operators—against one another. The special interests won. And students lost.

The good news is we know what we have to do in order to strengthen public education, so that it works for every child and all of our communities. Research and practice have repeatedly shown that we can improve a child's education by elevating the teaching profession and ensuring that every child has a quality teacher in his or her classroom; empowering parents with information and a role in the direction of their child's education; and creating accountable governance systems and fair and sustainable sources of education funding. Local school districts like New York City, Denver, Charlotte, and Washington, D.C., have shown great success in improving outcomes for children. They did so by enacting policies that removed bureaucratic rules and reformed the antiquated system of compensation that keeps good teachers out of the classroom. They have empowered parents by giving them more information and meaningful choices. They have moved dollars out of administrative central bureaucracies and into the classroom. Student learning has dramatically improved.

We can improve our public education system. The solutions will not be easy or quick. They have to be sustained, well financed, and purposeful. But it's absolutely possible. What do these changes look like?

Start in the classroom. We know that teachers are the number one in-school factor in determining the learning of a child. So we have to evaluate teachers through a rigorous system that measures how effective they are at ensuring that kids learn. We should then reward the best teachers by respecting them and paying them commensurate with their value in society—as the most important professionals in the community. We were able to establish a process in Washington, D.C., where the top teachers could earn as much as $140,000 a year, with bonuses based on their success in the classroom.

Staffing decisions in schools will be made on effectiveness, not seniority. Professional development will truly enhance our teachers' practice and enable them to share best practices. Teachers will know what the expectations of their practice are, and they will have the freedom to innovate as long as they produce results.

When teachers walk into their classrooms they should have all of the supplies, equipment, and books that they need to execute engaging instruction. They should have the technological tools that they need to track the academic achievement levels of every individual student so that they can monitor their ongoing progress. For the classroom of tomorrow, technology is an *essential*. Today there are handheld devices that allow teachers to do immediate assessments of their students. Based on that data, teachers can generate reports noting which children are in need of interventions or enrichment. Individualized homework can be tailored for each student depending on what skills they need to work on. Computer software programs allow students to move through material at their own pace, differentiating based on their level, so that every student is being challenged. We have to make these advancements available to every teacher and also embrace them as a profession. They will allow us to serve children better.

Educators also need access to curricula, plans, and best practices that allow them to implement high-quality lessons for their students and modify their instructional practice based on the needs of their students. Imagine a third-grade teacher whose class is working on fractions. She opens up her laptop that the school has provided. She ventures into a teacher portal that the district has set up to assist educators. The teacher types "adding fractions" into the search engine. Up pop links to lesson plans that various teachers in the district have used to teach the skill of adding fractions. They are sorted by grade level. Each lesson is rated by a certain number of stars, ratings other teachers have given the plan based on how well it was written and how well it worked in their classroom. There are also links to videos of master teachers presenting lessons on adding fractions. In these videos teachers can hear narration by the master teacher, who is explaining what happened in the room, and why she did what she did. There's also a message board that teachers can use to comment on the video and share ideas.

Teaching is sometimes a lonely profession. It doesn't have to be that way. We can build structures that allow teachers to grow their practice and engage in meaningful sharing with other educators within schools and across the country. We have to invest in developing those structures if we want teachers to fulfill their potential.

If we can bring about these changes, students will be excited about coming to school every day, because they know they'll be challenged and engaged. School will become the place where they can grow not only academically but also physically, through robust athletic competitions and activities. Art and music offerings must be mandatory in every school, so students gain important skills and knowledge beyond academics. In tough economic times, like the ones we are facing today, school districts often move to cut art and music programs first. They are seen as nonessential. We simply can't allow that to happen. All children must have access to a broad-based curriculum. Art, music, and PE are not "nice-to-haves"; they are must-haves. Studies show that achievement on test scores goes up with a broad curriculum, rather than a narrow one. That's why we tried to ensure that every school in D.C. had access to an art, music, physical education, and library professional. Debate and chess teams, orchestra, dance companies, robotics, and gaming programs should sit alongside the traditional athletic programs. Students will grow in social skills, too. We are building character skills such as discipline, effort, and hard work. When we engage kids fully, they will both respond and thrive.

We also have to acknowledge that the lives of children have changed significantly, which means the role of the school also has to evolve. Thirty years ago schools were responsible for teaching reading, writing, and arithmetic. If you delivered the material, you were doing your job as a teacher. Not anymore. Ask any teacher, and he will tell you that at times he feels like a guidance counselor, social worker, nutritionist, and sometimes parent for many of his students. With a new understanding of how difficult it is to be an effective teacher in our changed American culture, we have to do everything we can to recognize and reward the best teachers. They are our country's heroes.

We must also recognize that parents deserve options in choosing the right schools for their kids. No family should ever feel as if their sons or daughters are trapped in a failing school. Successful charter schools should be allowed to flourish and grow to scale, with our assistance rather than barriers. Low-income families should also be able to access vouchers to attend private schools. We should care less about whether a school is public, private, parochial, or charter. The measure that matters is whether it's an effective school—or not. To that end, we should have structures and systems that give parents and the public real and meaningful information about how all of our schools are performing and an accountability system that shuts down failing schools.

The average parent with a child entering school should have ample access to information about their options. Ideally, parents should be able to log onto a website, input their address, and search schools that are a possibility for their child by proximity to their home, curriculum/course offerings, or theme. Information should be available about the academic achievement levels of the students, listings of the program of study and extracurricular activities, teacher-parent retention and satisfaction rates, and other available programs at the school. Parents would be able to view a virtual tour of the school and hear testimonials from other parents about the quality and qualities of the school. If they wanted, they could schedule an in-person tour or have their child attend a day at the school in the grade to which they are about to enter. Having assessed this information, families would then rate their choices of school in order. But unlike current lottery systems, which have far too many applicants for far too few spots, mutually agreeable matches would be the norm.

School funding will no longer be based on formulas. It will

be distributed based on both need and performance. We should have complete transparency of the taxpayer dollars that are being spent on education so we can stop spending money on things that don't work (or benefit only adults) and focus on the things that do. That means we have to shift more dollars into the classroom and schools, where they'll have the greatest impact, and away from bloated bureaucracies and mandated spending requirements that don't produce results.

To restore the competitive spirit, we need to have high expectations for all children. We have to fully acknowledge the challenges that we face, yet not let those serve as an excuse for a lack of achievement. We have to ensure that all students who graduate from high school or college are ready and able to compete in the global marketplace.

And since students know better than anyone what is working, they should also have a say in evaluating and rating their teachers and schools.

Teachers deserve a greater voice and role in the education reform debates. We can't do anything without a significant number of teachers behind us. If the unions can reform themselves, that would be great. They should spend far less time protecting ineffective teachers and far more time developing and investing in the best. They should stop fighting change (and denying that they're fighting it) and come to the table willing to have the tough conversations. Union leaders and reformers have to have real and meaningful conversations instead of staking out polarized positions with kids in the middle of the battle. If unions can't come along, it shouldn't stop us. Teachers can no longer close the door to their classroom and hope that things get better. They have to take an active part in the reform, with or without union involvement. Everyday classroom teachers must be front and center.

We have to begin aggressively identifying and electing candidates for public office who are able to withstand pressures from special interests in order to serve the interests of children. Every-day citizens have to make education their number one priority. They need to be knowledgeable about school reform and hold their elected officials accountable for their votes on the subject. Bowing to pressures for political reasons ought to be a case for ousting those officials from office.

The inevitable question is, How will we pay for it? It's a valid one. For decades, the education establishment has been arguing that we need more money to fix the schools. Whether we are in lean times or prosperous ones, the same dance seems to occur around budgeting time every year. The school districts argue they need more money, and the government doesn't seem to have enough.

A hard look at the data here is important. The bottom line is that over the last three decades we have more than doubled—almost tripled—the amount that we are spending per child on public education, controlling for inflation. Yet the results have remained stagnant. When we plot the spending on education and academic achievement levels of countries across the globe on a graph, we are in the quadrant where you don't want to be. We spend more than almost every other country, but our achievement levels are not high. Countries like South Korea spend about half of what we do per student.

The days of claiming that all we need in order to fix education is more money have to come to an end.

I have said and will continue to say that our reforms require investment. But that doesn't necessarily mean they require huge infusions of new cash. The bureaucracy doesn't work. We can throw good money after bad, but we won't get a different result in the classroom until we start spending taxpayer dollars in education more wisely. Only when we fix the fundamental flaws in the system should we begin to invest more money.

How? First, we have to mandate total transparency. Every parent, teacher, and taxpayer should be able to see how public dollars are being spent. This means that a district would have to report how much of its budget is going toward classrooms, compared with the central office bureaucracy. Are we paying for bureaucrats to go to conferences in Las Vegas versus children being able to go on a field trip to the nation's capital? All of that information should be accessible.

We can begin by making the hard decisions to move dollars away from the programs that, while beloved, aren't producing results for kids. Let me give you an example. Right now we spend about $18 billion a year paying teachers for having their master's degree. Research shows that teachers with master's degrees—except those in math and science fields—do not have better student achievement outcomes. Eighteen billion dollars! For something that is not producing better results for kids. That money could be spent much more effectively. So could many other dollars being spent on everything from after-school programs to class size reduction initiatives at higher grade levels. That doesn't mean we shouldn't have after-school programs. We need them. But we should be funding only those programs that show a measurable benefit to children.

We also have to move a greater percentage of the dollars we spend into the classroom and school. When I took the helm in the Washington, D.C., school system, we were spending more money than almost any other jurisdiction in the nation, and yet our results were dismal. The same can be said for cities across the country. Newark, New Jersey, spends about $22,000 per student. One would think they'd have a model education system. Instead it's one of the worst in the nation. These districts are clear examples of why more money doesn't always get us better results. The funds are not being spent well. There is no reason why teachers in D.C. or Newark should want for anything, yet throngs of them will tell you that they often lack the basic supplies and books they need to teach.

In D.C., this meant cutting the central office from more than nine hundred employees to fewer than five hundred. It meant improving the services and programs for special-needs students to stop the costly lawsuits and the court-mandated tuition payments to private schools. If we are going to spend more money than any other country in the world, then let's make sure that money is felt by students, parents, and teachers every day.

And finally, we should ensure that every additional dollar that is put into education is accompanied by the policies necessary to reform the system. This should include federal dollars, which are currently largely distributed by funding formulas. Under those formulas, each jurisdiction is allocated a certain number of dollars based on the number of students it has, and how many of those students are low-income, special education, et cetera. There is, however, little to no accountability for those dollars. Instead, federal dollars should be given to states based on their willingness to adopt and implement reforms, similar to President Obama's Race to the Top initiative.

If we want to stop the cycle of spending more money for the same, dismal results, we have to reward reforms that produce good results.

HISTORY TEACHES US THAT the only way to effect radical change in an entrenched system is through grassroots activism. There's only so much that people will do for other people's children or the greater good. People become active when something significant in their own lives is at risk or under attack. Right now, Americans need to understand that this is not someone else's fight. This is about the soul of our nation and the future of our children.

I'm often asked when I will be satisfied. Maybe we should never be satisfied. But I'll think we're on the right track if:

- Every child has a high-quality teacher in his or her classroom. That every teacher has the confidence that he or she will have the resources and professional feedback they need to succeed, and understands that he or she will be treated like a professional so that they are judged based on their results.
- In the hallways of power, decision makers know they will be held to account for doing right by children. That they make decisions based on the best interests of students and not the special interests, based on the advancement of learning and not the advancement of power. That they spend dollars on education rather than bureaucracy, on what works rather than what doesn't.
- And all parents know that they will have the tools and power to hold all of us accountable.

To what end? What is possible?

America is the greatest nation in the world. We should have the greatest education system in the world to match. I believe it is possible for the United States to move from the bottom third on international tests to the top third in a ten-year time span. It's doable. It's been accomplished by other nations. Finland educated and exalted teachers. Germany made improvements to public education a national priority after reunification, and its students responded by moving to the top third of international rankings.

Elevating our children into the top third is possible only if we make education, teachers, and students the priority of the entire nation. That means acknowledging that our system is broken, but that its radical improvement is within our grasp. It means setting aside other issues, knowing that education is the key to the comeback of America and its economy.

It means putting the interests, dreams, and future of our children at the forefront of our country's collective efforts.

It means putting students first.

Acknowledgments

So many people made this book possible. It was truly a group effort.

First, thanks go to my husband, Kevin Johnson. I couldn't ask for a more patient and supportive partner. You push me to be a better person, a more effective leader, and a more thoughtful advocate. Your passion for kids and public service inspire me every day, and you set a high bar for what hard work looks like. Your strategic advice and insights are second to none, and when all else fails, you make me laugh.

To my daughters, Starr and Olivia. Thank you for allowing your mom to be away more than we'd like so that we can take on this important work. While I know it's not always easy being my daughters, you handle it with great aplomb, and moreover, you've become impressive education reformers yourselves!

Next, to my mom and dad. While all of your friends are enjoying their retirements on the golf course or the beach, you've taken on the duties of chauffeuring the kids around and attending field trips. Dad, you taught me about social justice and to fight for the underdog. Without that, I wouldn't have chosen this course.

Mom, without your help, I would not have been able to take on the jobs I have. Thank you for your sacrifices.

To my brothers: Erik for helping me start StudentsFirst and serving as my attorney on this book, and Brian for always supporting my efforts and keeping me humble.

Much love to Jason, Alissa, Ann, Myung-Seok, Young-hae, Stephanie, Ted, Namhee, Sungjin, and Mitchell for always being on my side. Appreciation to Denise Merano and Dana Peterson for making my and my husband's lives better every day. And to Mother Rose and Shawn Branch, who are my biggest cheerleaders and defenders!

There were many people at StudentsFirst who helped with the book, but special thanks go to Dominique Amis, Dmitri Mehlhorn, Enoch Woodhouse, Tim Melton, Matt David, Mike Phillips, and Brian Wanlass. Each of you added to the book in different ways, and I appreciate all of your help.

To my colleagues from Harlem Park Elementary: Michele Jacobs, Deonne Medley, Andrea Derrien, Chris Isleib, John Wagner, Bertha Haywood, Rhoda Jones, Pam Saunders, Neva Camp, Everlyn Strother, and of course, Linda Carter. You made me understand what great teachers do and look like. To my students and their parents, you helped me to see what is possible in this world. My experiences with you are what have shaped my entire career. You showed what is possible when adults believe in children.

To the leadership and staff at The New Teacher Project. The work that you do is some of the most important in the country. Ari Rozman, Tim Daly, Karla Oakley, Jessica Levin, Victoria Van Cleef, Karolyn Belcher, Robin Siegel, Roger Schulman, and Bruce Villineau, you are one of the best teams a person could have asked to work with. You taught me a tremendous amount.

I can honestly say that this book and story would not have been possible without my fearless colleagues at the DC Public

Schools: Kaya Henderson, Richard Nyankori, Lisa Ruda, Jason Kamras, Jim Sandman, Erin McGoldrick, Abigail Smith, Michael Moody, Carey Wright, Noah Wepman, Cate Swinburn, Peter Weber, Peggy O'Brien, Tony Tata, John Davis, Billy Kearney, Dwan Jordon, Anthony deGuzman, Chad Ferguson, Susan Cheng, Pete Cahall, Brian Betts, Bill Wilhoyte, Scott Cartland, Angela Williams-Skelton, Joyce McNeil, Dave Anderson, Errick Greene, Barbara Adderley, Clara Canty, Tim Williams, Willie Lamb, Reggie Ballard, Mafara Hobson, Kaitlin Murphy, and last but not least Margery Yeager. Each of you took on one of the most daunting tasks imaginable, and you worked at it every day with dedication, fervor, and an unshakable belief in children.

Thanks to my agent, Simon Green, and my editor, Tim Duggan, along with his assistant, Emily Cunningham. George Parker, Kahlil Byrd, Hari Sevugan, and Eric Lerum were integral to the book by reading drafts, giving insights, and generally making it a better read. Harry Jaffe's writing guidance was essential.

To my best friends, Layla Avila and Liz Peterson. You keep me sane, happy, fed, and looking cute! You are wonderful aunties to my children and the kind of BFFs every girl needs.

To my teachers Susan Zaliouk, Chuck Lundholm, Beneth Morrow, Sam McCoy, Margaret Blackburn, Karen Horikawa, Jane Bishop, Laszlo Koltay, Mari Dorfmeyer, Al Getman, Bob Russell, Ken Meineke, Ron Euton, Sandy McPeck, David Burkett, Jenny Barthold, and Hope and Peter Stevens. You ensured that I got the great education that we should aspire to for all of our nation's children.

To the members of the D.C. government who were so supportive of our efforts: Victor Reinoso, Dan Tangherlini, Peter Nickles, Neil Albert, Joanne Ginsburg, Bridget Davis, Kate Gottfredson, Cathy Lanier, Allen Lew, Jesus Aguirre, Carrie Brooks, and Tene Dolphin.

Much thanks to those in D.C. who supported me from

beginning to end: Beth Dozoretz, Katherine Bradley, Mark Ein, Jim Joseph, Don Graham, JoAnne Armao, Mary Sidall, Tijwanna Phillips, and "the clock lady," Lenore Moragne.

To Adam, Steve, and Mary Weiss, Gretchen Verner, Patrick Day, Peter Chung, Melissa Williams-Gurian, Jenny Kim, Donald Kamentz, Chris Bierly, Wendy Kopp, and Jewel Woods—you all shaped my views on the world and life for the better.

In my research, I relied often on *A Change for Every Child: A History of Toledo Public Schools*, by Robyn Hage and Larry Michaels; *The Bee Eater*, by Richard Whitmire; and *Dream City: Race, Power, and the Decline of Washington, D.C.*, by Harry Jaffe and Tom Sherwood.

And finally, I owe a debt to my mentors: Joel Klein, thank you for having more confidence in me than I do in myself at times. You are my hero. To Kati Haycock, who taught me to be fearless and speak my mind. You are my role model. Fred O'Such, you believed in me when few others did. To David Coleman, who forces me to think deeply about everything, no matter what the topic.

And to Adrian Fenty, who is the most courageous politician I have ever met. Your leadership on education reform has benefited the children of the entire nation. We owe you a debt of gratitude.

About the Author

Michelle Rhee is the founder and CEO of StudentsFirst, a political advocacy organization for education reform. She served as chancellor of the Washington, D.C., public schools from 2007 to 2010. She is also the founder of The New Teacher Project and a former Teach For America corps member. She divides her time between California—with her husband, Kevin Johnson, the mayor of Sacramento—and Nashville, Tennessee, with her daughters, Starr and Olivia.